Private Dwelling

What do housing professionals, architects, estate agents and town planners do when they go home at night? Presumably they do the same as the rest of the population. They indulge in that ubiquitous and unique activity called dwelling. They use the housing planned, designed, managed, bought and sold by professionals for uses specific to themselves: and while they are doing it, so is everybody else.

Housing is something that is deeply personal to us. It offers us privacy and security and allows us to be intimate with those we are close to. This book considers the nature of privacy but also how we choose to share our dwelling. The book discusses the manner in which we talk about our housing, how it manifests and assuages our anxieties and desires and how it helps us come to terms with loss.

Private Dwelling offers a deeply original take on housing. The book proceeds through a series of speculations, using philosophical analysis and critique, the use of personal anecdote, film criticism, social and cultural theory and policy analysis to unpick the subjective nature of housing as a personal place where we can be sure of ourselves. The book will be of interest to students, academics and researchers in housing, architecture, and planning as well as social theory and philosophy.

Peter King is a pioneer in the area of social philosophy and housing. His main research interest has been to differentiate how housing is used at the individual level from the manner in which it is perceived as a social or collective entity. He is the author of five previous books, which explore various aspects of housing, including *A Social Philosophy of Housing* (2003). He is a Reader in Housing and Social Philosophy at the Centre for Comparative Housing Research, De Montfort University.

Housing, Planning and Design Series

Editors: Nick Gallent and Mark Tewdwr-Jones,
The Bartlett School of Planning, UCL

This series addresses critical issues affecting the delivery of the right type of housing, of sufficient quantity and quality, in the most sustainable locations, and the linkages that bind together issues relating to planning, housing and design. Titles examine a variety of institutional perspectives, examining the roles of different agencies and sectors in delivering better quality housing together with the process of delivery – from policy development, through general strategy to implementation. Other titles will focus on housing management and devlopment, housing strategy and planning policy, housing needs and community participation.

Housing in the European Countryside
Edited by Nick Gallent, Mark Shucksmith and Mark Tewdwr-Jones

Housing Development: Theory, Process and Practice
Edited by Andrew Golland and Ron Blake

Private Dwelling: Contemplating the Use of Housing
Peter King

Forthcoming:
Decent Homes For All
Nick Gallent and Mark Tewdwr-Jones

Rural Housing Policy
Tim Brown and Nicola Yates

International Perspectives on Rural Homelessness
Edited by Paul Milbourne and Paul Cloke

Private Dwelling

Contemplating the use of housing

Peter King

Routledge
Taylor & Francis Group

LONDON AND NEW YORK

First published 2004
by Routledge
2 Park Square, Milton Park, Abingdon, Oxfordshire OX14 4RN

Simultaneously published in the USA and Canada
by Routledge
270 Madison Avenue, New York, NY 10016

Routledge is an imprint of the Taylor & Francis Group

© 2004 Peter King

Typeset in Galliard by
HWA Text and Data Management, Tunbridge Wells
Printed and bound in Great Britain by
TJ International Ltd, Padstow, Cornwall

British Library Cataloguing in Publication Data
A catalogue record for this book is available from the British Library

Library of Congress Cataloging in Publication Data
King, Peter, 1960–
    Private dwelling : speculations on the use of housing / Peter King.
      p. cm.
    Includes bibliographical references and index.
  1. Housing. 2. Housing–Psychological aspects.
  3. Functionalism (Social sciences) I. Title.
    HD7287.K559 2004
    363.5–dc22   2004001851

ISBN 0–415–33620–1 (hbk)
ISBN 0–415–33621–X (pbk)
ISBN 0–415–42140–X (e-book)

To no. 78 and its contents

Contents

Preface and acknowledgements

One of my obsessions has been to state, over and over again, that housing is a means rather than an end in itself. By this I mean that housing is something that we use rather than just have: its importance is that it allows us to do other things. This simple fact, which we all implicitly accept in our daily lives, is all too frequently forgotten when housing comes to be discussed by academics, commentators and policy makers. There is just far too much emphasis on the production and consumption of brick boxes, and not enough appreciation of what we need them for.

Of course, one of the main problems in developing such an appreciation is that much of what we do in our little brick boxes we seek to keep private, and we want to share it only with those we know well. What goes on behind closed doors is really not a matter for public observation. But this does not mean it is not significant or important, merely that it is not to be shared with those we do not know or care for. Just because we cannot see something does not mean it is not there, nor that it is not of considerable import. And we know this precisely because we all experience it as such. We all have ends and interests that we have chosen, as individuals, as couples, or as families. We make use of our housing in order to achieve these ends. Housing can therefore be seen as a tool, albeit a complex and expensive one.

Having been obsessed by this simple idea, and frustrated that it appears to be beyond (or beneath)[1] the understanding of many, I decided to set about exploring what it actually means to use our housing: what do we use it for or to do, and therefore why is it so important to us? In doing so, I hoped to point out just what it is that other thinkers have been missing. The result of this is the speculations that follow. I have tried to consider some of the important aspects about housing, or what I have termed *private dwelling*. I have looked at the importance of privacy, how we describe our dwelling, how we share it, and how it is created and modified by desire, anxiety and loss. This is not a complete picture, merely a start, and many may disagree with my choice of topics.

What has conditioned my choice of topics for these speculations is the method I have adopted in exploring them. Many people who I have spoken to about this project have asked about method, particularly whether I have undertaken fieldwork, interviews, observations, etc. When I have told them that instead these speculations are conceptual and rely on anecdote, film criticism and other apparently unscientific methods – on what we might refer to by the old-fashioned notion of *critique* – some have looked askance. However, I want to suggest that my method is crucial to the subject under discussion. Private dwelling is both ubiquitous and unique – we live as separated households, but we all do this – and so, it seems to me, we should consider the subjective use of housing *subjectively*.

Of course, the housing literature has become increasingly aware of the subjective experience of housing, with academics such as Craig Gurney, Keith Jacobs and Tony Manzi doing some interesting and innovative work. More generally, I would point to the compendious study of the structuring of urban space around the public/private dichotomy undertaken by Ali Madanipour (2003). This book's content is perhaps the nearest to my speculations, although Madanipour's scope is wider than mine, taking in the whole range from the deeply personal to the anonymity of the city. In addition, he has considered seriously the problems of a 'first person' or phenomenological approach, which relies solely on the subjective or interior aspect of human consciousness. Instead he seeks to develop a dynamic approach that incorporates the first person with the 'third person' or scientific approach. His method is thus rather more 'traditional' (or respectable) than that used here. Indeed there is rather more third than first person in evidence. My main criticism of this work, along with that of many who write on subjectivity, is precisely that it tends to use an objective social science approach in order to consider subjectivity.

Many academics would perhaps see no fault in this, and there certainly is a need for this 'objective' approach in developing a truly comparative basis for the subjective understanding of housing. But my fear is that we can only undertake an objective study of this private level of experience by intruding into it to such an extent that it is altered or even destroyed.

By way of analogy (and only analogy) I would suggest that a type of *uncertainty principle* is at work here, whereby the observation of this micro level activity alters it and creates new patterns and formations that would not be there were it not for the observation.[2] What is called for, then, is a different approach that relies on observation from the inside itself. In this way we can hope that it is left undisturbed. This involves a subjective description of housing, even if it involves eschewing methods that might help us gain a broader perspective. In essence, then, I am asking that these speculations be judged according to their content and the procedures whereby they have been arrived at. As Madanipour (2003) correctly states, phenomenological accounts will be incomplete, *but they are still necessary*. They are necessary to complement the equally incomplete third person or scientific approach, described by Madanipour as 'left outside' (p. 3). First person narratives, for all their faults, are the only means to get inside the private sphere.

There is a further reason for adopting this approach, and this relates to the fact that much of what we do in our dwellings – what we use housing for – is quite banal. Our private dwelling is uneventful, mundane and ordinary. What is more, we actively seek (as it were!) to maintain it as such. But the banal and mundane nature of our dwelling means we do not see the need to quantify and qualify, to sift and divide, to determine and essentialise what we do. Rather we just get on with it: it is how we live *now*. It strikes me that the best way of grasping this quotidian sense of how we live is through a phenomenological approach, just as writers such as Gaston Bachelard (1969) have done earlier. This is because it allows us to pick out the tiny details of our own dwelling, apparently insignificant to anyone looking in, but so important to us.

Of course, I might be accused here of attempting something different from what I have criticised. I am not undertaking here a study of subjectivity but writing subjectively. I might therefore be accused of mistaking method for content. On one level this is indeed the case, but it is an entirely necessary conflation, in that what I am considering here is what we do in housing on the basis of what *I* do and think. The method – the use of the material – is exactly what is important here, just as the use of the entity is more significant than the entity itself.

This does mean that what follows is neither scientific, nor free of bias. I cannot claim that this is definitive, and indeed it would be absurd even to try. My method is then as speculative as some of my conclusions. In that sense, what use is it? At the risk of being glib, I want to suggest that these speculations are useful – or if you want, relevant – for those interested in these types of studies, *and only them*.[3] I have written in this way because I found it interesting and enlightening. I have no illusions that this will be shared by all or even many, but I hope that some will find it worth persisting with. And some might even find elements within it that are illuminating. But if not, I would not seek to persuade them that they are misinformed or disingenuous – doubtless they have their own ends to be getting on with. I promise to leave them alone – if they will do the same!

Another doubt that some may have – and I have periodically had myself – is whether this is really an academic approach at all. Do the contents of these speculations constitute a properly rigorous academic study? There are several responses we can make here. Some may see that these speculations are not rigorous, and were they to offer reasons to support their view I would happily engage with them. Others may suggest that there are already many different and diverse approaches, and as housing studies does not of itself constitute an academic discipline with its own formalities, methods and theories, why not use something different? This, not unnaturally, is a view I would happily concur with. However, my defence of choice would be to argue (as I do in the introduction) that this method is by no means as different and unusual as it appears, and is already commonly used in philosophy, health studies, feminist discourse and cultural studies.[4] Whilst I have found little akin to these speculations in the housing literature, there are many examples in other subjects and disciplines.

A final point about the style and content is that, unlike most other writers and academics on housing, I have not seen my aim here as being to change anything. To my mind, the great virtue of dwelling is that it insulates us from transformation and change. What I have sought to do in these speculations is to try to describe why this is so and to understand why it is sometimes better to leave alone.

But that is enough self defence (after all no one has to read it!). I have many people to thank who have helped and assisted me in this project. Nick Mills took time off from his own research to read and comment on a complete draft as well as some chapters through successive iterations. Other colleagues from the Centre for Comparative Housing Research have read and discussed parts of this book with me, particularly Deborah Bennett, Tim Brown and Jo Richardson. Other parts of this book have been presented to CCHR seminars, which gave me the opportunity to defend my views and to extend them under criticism. I am grateful for all the support I have received from my colleagues. The support and sense of collegiality within CCHR has been a continual help both on this project and on others I have undertaken.

I am grateful to have such a responsive editor in Michelle Green at Taylor & Francis, who has been supportive of this rather eccentric project. Likewise, I need to thank the series editors, Nick Gallent and Mark Tewdwr-Jones, for their encouragement and support. I would also like to thank the anonymous reviewers who commented on this project at various stages, all of whom made useful and helpful suggestions.

My family has assisted me greatly in the writing of this book. My daughters, Helen and Rachel, have asked me continually about the project – 'are we really in it, Daddy?' – and have been able to comment on some of my wilder ideas. My wife, Barbara, has assisted in this book almost beyond measure.

She has offered a reality check where necessary, and has continually challenged me and so forced me to defend many of my ideas. This has led to the jettisoning of some observations and the strengthening of others. In addition, she also undertook the daunting task of proof-reading my final draft and she has thus prevented me from committing many errors in style and grammar. Unlike any other book I have written, these three people have been intimately involved in the gestation and completion of this one. They more than anything, or anyone, have validated this whole project and they deserve more love and care than I have been able to show.

And finally, a couple of words on the photographs used in this book. First, I thank my brother, Graham, for preparing the images and scanning them onto disk (and for refraining from being excessively patronising to his big brother). Second, I originally had no intention of including any images in the book at all, but two of the anonymous reviewers suggested that they would be useful. Having agreed to include some, and having already finished a draft of the book, I was initially at a loss to decide what images to use. It soon became clear to me though that my subjective approach should be extended to these as well. Hence the images included have been taken by me (with the exception of a drawing by my daughter that appears in chapter 5) with the aim of highlighting, perhaps somewhat elliptically at times, some of my main themes and ideas. They are, then, of a piece with the text. The photos have no pretensions towards art – or even competent photography! – but I hope that, like the words around them, they have some use.

Peter King
January 2004

Introduction
Looking out and looking in

To speculate is to take a risk: it is to indulge in conjecture without full knowledge of all the facts. We are not entirely sure of our ground, but still feel a need to address the issues. The problem is that we are not really sure that we can answer the questions that are posed. Instead we can only frame the questions as acutely as possible, and hope that, as part of the process, answers of some sort will emerge. Yet, at the same time, we are not really sure that there is an answer out there at all. All we can do is speculate, and, in doing so, hope to accumulate. For this is the whole point of speculation: we have to take a risk if we are to achieve anything. This, however, presumes that we know what we are seeking to achieve, of where we want or expect to go. Yet those who speculate are not always so aware of their circumstances or the possible consequences of heading off in any particular direction. They are half-blind to any outcome, unknowing of what they may meet upon their journey.

All they know – or think they know, or want to believe – is that the rewards of any speculation can be great; that the greater the risk, the larger the reward. Long journeys do not always end in disappointment and one day someone will find the proverbial pot of gold. And we believe that the bigger the punt – the more we are prepared to speculate – the more we are likely to win. We may fall further and harder, but just sometimes the flight is truly spectacular.

I cannot, of course, claim a spectacular flight (and not even a gentle landing). One of the problems, and the thrill, of speculating is precisely that we do not know whether we will soar or fall painfully to earth. All we know is that the risk is there and that it is worth it. And we believe this not because of any special knowledge, but for the very reason that we do not know where we are to end up. Perhaps then, what is most important is the risk itself; what matters to the speculator is the very act of speculating. Success will validate our actions, and provide more latitude to speculate again. But this is not the real purpose. Is not what we want – and I am speculating here – to stretch ourselves and to find where our limits are?

Every dwelling tells a story …

This is, I think, what I am attempting here. What I present in the following chapters is a series of speculations on how we use our housing. I look at what we do with it, what it means to us and just why it is so significant. My aim is to present a series of questions in the belief that this will elucidate how we live in our little brick boxes.

The first question is just what do we mean when we talk about the use of housing? What does *use* mean in this context? Raymond Studer (1993) states that 'Use suggests overt behaviour, the employment of objects and ideas to facilitate an action' (p. 30). Use is, he argues, a manifestation of '*effective* behaviour' (p. 30): it is behaviour intended to achieve some particular effect. Likewise, Guido Francescato (1993) suggests that the term is 'often taken to mean engaging in "activities"' (p. 42). The term, then, tends to 'imply action or overt behaviour' (p. 42). According to this view, use is suggestive of intentional actions. We use our housing to do things in. But Francescato considers this too restrictive a view, and what he seeks to do is broaden the notion by linking use with *meaning*. Following Roland Barthes, he suggests that the use of any object involves communication, through the sending of a signal to others. We broadcast signs through the use of our

... and carries a meaning of its own. Much of this meaning is secret and upon which we can only speculate

housing, as we do when we use any object. This communication creates meaning. Hence the dwelling might offer a sign of its functionality by sheltering us from the weather. But what Francescato calls a 'social semantization' (p. 43) also comes into play, offering new aims and intentions for the dwelling. As an example he sees that a dwelling can come to symbolise a certain social status within a community. Certain house types, or housing in particular locations, can communicate information about the occupiers. In a similar manner, he suggests that programmes of government action – where housing is used for certain social and political objectives – might operate as signs of status.

So the use of housing involves certain social symbols or signs as well as being a series of conscious actions. What is important here, of course, is that the social signals need not be consciously designed or intended for them to operate. What this suggests is that use and meaning are closely interrelated. As Studer states, 'It is difficult to imagine an environment that could be either highly meaningful and completely useless, or quite useful but meaningless' (1993, p. 30). So what matters is not just what we intend and what actions we take, but how these actions become meaningful *and* how the manner in which we and others perceive our housing leads us into certain actions and beliefs. Use is then as much about the symbols we create – and therefore others react to – as it is about explicit actions. We cannot separate out use from meaning, and this is because use creates meaning and we use things because of what they mean.

This being so, let me start then with a silly question: *who uses housing?* – a thoroughly banal and stupid question, we might say. The answer is so obvious that we cannot even be bothered. We should stop wasting time and get back to the important stuff about building, developing and implementing policies, and dealing with real world problems. Life – or at least the working week – is just too short for this naïve navel gazing. The important thing, surely, is to ensure we build houses; what happens then can take care of itself.

And yet … like many silly questions – like those apparently naïve questions asked by children of their harassed parents ('Daddy, why are there wars?') – there is something just under the surface that snags us and bring us up short. So just what answer would we give? What is the first thing that comes into our heads when asked who uses housing? Is it 'the owners', or is it 'tenants', or 'the residents', or perhaps is it 'I do' or 'we do'? The answer we might give to this silly naïve question is, I believe, important because it points to where our priorities and interests lie. Our answer might show whether we see housing as being about the allocation and distribution of resources, about maximising a given stock of dwellings, or about what you and I can do in private. It might say whether we see housing in collective or personal terms. Thus we are quickly led to some pretty significant issues at the heart of both housing policy and the manner in which we relate to each other.

What affects the answer we make may well depend upon our interests, and more particularly our relation to housing. For the purpose of this discussion I want to distinguish between two categories of human beings, on the basis of how they relate to housing. First, there are those who work in housing and related professions, including those who undertake research, analysis and commentary on housing issues. This category contains people whose livelihoods depend on housing. Let us call them *housing experts*. In the second category are all those persons who currently live in and habitually use housing, and all those who want to. We can refer to these as *human beings*. We can admit that the first category is a subset of this second universal grouping. What is more, the first category is likely to be a very small one when compared to the larger group. There are not many of us who earn a living through the construction, management and planning of housing, or by talking and writing about it.

The problem is that those in the first category often appear to forget, or at least ignore, their membership of the bigger group. They bracket or separate out their membership of the larger grouping. The fact that these people also live in housing, and that they might in fact go home at night to get away from a day entirely concerned with housing[1] appears to escape them.

Those who work in and comment on housing bracket out significant elements of their own housing, as being irrelevant and unrelated to their professional life of managing, building, commenting on and researching into housing. Is this about being objective, of getting away from the normative as Bo Bengtsson (1995) has suggested? Is it an attempt to rid themselves of any perceived personal bias? Or, more likely, is this business of living in housing seen as such a mundane activity, as so quotidian, that it is taken as having no intrinsic worth in itself?

But what if the reality about housing is the other way around? What if the actual living – the day-to-day use of our housing – is the important bit, but that housing professionals and commentators just have not yet had anything interesting to say on this? Their concentration on standards, aggregates, costs, access, targets, levels of provision and so on is just irrelevant to what is important for the vast majority of those in the second category. What if these housing experts actually go home at night, not to get away from housing, but like all the rest, to properly connect with it?

One common explanation for the professionals' view is that it matters more. There is a grave problem they have to face up to *now*. Professionals and commentators concentrate on imperatives and see anything else as a luxury, or worse, as a distraction. Their argument might run something like this: 'with limited time and resources we need to prioritise. We need to be useful, and not concern ourselves with abstractions and concepts that do not affect actual housing conditions'. The implication is that researchers should concentrate on something more practical, say homelessness, instead of abstract debates about meaning and how we live.

But if one wishes to use this reductive argument, why stop here? Instead of writing about homelessness, why not actually do something practical like run a soup kitchen, lobby Parliament, give money, etc.? But again, why stop there? Surely it is more useful still to manage housing, or even more, why not actually build the things, or give half your belongings away to someone who needs them more? What could be more useful than this? Why bother to write books at all when there are still people on the streets?

Reducing arguments to their basics can indeed be useful, but not always in the manner intended by the proponents of the argument. Quite properly we consider nothing could be more important than getting people out of shop doorways and subways and into decent housing. Yet why do we think this? Another naïve question certainly, but we only need to consider it for a moment before we begin to appreciate that we are returning to our initial question, and this time it is loaded with much more significance: 'who uses housing?' leads to 'why do they need to?' which goes straight to 'what happens if they don't?' and so we are back scouring the streets with our soup bowls and blankets! Perhaps what we need to appreciate is that 'naïve' and 'fundamental' are not opposites.

What we also need is a more considered view that asks what something is useful *for*? Theoretical studies of housing are useful precisely to those theoreticians interested in housing. This places no moral claim on others, but then nor does it place any claim of significance on the part of the theoreticians of housing. Ultimately something is useful if enough people think it is. But it is still only useful *for them*. In any case, persuading someone not to write theoretically will not inevitably lead to a different sort of book, more soup kitchens, or even any new houses built. All it will do would be to stop someone writing. To my mind, the important issue is that writing books does not prevent anyone from helping in a soup kitchen or any other sort of involvement in housing. Nor does running a soup kitchen prevent book writing.

So what matters more depends upon what we want and where we stand. Nothing demonstrates this more clearly than the relatively low political significance given to housing issues in most Western countries. Where housing is taken seriously and given attention by politicians and the media, it is not the homeless or social housing allocations that interest them, but house prices and owner-occupation. What appears to grab the attention is how affordable or profitable one's own house will be now and in the future. We can criticise this view, as I do throughout this book, but I think it does tell us something about housing and how it is viewed, and therefore that most commentators are missing the main point. What matters to most people is what they can do with their housing. The two important words here are 'do' and 'their'. The importance of housing is the manner in which it is used, and furthermore what is used is particular to that household. We can consider housing collectively, but at the level of use it is a personal matter.

There is an iconography attached to housing that transcends the manner in which professionals and commentators conduct their discourses. This iconography is of that place which is *mine* or *ours* (where the 'we' in question is a family or small band of intimates). This is housing in the subjective sense of 'a place of my/our own'. But this has nothing to do with tenure – this book is not another paean for home ownership. It is rather about the recognition that the important thing we seek is a condition of privacy, security and intimacy, and this can only be achieved by housing of our own, or rather by what I shall refer to as *dwelling*.

Therefore when considering housing we need to be aware that usefulness is use *for* something. And *that* something is not defined externally, or collectively, but individually within the dwelling. It follows then that if we are concerned with the subjective, then approaches that rely on the subjective might be the most appropriate. Indeed why should we expect traditional methods to help? What is needed here is a different approach for a different set of issues, one capable of giving naïve questions their full significance.

Writing about housing

But what approach would do to achieve this? What style would this involve and, crucially, would it be in any sense acceptable? I believe that such an approach is both possible and fruitful. This book seeks to explain and to use such an approach. However, what needs to be appreciated immediately is that its application would be quite specific and related only to certain types of analysis. Such an approach is relevant to describing housing at the personal level only and should not be seen as an alternative or competitor to other more traditional means of discussing housing.[2]

So then, what does this approach consist of? I would say it is essentially a style that centres on reflection of a self. Elijah Milgram talks of a style of philosophy based on the persona, which proceeds by rumination and reflection on the self rather than rigorous argument. He refers to this as 'the presentation of the philosophical self' (Milgram, 2002, p. 176). What we present, according to Robert Nozick (1989) is a portrait not a theory. We present a persona, or as Alexander Nehamas (1998) describes it, *a way of living*. We do not write of or about ourselves as such, but of a particular way of living out our lives. Like a portrait the correspondence to reality may not be exact, but rather it seeks to bring out the essence or elements of a character that are deemed significant. More specifically, it is where we describe the subjective philosophically, not as abstract ideas and concepts but as lived experience. This form of philosophising involves engaging with a form of life, with examining why we do the things we do, partly so that we can justify them, but also to allow us and others to understand what it is we have achieved. It is a form of thinking and discourse that is ideal for the consideration of meaning, of coming to terms with the fundamental significance of our subjectivity. We draw a picture to shed light on the way we live, and in so doing we express – or bring to light – the meanings we attach to that way of life.

This is a style of philosophy that has a long tradition, even if it now only forms a minority within the modern philosophical canon. Nehamas, however, argues that it is only relatively recently that philosophy has become theoretical, whereas the tradition of Socrates, the Stoics and others saw philosophy as essentially therapeutic – as clearing away the clutter and helping us to come to terms with the world around us *as it is*. Philosophy is not there to change us, so much as to help us understand our predicament – to see more clearly what is right there in front of us, and, of course, within us. It is to this style that Ludwig Wittgenstein (1953) sought to return philosophy by emphasising that it should not be about theory building, but an activity with the sole aim of describing the world as it appears. Importantly for Wittgenstein, this does not involve explaining and is certainly not concerned with transformation or change.[3]

The therapeutic approach when applied to how we use housing would provide us with examples of how we live and cope with our dwelling and the wider environment. These situations will frequently tend to be trivial and banal – we will not often be picking out the imperative cases – but then this is precisely what lived experience is like. It is not trauma and crisis, but mundane coping and quiet enjoyment (indeed we can see trauma and crisis as precisely where we cannot cope with the mundane and enjoy our privacy). What we should be concerned with is describing how we use the housing that we have (and, of course, what we want it for is to be calm and quiet). From these descriptions we might be able to posit some tentative understanding of the meaning that housing has as an artefact, an instrument and a series of relationships. When we have some understanding of how we live, we can then understand more fully the extent of the trauma and crisis that comes with the loss of our dwelling environments.

But there might be dangers in this approach. In particular, if we deliberately eschew some of the rigours of academic argument, can we expect to be taken seriously by other academics? Wittgenstein and others who wrote in this manner did not follow normal conventions, or even write in an academic style.[4] Wittgenstein's *Philosophical Investigations* is written in a broken text style as a series of (roughly) connected aphorisms, but with no attempt at argument, proof or refutation. Likewise, other exponents of this style, such as Emile Cioran (1998, 1999), write in an oblique aphoristic style that depends on analogy, metaphor, absurdity and exaggeration for its effect. Cioran's style is self-consciously literary with no pretensions towards science. So any studies on the private use of housing depending on this approach, even if they did not go as far as Cioran's approach, would not be based on general observation or be properly scientific. What they would depend on, as I do in this book, is insular reflection.

This leads to the obvious criticism that these reflections would merely be the thoughts and ideas of the author, with no merit or use beyond him or her. At one level this criticism is correct, and this book does not follow a scientific approach and has no pretensions as such. Many proponents of this approach would not see that as a criticism or a complaint, but almost as a compliment. Indeed, I believe seeing this style as a literary exercise is important at one particular level. The significance of good literature and drama is that it appears to us to be both meaningful and true. Indeed, it can sometimes be much more effective than the most weighty empirical study. So, to use the most hackneyed example, the 1960s television drama *Cathy Come Home* was far more influential than countless studies, reports and academic papers in highlighting the actuality of homelessness and poverty. This is because we can evince something personal from this fiction that strikes us as being true. Indeed, I would suggest that it is the very subjectivity – of a specific family breaking up and of a mother losing *her* children – that gives the film its huge emotive appeal and strength as a campaigning vehicle. This is the case even though we know that what we are watching is a fiction played by actors speaking words they have memorised. What is important here, I believe, is that we can link this fiction into our own experiences and imaginings – we can feel what losing the home and family we have might mean – and from that see the significance of the general issue.

We appreciate literature because of the acuity of its descriptions and the manner in which it puts across notions of meaning and significance. The biggest compliment we can give a work of fiction is that 'it is so true': to coin a phrase, 'it speaks to us of the human condition'. Thus what is important here is the reception the study has and not its theoretical and methodological rigour. Think of the manner in which novelists conjure up an image for us, for example, Céline's construction of the decadent and destructive domesticity of the Dutch pawnbroker, Titus Van Claben, in *Guignol's Band* (1954). Céline creates an image of sullied materials piled up amidst clutter and filth. Van Claben is described as 'a potbellied sneaky-looking hippo, stuck away in his filth and semi-darkness' (p. 144). He lived amidst 'mountains of junk' where 'Everything was itching to fall down' (p. 147). Céline describes Van Claben on his bed, helped by Delphine, his housekeeper:

> He never left his premises, never got undressed, he kept all his clothes on, his cloaks and his turban, he buried himself as is beneath the pile of sables,

sealskins, minks ... he slept with one eye, always worried about robbers ... Protected against drafts by the huge tapestried portiere, I still see the gigantic thing that cut the whole place in two, the 'Prodigal Son'...

He'd cough, sniffle, wheeze ... he was really going to catch cold ... He was sore at Delphine ... It was just about over ... The two or three big valleys of junk just about under control ... shakily stacked against the walls ... Delphine would shut the blinds, Titus would light the globe, his water-lamp ... poke at the Greco-Byzantine incense burner ... swinging from the ceiling ... when it sizzled, smoked hard, he'd take a deep sniff ... he was ready for business!

(Céline, 1954, p. 154)

This construction is evocative of decay and decadence, of a cynical venal old man living within piles of useless junk he is unable to part with. But his picture is also of an attachment to the dwelling, of an unbreakable bond with a place.

But what is interesting here is just how do we build on these images given to us by Céline? From Céline's words, put together as they are in snatches, as if they have just occurred to him, we develop a mental picture of our own, that has colour, dimension and scale; it has substance, in that the filth and decadence are very nearly palpable. From this we construct the scene: we visualise it in our mind's eye as a site that resonates with meaning. It is a scene of corruption and decadence, of darkness and decay.

We may not construct this site as Céline himself imagined (or experienced) it – and indeed others may imagine it differently – but it is recognisable as dwelling. Do we therefore carry within us some sense of material dwelling that allows us to put this picture together? This might be like an identikit photo, or more properly, because the image is not actually of any existing thing, a montage. We use the various parts of our experience of housing and our imagination: we draw on our own knowledge, perception and aspirations of dwelling in its varied forms. Yet the picture we derive – as is the case when we dream – is a *new picture*, which matches nothing we have actually experienced. We have created a new whole, something that goes beyond our experience and imagining. Thus, like the novelist, we too can create a new dwelling. This creation is not out of nothing, but is rather out of our own experience. We build on our own experiences of housing and from this create new unique images with the help of the author.

Jerome Bruner (2002) makes an interesting suggestion in his discussion of stories and their importance to us. Bruner suggests that a fictional narrative gives 'shape to things in the real world and often bestows on them a title to reality' (p. 8). Stories, as it were, 'create' a sense of reality by pulling together elements of our experience and imagination and giving them a palpable quality. He uses the example of Charles Dickens' creation of the character of Mr Macawber, who is now seen as the exemplar of a particular type of person. We all recognise elements of Macawber in others, and we thus find ourselves using a fiction to identify real psychology and social relations. Likewise, Céline's drawing of Titus Van Claben in his shabby clutter creates a model or archetype for us to recognise the reality of this form of existence.

Katherine Shonfield, in her book *Walls Have Feelings* (2000), uses fictions (mainly film, but also novels) to explore the architecture of cities. She suggests that a number of 'analytical possibilities exist in using fiction to decipher space' (p. 160). First, she suggests that we can often understand those realities that are ineffable and hidden from view through symbols and allegories. Following Walter Benjamin, she suggests that allegory can help us to subvert and 'penetrate through the received wisdom of the technical' (p. 160). Second, fictions present us with a narrative or story of how space is used. Space has a narrative effect that serves to develop the narrative itself. Fictions, such as the film *Panic Room* discussed in chapter 7, demonstrate how space can drive events, and this instrumental quality is palpable for us. The space can, in effect, be a character in the drama.

Third, Shonfield sees that fictions can present what she terms 'structural pattern'. We seek to put a pattern onto the 'disjunctive' nature of modern urban living, and in doing so we can transgress the standard perception of the use of space. Her view seems to be that we can suspend our disbelief when watching or reading fiction whilst retaining our knowledge that it is still a fiction. For the duration of a fiction we can believe it as absolutely true, but then know it to be false upon its completion. But, as a result, we are able to see that there are other possibilities beyond the technical solutions of experts:

> The transgressive role of fiction means both that, like feminism, it legitimates architectural and urban insights and experiences of the non-expert (as manifest in films and novels), and that specialist knowledge itself is subjected to a wider structure than its own self-validating technical terms. This allows fictional insight to be considered on the same terms as the insights of the non-expert.
>
> (Shonfield, 2000, p. 161)

For Shonfield, fiction offers the possibility of opening up professional and technical discourses to a wider appreciation. This has possibilities to subvert the pieties of professionals, but it also offers much to professionals themselves.

She holds that 'culture at large evidences an untapped spatial and architectural understanding', and that 'The site of this understanding is in its fictions' (p. 173). What such an understanding would allow for is a debunking of the notion that professionals have a "superior" comprehension' (p. 173), but would also show that this technical aesthetic too has fictional origins.

So we have much to gain from looking at housing, or dwelling, in a subjective manner. This then is my starting point: that housing is best understood as a personal entity, based around particular narratives. What I want to do then is take up Bo Bengtsson's point about the neglect of the normative, and radically extend it to consider housing as something deeply personal. As a result this book is episodic and does not attempt to give a complete picture of dwelling. It is fragmentary and at times allusive. Some of the comments are based on personal experiences, simply because there is no other source that can deal with the personal experience of housing. The book also uses what might be seen as non-conventional approaches, or ones that are not common to housing research. However, we only have to look at the growing influence of thinkers such as Slavoj Žižek (1999, 2000, 2001) to see that this approach is quite acceptable in philosophy and social theory. The use of film criticism, anecdote and speculation is more common here and seen as offering insights that traditional methods cannot offer. This is not, to reiterate, an attempt to provide an alternative, or suggest that these older methods are redundant. Rather this is a different approach to what is a different subject matter. Of course, others have written on discourse in housing, and on the nature of the home from various perspectives. My aim is not to suggest this work is of no significance, or even that my work should supersede it. Instead, what I am suggesting is that this book takes an original approach that considers the subjective use of housing through subjective means. Whether this is itself significant is for others to determine. All I have done is to present my views as persuasively, engagingly and imaginatively as I can.

What we are looking at

The speculations in this book are not presented as a complete survey, nor do they have any particular narrative flow. Apart from chapter 1 defining dwelling, the rest could pretty much be read in any order. This, however, is not intended as some too-clever-by-half attempt at postmodern irony. But rather it strikes me as virtually impossible to write a compendious description of dwelling and keep it to manageable proportions. I have therefore just looked at those parts of dwelling that interest me particularly. These were the things that occurred to me as I considered what dwelling meant. Inevitably this was what dwelling meant to *me*. So this is very much a subjective coverage of the use of housing, and is intended so to be.

Chapter 1 develops a definition of dwelling, differentiating it from both the notions of 'house' and 'home'. We need to know what meaning housing has as a subjective entity. This can best be explained by exploring the phenomenology of dwelling. This approach relies on the thought of Gaston Bachelard, Martin Heidegger and Christian Norberg-Schulz who have all sought to place the search for meaning at the centre of their discourses on space, building and architecture. Out of this thought we will arrive at a definition of private dwelling that does not ignore the social significance of living within communities, but which stresses the significance of dwelling as a subjective experience. Chapter 2 considers the nature of privacy and the possibilities it offers to households, as well as the limitations to privacy. Privacy is distinguished from isolation: how is it that we can be alone in a crowd, yet harassed by someone we never see? How can dwelling protect us from intrusion, but what are the pitfalls of separation? This chapter will emphasise the importance of security and intimacy as the key purposes of private dwelling.

Chapter 3 looks at the physical, ontological and emotional structures of dwelling. Beginning with Walter Benjamin's description of the dwelling as akin to a compass case lined with velvet, the nature of the dwelling as a physical structure and series of mechanisms will be explored. Three things are dealt with here: first, how the dwelling is a receptacle that both encloses and enframes households; second, that the proper function of the dwelling is to ensure complacency so we can set about achieving our ends and interests; and third, that the dwelling should also allow for a stable existence. The consequences of dwelling not fulfilling these three functions are considered. The discussion centres on whether dwelling is more than a physical structure, and if so, what functions it has.

The manner in which we discuss housing is important, and this issue is turned to in chapter 4. What do we mean when we use terms such as 'home' or 'quiet enjoyment', or phrases such as 'make yourself at home'? Accordingly, I consider the ways in which dwelling is described and what are the implicit and explicit meanings attached to these statements. An important element is the way in which language is built on conventions, which in turn can be further substantiated by language. How this ordinary language approach links into housing discourse is also touched upon.

In understanding the private nature of dwelling, we need also to consider how we share it with others. Many of us live alone, but even more of us live with others. But even single-person households have to relate to others, be they neighbours or the wider community. Accordingly chapter 5 looks at sharing, learning and protecting. Dwelling is where we live with others, and of particular importance are the relations between parents and children. Children are socialised and learn within the dwelling. We are able to experience intimacy as a secure bond because of dwelling. Sharing also draws out the limits of privacy and therefore we need to understand how our responsibilities to others impinge on our personal autonomy. This chapter will consider the growing presence in our dwellings of the Internet and the ability we have to use our privacy to exclude others, but also to exploit them. The manner in which we share much whilst remaining apart will be considered, particularly with relation to television. The crucial concept here is that we experience shared interests in private.

We need a dwelling, but it is also something that we desire. Accordingly I turn to this issue in chapter 6. Dwelling is both a site of desire, and something we desire in itself. The privacy of dwelling allows us to dream and fantasise in relative security and freedom. It also allows us to exercise our desires by providing us with private space. Yet we also desire that our dwelling represent something to others, in terms of status and as a commodity. Therefore the role of commodification, ownership and consumption needs to be considered in terms of how it impacts on authentic use of dwelling. Furthermore we desire dwelling itself. So dwelling can be an object of desire as well as a site for its fulfilment. It can also protect us when we fall short of our desires. This chapter questions the connection of desire with transformation made by post-structural thinkers and argues that dwelling can be seen as sanctuary from desiring, but also where desiring is safe. But dwelling is also a site of anxiety. This is explored in chapter 7, initially by a discussion of David Fincher's film, *Panic Room*. This allows us to deal with issues such as invasion, protection, security and the impotence of domesticity in the face of extreme threats. The chapter then considers more mundane anxieties associated with dwelling based around conventions of décor and status. But dwelling can be seen as offering security and therefore as where we hold off anxiety. How children view their dwelling is again considered here. Dwelling, it will be shown, can both assuage anxiety, as well as being the cause of it.

Dwelling is where we can share and be intimate with those we love, but this means that the stakes are high. What becomes of us and our dwelling when we lose those we love? What role is played by dwelling in helping come to terms with this loss? These issues are considered in chapter 8, using Krzysztof

Kieślowski's film *Three Colours: Blue*, C. S. Lewis' autobiographical fragment *A Grief Observed* as well as my own experiences of loss. It looks at how dwelling is de-animated by loss, and this may lead us to withdraw from the world around us. How we deal with loss and what role dwelling can play in this is considered here. Loss shows both the implacability and neutrality of dwelling by making manifest the importance of meaning within the dwelling environment. Accordingly the implication of losing the dwelling itself is commented upon.

In the conclusion to this book I make some attempt to draw these speculations together. I try to suggest what it is that dwelling does for us, but also consider the negative aspects. I shall stress that what we need dwelling for is to conserve and protect our intimacy. To do this we have to stop. Dwelling is what I refer to as *the stopping place*, where we fill up on memories. In this sense, dwelling is not concerned with transformation, be it social or personal, nor is it merely a concern with consumption. Dwelling is both unique to us – it is always *mine* – and ubiquitous, in that we all do it. Thus my closing comment is that this offers an alternative prospect for social solidarity: what we have in common is that we all dwell.

What will quickly become apparent is that the aspects I have covered overlap somewhat. At times it has been an almost arbitrary decision to put certain issues into certain chapters. So, despite having a chapter on language and conventions, these issues are also considered in the chapters on dwelling and sharing. The only way of avoiding this would have been to include some rather large and amorphous chapters. But this also indicates the problem of developing a particular narrative flow in this book: this is a story with no middle or end, but perhaps merely a series of beginnings. The result then is a series of speculations that operate rather like Edmund Husserl's concept of the lifeworld referred to throughout the book: a series of overlapping circles, rippling out, some subsuming others and forming larger waves, whilst others move further apart (Husserl, 1970). This book then is very much like that: a series of speculations that overlap, reinforce each other and support or at other times clash with each other. However, the whole is, I hope, effective and offers some clarity to the issue of how we live privately, usefully and meaningfully in our little brick boxes.

Chapter 1
What is dwelling?

Ambiguity on purpose

Dwelling is a nebulous concept. It is one of those words we use in different ways, and to mean different things. We can talk of *a* dwelling or *these* dwellings, but also of the *act* of dwelling: we can talk of things and of actions. It is a word with a long history: Parliament passed several acts in the nineteenth century dealing with dwelling houses for the poor. It has a distinct biblical context: Yahweh, the God of the Old Testament, dwelt in the Ark of the Covenant and later in the Temple in Jerusalem. The word is also used in a technical sense, to define a residential property.[1] There is then a difficulty in defining a word that is used in so many different ways.

Yet this very ambiguity might be useful to us. First, it points to the ubiquity of the thing underlying the concept: dwelling might be important if it is found so frequently in different contexts. Second, it might allow us to connect up what would otherwise be seen as incongruent areas, such as the theological with the architectural. As we shall see throughout this book, we need a concept that allows us to draw from many areas, as this is precisely how we lead our lives. We are concerned at times with matters theological and at other times with the plumbing. This may appear flippant, yet our lives do shift from the mundane to the sublime, and we need both a receptacle and a conceptual frame in which to unite them. Third, a lack of precision allows different meanings and emphases to be elided together into something that still retains some general meaning. So it is useful to say that we all dwell, yet our particular dwellings differ markedly. Modern Europeans live differently from Bedouins, and from our ancestors a thousand years ago; I do things differently from my neighbour, and my wife does things differently from me. This is just as it should be. Yet we are all doing, at the most general level, the same thing. Dwelling allows this generality to be said.

What is fascinating about dwelling is not just its ambiguity, but the fact that it operates between two poles – the ubiquitous and the specific: the mundane and the unique. Dwelling is something we all experience, but it is not something that we necessarily experience together. For each of us dwelling is unique, in that it is something we do by and for ourselves. We all dwell, but each of us does it separately.

It is this ambiguity that I am most interested in and wish to explore in these speculations. However, I wish to be somewhat narrower in my discussions than the concept of dwelling would otherwise allow. Whilst I shall offer a fuller definition of dwelling in this chapter, this is only to give full resonance to the term and to put my main topic into focus. My priority is to consider how we dwell privately, and hence I am particularly concerned in this apparent dichotomy between the mundane and the unique: between the fact that dwelling is something we all do, and the counter fact that how I experience dwelling is different from how others experience it, including to an extent those with whom I share my dwelling. What I wish to consider then are two key epistemological questions to do with dwelling. First, how do we *respond* to the physical box we call the dwelling? In others words, what is the relationship with the physical entity of a dwelling? The second question is, how do we *regard* this relationship: what significance do we give to it, and in what sense or senses does it transcend the physical? In short, why it is so important to us on a number of levels?

Yet, answers to questions such as these that can be framed in different ways, and which themselves depend on other questions, are likely to prove illusive, and such an illustration is offered in a wonderful quote in David Schmidtz's book on Robert Nozick. He is discussing the idea of philosophy as persona in relation to Nozick's frequently misunderstood book, *The Examined Life* (1989). Schmidtz states that 'Life is a house. Meaning is what you do to make it a home' (Schmidtz, 2002, p. 212). This simple statement, which does not quite veer into sentimentality, makes clear the distinction between objects and subjects: between things that allow us to do and be, and doing and being itself. But this quote is also useful for connecting dwelling with a more general sense of how we live. We seek to do meaningful things and most things are meaningful because of what we do. Dwelling is that activity that contains this meaning, but what we do it in is a dwelling.

Yet, we need to remember that policy makers and professionals do not talk about dwellings, nor do they concern themselves any more with housing: they are concerned with *homes*. Both private developers and social landlords build homes and not houses; for them there is only one level, with any nuance between dwelling, house and home occluded into the one entity.

But the problem goes deeper. Not only is it one of misdescription, but also it ignores that the full functions and uses of dwelling cannot be created by housing policy. Policy can only achieve the basics – the brick boxes – and even there it may fail. Indeed it is hard to see what role any public agency can play other than to provide enough brick boxes and ensure people can afford them. Of course this is not a particularly negligible role – we can do little unless the dwellings are there first – but it is still a *limited* one. The problem is that politicians, policy-makers and practitioners either do not appreciate this or simply refuse to accept it.

But there is a further thing they refuse to accept: that dwelling can actually be impeded by policy. This is usually a result of the introduction of policy into areas where it is not applicable, where housing practitioners are not, and cannot be, expert. This is the level of relationships within and outside the dwelling: with how we use our housing. Outside interference will either be arbitrary, based on the whim of the person intervening, or overly standardised, as a result of a general policy. But it can be no other: there is no possibility of policy or even an individual practice being so fine-grained as to actually articulate the varied needs and choices of all, or even many, households. Housing policy should then restrict itself to the provision of brick boxes and leave what goes on inside them to the users.

Housing policy does not, because it cannot, engage with *how* we live. There is little it can do about how we use housing, without destroying that use through its interventions. Rather policy should be concerned merely with the 'what' and the 'where': with production and standards, access and control. These are important issues, but there is something equally important missing from the totality of housing as a practice. This gap is to do with the subjective – with the individualised, personal relationships that *we* have with *our* dwelling. Once a dwelling has been built it remains a mere thing. Only when it is occupied does it take on a meaning and significance beyond this physical structure: only then, so to speak, does the house become meaningfully a home.

But just what is it that our housing does for us? What functions does it perform? What does it allow us to do? Now most assuredly, these are questions capable of a glib response. Houses are for living in, aren't they? They provide shelter and security. We might suggest that housing is related to status and social value, and thus we can use tenure and style (detached or semi-detached, terrace or mews, single or double garage, and so on) as measures of success. Like all glib answers, these contain within them an element of common sense and speak at least a partial truth. So, of course, houses are for living in; they do help to make us secure and safe.[2] But glibness will only take us so far. Our relations with and within our housing are complex and multi-dimensional.

What is more, these relationships differ from person to person. Therefore glib answers, because they seek an instant judgement, miss many of the nuances and subtleties of our lived experiences within dwellings. One can submit to glibness because of the very ubiquity of dwelling – we all do it and we all know what it does or ought to consist of. Yet the superficiality of our scepticism is evident as soon as we start to consider what it actually is that we do. It is the very subjectivity of this common relationship, with its self-generated aims and interests, that brings us up sharply against a dilemma.

What is needed therefore is a more considered answering of the basic questions concerning the use of housing and its significance. What we need is some mechanism whereby we can unpick the complexities of dwelling as a subjective experience. This can be achieved, I believe, through a consideration of descriptions of dwelling and the use of these descriptions in particular situations. What is sought, therefore, are those universal notions of significance common to all dwellings that can be derived from a close analysis of lived experience, to draw out the *concepts* upon which the significance of housing is made manifest. These studies need to be specifically based on actual activities within dwelling. As such, we need to consider concepts such as privacy, sharing, the way we describe and discuss where and how we live, our desires for it and within it, and the anxieties that go along with possession and yearning. This is what these speculations seek to explore, not in any definitive or prescriptive manner, but to open up dwelling as a place of possibility and enquiry free from the dictates of policy and practice. But first, dwelling needs to be defined more fully. A precise definition is neither possible nor wanted – it would limit possibilities – but we do need to be clearer about what it is we are describing.

The phenomenology of dwelling

Housing is more that mere possession. It facilitates or restricts access to employment, family, leisure, and the community at large. This is partly a question of affordability and location, but it also relates to notions of identity, security and the significance of place. What determines how we view housing, therefore, is how we dwell. This shows immediately that there is a distinction between housing and dwelling. Indeed housing, properly speaking, is a subset of dwelling. Dwelling encloses housing, but much more besides. But this is to get ahead of ourselves. We need first to look at these two notions at a more basic level.

Both the terms are ambiguous, partly because they can be used as a noun and a verb. However, there is a distinct qualitative difference between the two terms. Housing, as a noun or verb, cannot be separated from the physical structures called houses. It is, of course, the collective noun for these entities. But even the activity of housing is limited to management and control of these physical structures. However, we can see dwelling as meaning far more than the general physical space meant for personal accommodation. To dwell means to live on the earth and can refer to diverse activities such as human settlement, the domestication and taming of nature, and the creation of permanent social and political structures (markets and urban space) as well as the private inhabitation of space (Norberg-Schulz, 1985). Tim Putnam (1999, p. 144) believes 'Dwelling is at the core of how people situate themselves in the world'. Dwelling is where human beings inhabit space in the broadest sense. It collects up physical and broad sociological factors but also those psychological, ontological and emotional resonances we experience within the context of our personal physical space.

But we need to make a further distinction between the two terms. Inasmuch as housing relates to, and is inseparable from, physical objects, many of the concepts we connect with our dwelling, such as privacy, security and intimacy, are intangibles. These are not things we can touch, but we experience them, as it were, as by-products of the relationship between our dwelling and ourselves. It is not the dwelling that gives us these things of itself, but the manner in which we are able to use it and how it relates to a wider series of meanings.

Dwelling has a public and a private dimension. Christian Norberg-Schulz (1985) makes this distinction by differentiating the public dwelling of institutions and public buildings and the private dwelling of the individual house. Likewise, he recognises that the process is undertaken by the community at large and the individual household. Such a distinction is derived from the later thought of Martin Heidegger, in particular his essay 'Building, Dwelling, Thinking' (1971). In this essay Heidegger equates dwelling with building: for humans to dwell means they build structures for themselves. In turn, he defines building, through its etymological roots in Old English and German, as related to the verb 'to remain' or 'to stay in place' (p. 146). Dwelling as building is thus more than just mere shelter, but is a reference to the settlement by human beings on the earth. Indeed for Heidegger, dwelling is humanity's 'being on the earth' (p. 147). Heidegger is prepared to see dwelling in the broadest sense, as human settlement in general. Dwelling is the house, the village, the town, the city and the nation in their generality – it is of humanity taking root in the soil.

Norberg-Schulz takes Heidegger's phenomenological approach and extends it into a discussion of the meaning and nature of dwelling which is both more thorough and less metaphysical than Heidegger's description. According to Norberg-Schulz, dwelling refers to spaces and places, both in terms of how they are used and what this use means to individuals and communities. Dwelling, he suggests, means three things. First, it involves meeting others for the exchange of products, ideas and feelings, where we experience life as a multitude of possibilities. Second, dwelling means to accept a set of common values. It is through this that we can share. We dwell through establishing and operating conventions. Third, it is to be ourselves, where we have a small chosen world of our own: it is our private place where we can withdraw from the wider world. These three meanings are, of course, interrelated. We are able to be ourselves through the security of a common bond within a community of like individuals able to freely meet and exchange. Norberg-Schulz recognises this when he states that, 'When dwelling is accomplished our wish for belonging and participation is fulfilled' (1985, p. 7). Thus an important linkage between the public and the private is enacted through dwelling. The security of dwelling gives us the ability to participate within the community. Dwelling identifies the individual with the community, using place as the reference: 'The particular place is part of the identity of each individual and since the place belongs to a type, one's identity is also general' (p. 9). In stressing this linkage between the public and the private Norberg-Schulz is recognising the crucial sense of dwelling whereby we are

Dwelling consists of a series of connections, a mix of public and private space

part of a place and that place is part of us. He goes on to define four modes of dwelling which show the extensive nature of this concept (see Table 1.1).

First, he describes the idea of 'settlement'. This is the mode of 'natural dwelling', where humans develop, use and exploit the natural environment. We can equate this to the process of the domestication of nature and its subsequent development as a predeterminant of stable civilisations (Hodder, 1990). Accordingly, we can add the domestication of nature to the three meanings already stated by Norberg-Schulz. Second, he describes the mode of 'collective dwelling', where human interaction takes place in the medium of urban space. This is where the first meaning of dwelling is fulfilled, as people interact to exchange products, ideas and feelings in towns and cities. Third, Norberg-Schulz defines the mode of 'public dwelling'. This is the forum where the common values, as articulated in his second meaning of dwelling, are expressed and kept. He identifies this mode of dwelling with the institution, be it political, social or cultural. Finally, he defines the mode of 'private dwelling', as exemplified by the house. This is where we are able to be ourselves. It is 'a "refuge" where man gathers and expresses those memories which make up his personal world' (p. 13). This, then, is where we can withdraw from the world to define and develop our own identity. Norberg-Schulz's conceptualisation of dwelling is able to encompass historical, philosophical, psychological and social dimensions. In so doing, he demonstrates the nature of the 'belonging and participation' which dwelling brings. He shows how dwelling is the security (private dwelling) to participate in, and withdraw from, a stable agreed culture (public dwelling) where social interaction (collective dwelling) is facilitated within, and co-determined by, our environment (natural dwelling).

Table 1.1 A taxonomy of dwelling

Mode of	Built form	Meaning
Natural	Settlement	Domestication of nature
Collective	Urban space	Exchange and social intercourse and interaction
Public	Institution	Common values
Private	House	Withdrawal and definng of identity

Norberg-Schulz goes on to consider the meaning that dwelling gives, and is given by, the individual and the community. He does this through the articulation of two concepts, *identification* and *orientation*. Identification is to experience a 'total' environment – where the four modes considered above are present – as meaningful for what it is. He is here associating dwelling with the phenomenological concept of the *lifeworld*. This concept, as initially defined by Edmund Husserl (1970), refers to the meaningful world of things into which individuals are born. Husserl suggested that the lifeworld can be seen as a series of overlapping circles, beginning with the *homeworld*, and rippling out into the social world. The lifeworld then consists of those things that surround each person, yet are implicitly accepted without conscious thought. David Pepper (1984) defines the lifeworld as the world of familiar ideas, experiences and objects, like the furniture, 'on which we do not consciously bring to bear our thought processes but in whose sudden absence we could feel disturbed, as if something were wrong' (p. 120). We only recognise this lifeworld by thinking 'consciously and descriptively about things we do not usually think of in this way in order to bring them from the back to the forefront of cognition, and make explicit what was implicit' (p. 120). Short of their absence then, we must actively strive to recognise their significance; we identify with them only implicitly through their taken-for-granted presence. Pepper goes on however, 'And since the "lifeworld" is a personal thing, varying from individual to individual, we cannot induce law-like statements about it' (p. 120).

The notion of the lifeworld, and of identification, relates to Heidegger's notion of things as being *ready-to-hand* (Heidegger, 1962). This is where a thing is transparent to consciousness provided it fulfils its prescribed function. The thing is *equipment*, an extension of the person using it, and thus unnoticed as *present-to-hand*, as a substance with distinct properties. The things which form our lifeworld therefore are equipment ready-to-hand. Only once there is a problem with them, so that they are *unready-to-hand*, do we become conscious of these things as present-to-hand, short of a conscious deliberate act of abstract thought to focus upon these things. We use the things around us as extensions of ourselves and not consciously as distinct entities separate from ourselves.

Heidegger makes use of the lifeworld concept in 'Building, Dwelling, Thinking' (1971), when he states that dwelling 'remains for man's everyday experience that which is from the outset "habitual" ... For this it recedes behind the manifold ways in which dwelling is accomplished' (p. 147). Heidegger sees dwelling as habitual. It is the implicit, familiar, seemingly unchanging routine of habit. But more than this, it is hidden from consciousness behind the varied ways in which it is undertaken and achieved. Our everyday experience – which is of dwelling on the earth – hides the significance of dwelling. We are too busy dwelling – concentrating on those matters close to us – to see the full significance of what these very acts enclose.

This lack of cognisance of what we are doing is of itself interesting. Is the fact that we seldom ruminate (I could say dwell!) on our dwelling, and on how we live, a sign of its triviality or of its importance? If something is important to us then we might expect it to bear heavily upon us and involve us in some form of cogitation and decision making. Those things that are trivial we can readily cast off without much, if any, thought. In contrast, that which is important to us will bear heavily on our consciousness. But if the notion of the lifeworld has any merit, this would not appear to be the case. Something can be of crucial importance, but without being noticed particularly as such. Of course, this is all based on the supposition that triviality and importance are necessarily opposites. Yet this is clearly not the case: we consider many things we have as trivial – good health, a job, a full stomach – until they disappear. It is only then that we appreciate their significance. Perhaps we should say that we seldom dwell on dwelling because it is *both* trivial and important. It needs to be there for us to live well, but it also needs to be in the background and be mundane and uninteresting, so that we can pursue our aims and interests: so we can undertake those things beyond the everyday. Perhaps then the real virtue of dwelling is that it releases us from subsistence: from an existence based around its own maintenance.[3]

The significance of the lifeworld, and thus identification, for Norberg-Schulz is that these things give meaning to our surroundings. They allow us to identify with the world, but in an implicit, non-conscious manner. He states that identity consists of an 'interiorisation of understood things' (1985, p. 20). Things are understood by their implicit use, and give meaning by linking individuals to the world around them. Things are then an extension of a person, having been interiorised, or to put it otherwise, these things are personalised. According to this reasoning, human beings identify with the house, institutions, the city, the nation, nature, and so on because of their embodiment of 'existential meanings' (p. 19). They imbue one with a sense of belonging that Norberg-Schulz sees as being ontologically necessary. This belonging is derived from the house, for instance, being in the implicit relation of equipment ready-to-hand. It is what it does, or allows one to do – the process of *gathering in* meaning, to speak in Heideggerian terms – rather than what it is that is important.

Norberg-Schulz's concept of identification is complemented by that of *orientation*, which is concerned with exteriorisation into things and into places, rather than interiorisation. Orientation 'implies structuring the environment into domains by paths and centres' (p. 21). It is the aspect of dwelling that deals with the 'spatial interrelationship' (p. 15) within dwelling. He states that we need to orientate ourselves within a space constituted by things. It is where we have known pathways outwards from this centre into the world. The centre 'represents what is known, in contrast to the unknown and perhaps frightening world around' (p. 22). The dwelling then can be seen as the centre of our personal life. It is what acts as the focus, and the secure footing, from which we set forth into the world. The institution is likewise the centre of our civic life, where we are 'somewhere as somebody' (p. 51). In this case, it is the place which makes our life visible to others. Orientation is thus the sphere of dwelling that locates us in a place, giving us a focus. Yet it is also where we have well-worn routes from the personal – our dwelling – into institutions, the city and the natural environment. These paths are a focus of architectural significance, but are also existential routes where the personal links into the public. So we are not conditioned by things and structures but by the meanings we give to them. Norberg-Schulz argues that humans may be conditioned by a place, but this is because of how they identify and orientate towards that place, not because of its particular physical structure. What matters is how we identify with our dwelling as a meaningful thing and how it acts as the central point from which we set forth into the world.

Private dwelling

We have seen how our private dwelling is connected up to the social world and how it is necessary for us to have this homeworld in order for us to be able to orientate and identify with institutions and with other human beings. But what of private dwelling itself? Does it offer us more than connection to the social? Norberg-Schulz sees the house as the place of familiarity, where life is implicit and habitual: 'In the house man becomes familiar with the world in its immediacy; there he does not have to choose a path and find a goal, in the house and next to the house the world is simply given' (1985, p. 89). This is a place where we are accepted and accepting, where we have a measure of control over our environment. We are able, to an extent, to put down or ignore any social role or responsibility we may have. The confines of the home can be seen as liberating, in that they separate us from the public sphere. We are individuated by having this personal space. As Norberg-Schulz states, 'Personal identity, thus, is the content of private dwelling' (p. 89). Having this personal identity allows us to face up to the surrounding world. It offers us security in our location in the public domain. One is orientated, centred by personal space, it being one circle of the lifeworld, contiguous with, but separate from, all others.

However, the house also offers a retreat from the world, where one can disengage from the limitations imposed by fitting into a community. This withdrawal, though, signifies not isolation but intimacy. We are not able to obtain this intimacy in the public sphere, and nor would we want it. It is rather only in the privacy of the household, where our commitments are not mitigated by a diversity of public roles and obligations, that we can share in intimate relations with those we choose to be close to. Relations within the private sphere can therefore be characterised by love and care, rather than contract or civic obligation as in the public sphere. Our private relations are based on implicit voluntary commitments, as opposed to legal or formal conjunctions. So not only is there a physical division between the private and the public, but also a social and psychological separation in the sense of our relation to such space.

According to Norberg-Schulz, then, the private dwelling offers both security and identity. These notions are also addressed by Gaston Bachelard in his book, *The Poetics of Space* (1969). Bachelard, using both the techniques of phenomenology and Jungian psychology, develops the concept of dwelling by association with the notion of 'protected intimacy' (p. 3). This is to see the house as a refuge and as a stock of memories and images which are important to individuals. For Bachelard 'our house is our corner of the world' (p. 4). In phenomenological terms, Bachelard believes that the essential point when considering a dwelling is to, 'seize upon the germ of the essential, sure, immediate well-being it encloses' (p. 4). The private dwelling offers security and protection that gives us a sense of well-being. Thus it is what the dwelling does, and what it means in so doing, that is significant. Its intrinsic value is in the relationship of the household with the house. It is our residence in that dwelling that gives it its meaning. This meaning may be implicit, hidden by the habitual nature of the relationship, and thus only perceived – that is, as present-to-hand – when it is not possible to fulfil it. However, it is this relationship that differentiates the structure of a particular building and the home it may become, for as Bachelard states, 'all really inhabited space bears the essence of the notion of home' (p. 5).

Bachelard states that households experience their house in a particular way. It is not experienced in a narrative or a linear way, in the sense of what the house is, or was, has been, or may still be. It is not seen in terms of the history of the experiences within it. It is rather experienced in a cumulative way, as an ever increasing stock of images and memories. What is significant is what the house means because of what it allows us to relive, thus giving security: 'We comfort ourselves by reliving memories of protection' (p. 6). These images and memories also offer us a sense of continuity. This sense may be illusory or real, but within the confines of private space it is itself unbounded. Even the illusion of stability is significant, as it still centres the individual for as long as the illusion holds. Bachelard believes that the house serves this purpose: 'In the life of a man, the house thrusts aside contingencies, its councils of continuity are unceasing. Without it man would be a dispersed being' (pp. 6–7).

These notions of intimacy and protection from the public world are related together in Bachelard's description of *the refuge*. Bachelard defines this notion as being founded in the existential need for shelter. The house is 'a major zone of protection' (p. 31), that offers shelter from hunger and cold, that allows for well-being. But, well-being is more than physical survival. The house also provides for psychological and emotional well-being. Bachelard goes so far as to describe the house as a 'psychic state' (p. 72) that bespeaks intimacy. The house then is more than a physical structure, yet this does not detract from its significance. Indeed this significance comes precisely when the concept is developed from a 'geometric object' or a physical structure, into 'space that is supposed to condone and defend intimacy' (p. 48).

So, the importance of the dwelling is its meaning in the phenomenological sense, of that which is brought to consciousness. This presents itself as a universal, existential need, but because it is a need for intimacy, and the security necessary for intimacy, it is very much personalised. Private dwelling is also personal dwelling, where dwelling is individuated, whilst still remaining a common experience.

Transformation and tranquillity

But we need to consider another facet of dwelling. We have intimated, through the introduction of notions such as intimacy, security, orientation and identification, the sense in which dwelling connotes stability, a lack of change. It is this sense of dwelling that we need now to draw out more fully. It is an unfortunate trend amongst many writers on subjectivity to be seemingly obsessed with transformation or with transcending the current situation:[4] they are determined to change what we are. Why is this? Is it not difficult enough to understand subjectivity without trying to change it as well?

The problem, I would suggest, is an ideological one, and rests on the fallacy of applying a pre-existing theoretical model onto the item under study.

Private dwelling is a place of comfort, known only to us

The researcher arrives with his/her theoretical cloth already cut and then uses this to address the issue of subjectivity. In a sense then they already know the answer they require from the situation. But this is tantamount to saying that 'we may not know what subjectivity is now, but we know what we want it to be'. The transformation then becomes more important than subjectivity itself. This is precisely because one does not need to be concerned with what subjectivity actually is, merely with what it ought or ought not to be.

But this is precisely the process that Ludwig Wittgenstein (1953) warned against: how can we transcend or transform what we cannot understand, and therefore not even describe fully? Wittgenstein was adamant that what philosophers (and other researchers) should be involved in is *description*. Rather than seeking to change anything we should rather limit ourselves to representing what is actually there and then leaving it as it is.[5] However, ignoring this view, the 'transformers' seek to apply a rigid template onto subjective experiences that they do not yet fully understand. They can only see the problem in one particular way, and thus what they are really doing is converting the subjective into an objective condition upon which they can generalise.

One of the faults of academic study is to seek unity. This is first the belief that a complete answer or explanation is possible and then to strive to achieve it. It is thought that we can completely encapsulate an issue and consider it fully. If we have not achieved this yet, this is not a result of any fundamental epistemological problem but merely a matter of time and ongoing theoretical development.[6] Part of this ambition derives from a belief in rationality and logic: that we can construct a clear, precise and definitive argument that encloses the important aspects of the problem or issue, and then present some form of resolution. The aim is to pre-empt the unintended and ensure greater predictability. This according to the Popperian view of social science is the very purpose of enquiry (Popper, 1989).[7]

In short, the problem is one of *systematisation*. We believe that through the development of explanations we can define, codify and contain the phenomena under study. We can excavate the underlying structures or draw a suitably accurate map that reduces the problem to a contained system which we are then able to understand.

Yet what does this achieve, particularly in the case of private experience? Systematisation implies that boundaries and rigid rules are both possible and can be precisely stated. But reality is not nearly so precisely defined and bounded. We use terms and concepts and operate according to rules even where these are not clearly or precisely stated. Yet we still know what we mean and others (apparently) can understand us. We readily use phrases such as 'over there' and expect others to understand us: more specific to housing, we use words such as 'dwelling', 'home' and 'household' which we know are immune to precise definition (Kemeny, 1992). There are conventions which apply even without the pure specificity of logical propositions. As J. L. Austin asks, 'why if there are nineteen of anything, is it not philosophy?' (quoted in Stroll (2000), p. 166). Austin's point, which applies beyond philosophy, is to question why thinkers seek to base their arguments around a dichotomy or just consider one aspect of a problem and ignore the rest. Why do we assume that scientific enquiry should involve a simple 'either/or' and not be a complex mix and match? Why do we insist that life must be tidy?

I would suggest that this applies particularly when we discuss our experiences of housing, which are dominated by the subjective, the habitual and the tacit. Why then should we expect to understand this complexity through systematicity? Might we not achieve more through piecemeal description that picks out the manner in which housing is actually used, rather than seeking to enforce patterns and regularities on what are disparate activities? This relates to Ludwig Wittgenstein's conception of *philosophical description*

(Wittgenstein, 1953). Following Wittgenstein's philosophy we can argue that we know sufficiently well what housing means in order to use it without undue ambiguity *and without system.*

Wittgenstein's style of philosophy suggests that we should 'do it' rather than concentrate overly on how, or what, we are doing. But how is it possible to do this in housing research? Following Wittgenstein's method would involve a close description of what we actually do and say with regard to housing: to describe how we live and how we use our housing. Wittgenstein argues that we should not be concerned with explanation of anything, but rather with reminding ourselves of what is actually already open to view. The ultimate aim – if this is the correct phrase here – is to leave everything exactly as it is. So, according to Wittgenstein, we should not try to build a model or conceptualise, just describe what is actually going on.

The key concept in appreciating Wittgenstein's method is that of the 'game'. He uses this consistently as a metaphor or analogy to help understand ordinary language and everyday social relations. According to Wittgenstein, games are not bound by hard and fast rules or rigid forms of identification, but by what he terms a 'family resemblance'. Games form a family with common associations, with overlaps and commonalities, but along with important differences. Some games will look totally different (compare chess and rugby), yet have common features with others (winners and losers, skill, chance, conflict and its resolution, and so on). Thus, inasmuch as one can recognise members of the same family, one can recognise common features of games.

This idea of a family resemblance offers a way into looking at the use of housing. Housing differs in several important specifics when we compare cultures, classes, even individual households. Yet there are areas of common reference, of shared features, just as members of a family share traits such as hair colour, build, shape of nose and so on, whilst still being separate and distinct individuals. The resemblance in some cases will be striking, in others difficult to detect. Moreover the nature of the common traits might be hard to articulate. Yet we recognise the family resemblance as pertaining. Often we will see the resemblance instantly as obvious. Hence we associate them together with common words (consider notions of taste). Thus we can account for differences yet also for the use of common terms in ordinary language (Stroll, 2000, 2002).

Important to Wittgenstein's view is the priority of ordinary language over theory or any idealised perfect language based on logic. This relates to the tacit and habitual means by which we grasp concepts and associations. We are able to operate competently and fully without absolute precision in language. So we might say, 'Stand over there' and point roughly to a spot some distance away and know what it means. Likewise we understand what 'going home' means. Language, or our comprehension of it, operates on a 'good enough' basis related to conventions and associations that operate *along with* the words and propositions. Wittgenstein mocks the logician pointing out for us how to construct the perfect sentence – 'now this is what a sentence looks like' – as if we did not know. Hence, according to this view, we *know* housing is necessary because we are using it and that is enough. We do not need to be able to understand and articulate these conventional structures in order to operate them.

We have the common-sense conception of housing which operates within ordinary language. Part of this is based on the normative conceptions of what individuals ought to have and the consequences of their absence. Yet, this is to an extent question begging, as we need to see where these normative conceptions have come from. The important element would appear to be our own experiences of housing, which confirm the common-sense conception. For most people (i.e. those who are non-housing experts and commentators) what is crucial is their own experience of housing, in the sense of the role it plays in their lives.

Of course, this begs a further question of how we can make general statements about subjective experience. But should we really be looking for generality at all? Should we not instead be trying to attain a sufficient mass or body of work to allow us to make comparisons, synthesise across studies and to develop analogous procedures? These results will remain limited, but this is only proper. Understatement in theory is preferable and more sensible than overstatement, as well as being more open to rigorous examination and assessment. Ellis and Flaherty (1992) suggest that whilst we must be aware of any such bias, this should not invalidate the importance of recollections of subjective experience. One of the tests (a subjective one, of course) of such writing is its intelligibility in terms of the lived experiences of the reader. In this sense, the recognition of bias is useful in itself. However, Ellis and Flaherty stress the need to balance the particular with the existentially common, which of itself is an aid to understanding.

There is a more sinister danger here though, namely that, if we know what subjectivity *ought* to be, and we believe – as we will almost inevitably do – that it will benefit all individuals to achieve this, then it is but a short leap to forcing them into this mould. And any reluctance on their part to accept their transformation is merely a confirmation of its necessity; after all, if individuals were applying their agency properly they would know already how to behave.[8] Sadly, there are all too many examples of dictatorship arising from a call for freedom. Fortunately, when discussing dwelling, the stakes are somewhat lower and any imposition is unlikely to be fatal. However, this still does not justify imposing a preconceived judgement of subjectivity onto anyone. Rather we should never lose sight of the fact that protecting subjectivity is more important than understanding it. This suggests that we should not try to establish any particular model of dwelling, but rather be happy with the implicit, habitual nature of dwelling based around an individual's own formulation of their ends and interests. These may not concur with how we ourselves would want to live, but then this position is the one most likely to guarantee our own freedom to choose.[9]

But even if we are able to accept that stability is more important than transformation, why is it that much about personal dwelling is dealt with at a pre-critical and non-analytical level? In others words, why do we treat dwelling on a day-to-day basis so glibly? What is there to dwelling that allows the habitual and implicit to dominate? First, this level of housing phenomena is seldom seen as part of academic housing discourse, but is rather left for the domain of lifestyle and DIY. The subjective nature of housing is seen too frequently as a matter for dinner parties and TV programmes. It is either a form of self-aggrandisement, self-congratulation ('it cost only £40,000 and now look what it's worth!'), or else entertainment. Most housing academics ignore the subjective because it is felt there is little serious to say. It is just about luxuries and fripperies that do not matter. Perhaps even it is seen as bourgeois, the ultimate of sins. The problem, to return to the earlier discussion, is that social transformation is actually seen as less possible here. If one has a concern to transform society then one is more likely to go for the 'big picture': to attack the underpinning base rather than the fripperies and decorations. One might mock popular taste, and even deplore it, but there are more important issues to contend with. More charitably, it may be that academics feel there is too much to say about the public processes, structures and mechanisms that apply to housing. As Bo Bengtsson (1995) argues, there is a tendency to avoid the normative, with writers reluctant to draw on the personal. It might be that we should extend this beyond the merely political (Bengtsson reserves his comments to this level) and see this as a reluctance to deal with the aesthetic and phenomenological elements of dwelling as well.

But this answer is insufficient. It is not just academics who ignore the personal level of housing, but rather it is something we all tend to do ourselves: we are too busy living to consider the mechanisms that allow us to do so.

This raises the question of whether there is not rather something intrinsic to dwelling itself? For instance, both the personal dimensions of healthcare and education are analysed, so what is the difference? Is it the dichotomy between public and private? Is it because of the essentially private level on which dwelling operates compared with other welfare goods (perhaps this means we should stop referring to housing on the same terms)?

Yet this still cannot be the complete answer. This is because it is *our* health that concerns us and what makes health provision such a pertinent issue for public debate. However, the personalisation of dwelling – it too is ours and of immediate consequence to us – does not necessarily equate with public concerns over housing, except when there are crises such as the slump in the UK in the early 1990s.

The answer relates to the specific means of provision in each case. When we discuss healthcare we refer to both the process *and* the outcome: to the medical intervention and the derived sense of well-being and health. However, housing policy is concerned only with process – with the provision of dwellings, but not with how we use them. This relates to the dichotomy discussed by John Turner (1976) of seeing housing both as a noun and a verb – as things and as an activity based around those things. Healthcare naturally includes both the activity (process) and the thing (outcomes). The distinction here is essentially one of control. With dwelling, we can determine (partially, at least) the outcomes, but this is not so with health. We are able to control the activity of housing and it is therefore we who decide the process of dwelling. The process is constitutive of our everyday lives. This accounts for why we do not feel the need to analyse personal dwelling to the same level. We do not feel the need to analyse and assess that *which is under our control.* The process is ours and thus we accept it as the quotidian background to our aims and interests.

This also tells us why we concentrate on the public sphere in housing discourse. Public policy and discourse on housing are concerned with those who do not or cannot control their dwelling environments, either because they lack a dwelling, or it is unsuitable or unsustainable. Put in other terms, their need for housing is not currently fulfilled (King, 1996, 1998, 2003). Accordingly, much comment on housing is about those poorly housed or homeless households and on the provision that is (or ought to be) aimed to rectify their situation. Healthcare debates are more general to the population as a whole precisely because this lack of control (over both process and outcome) is a more general one.

But whilst this concentration on the public processes is both under-standable and necessary, it does have a denigrating effect on concerns for the personal. Because of a concentration on the vulnerable, those who concern themselves with the personal level, and thus with discussing housing from the perspective of the already adequately or well housed, are criticised as missing the main issues or concentrating on fripperies and luxuries.[10] Hence the other part of public housing discourse seems to centre around contempt or, at best, criticism of those who are currently well housed. This manifests itself in a concern for the poor standards endured by some and the com-placency (e.g. 'nimbyism') apparently shown by others in the face of these poor standards. An example of this is the manner in which the suburban semi-detached house has been demonised for the apparently bourgeois values it is purported to embody. Likewise the Right to Buy – a policy based around private interests of the user rather than public notions such as need, equity or social justice – has been excoriated.[11] This is redolent of the rather old-fashioned but persistent view that it is unacceptable for some (or even the majority) to flourish whilst others are languishing in poor conditions, as if it makes anybody better off to reduce the standards of those at the top.[12] In any case, those in social housing are as keen to protect the integrity of their environment as any other group. As we are constantly being informed by those who justify the crusade against 'anti-social behaviour', this is being demanded by the tenants themselves, who are sick and tired of having their (private) lives ruined by their neighbours who do not appreciate the side-constraint placed upon them to respect the rights of others.

So, consideration of health and education is greater precisely because we are not in control. The concern with housing is felt towards and *on behalf of* those not in control of their dwelling. However, most of us, most of the time, are in control and hence we do not have to reflect on our circumstances (and, as the example of 'anti-social behaviour' suggests, those who are not in control are capable of pointing directly to the problem).

What is important here is the level of predictability of housing as an activity compared with other elements of public policy. We know housing is predictable and that it can fit in with our lives: this is fundamental to understanding our relations to dwelling. We know we need housing and that we will continue to need it. We know all others are in a similar situation, and that this position will not change in the future, any more than it altered in the past. Levels of amenity may change and we may be more or less able to control precisely the activity (depending on factors such as age, income and incapacity). But we know we will need housing of some sort for all of our lives. This creates a level of predictability that can enhance the level of control, in that we develop a greater understanding of those things we are constantly engaged with. But also, and this is crucial to an understanding of dwelling, our continued involvement with housing creates a level of complacency, in that we become used to that which is around us and hence we are able to take it for granted. So we continually seek to make our dwelling environments more predictable. We might do this by making them more secure and thus preventing invasion and unwanted visits; or by financial arrangements such as fixed rate mortgages that create more stability for those on relatively stable or fixed incomes. But however it is done it is this predictability that makes housing so much more understandable and thus capable of controlling. This does not mean that dwelling does not change. What it does mean, however, is that for most of us, most of the time, when it changes it does so because of our actions. The dwelling alters because we wish it to and we can do so because we control it.

But what is it we do with this control? In other words, how do we use dwelling once we have it? The purpose of the speculations that follow aim to answer this question. But perhaps we can offer some immediate pointers by way of a conclusion to this chapter. Is not the purpose of control to protect? And so is not the principal aim of dwelling to preserve what we have? All the notions we connect with dwelling, such as privacy, security and intimacy, are concerned with preservation and conservation: about keeping what we have, and in the manner we wish to keep it. Dwelling is thus not about transformation, but tranquillity: it is not change we seek – to be 'better' people – but stability – to be the type of people we choose to be.

Chapter 2
Privacy
When dwelling closes in on itself

Policy and subjectivity

If we are interested in policy, it is likely that we would seek to know why certain policies succeed, whilst others fail. So, for those of us interested in housing, we want to know why, say, Tenants' Choice failed when the Right to Buy succeeded. Both these policies were intended to achieve the privatisation of housing and to diminish the stock of local authority dwellings, and give the residents more control.

The answer to this question, and to the more general one of housing policy failure, lies in the distinct, and mutually exclusive, perceptions of housing, as either a public or a private entity. The Right to Buy, which allows sitting tenants to buy their current dwelling at a discount, focuses attention on housing as a private entity, whilst Tenants' Choice, which allowed council tenants as a group to vote for a new landlord, retained the perception of housing as primarily public. The Right to Buy alters the relation between an individual household and *their* dwelling by vesting control with the household itself. However, Tenants' Choice, if it had actually been used,[1] would have left the relation between dwelling and household unchanged, merely altering the landlord. The tenants would now merely be beholden to someone else, and the fact they could choose to whom to be beholden would not materially affect their own level of control. Any power the tenants had would be lost as soon as they had voted; but this is precisely when the landlord's power over them would begin.

The distinction here, therefore, is that one policy concentrated on the use to which the household could make of the dwelling – it became an asset and something they could pass on to their children, use as collateral, sell for a profit, take a pride in owning, etc. – whilst the other was concerned with the ownership of a collection of dwellings. One policy, through allowing households to exercise greater control, succeeded, whilst the other failed to capture the imagination of tenants, largely because it would not change anything beyond who they paid their rent to. The essence of the Right to

Buy as a successful policy, therefore, was the fact that it played on the private relation between a household and the dwelling: it concentrated on the activity of dwelling itself and the facility with which the actors could control their environment.

Yet of course, looking at the policy in a different light, the Right to Buy changed the situation of households even less than Tenants' Choice. The residents stayed in the same dwelling and, on a day to day basis, used it in the same manner. As a functioning entity the dwelling worked no better or worse through a change of ownership and tenure. If this is the case, what then is all the fuss over the Right to Buy about? Have politicians and 1.5 million households become somehow confused, or have they misled themselves over the policy's significance? The answer to this lies in a further dichotomy that cuts across that of the public/private divide. This is the distinction between the *objective* and *subjective*. We feel we are capable of seeing dwelling objectively, when we see it as both private and public, and likewise we can apply subjective values to both. Take, for example, the private relation, which is most relevant in the case of the Right to Buy. Our private dwelling can be seen as objective, such as when we think of it in terms of its costs to us; its usefulness as an asset; when it ceases to function; as a sound physical structure; and as a shelter. We are capable of assessing whether it does each of these tasks well or badly. These are all qualities of dwelling that make it palpable. It is when dwelling is really housing. It is the solidity of bricks and mortar – a material entity.

But even here, the tests we might use to judge success or failure are always in some way comparative: we might judge the dwelling better or worse than another in an ordinal sense, rather than being able to place it on a cardinal scale. But it is not just a case of being better *than*, but better *for*. A dwelling is objectively better because of what we seek to do in and with it and not because of any intrinsic qualities: or rather, its intrinsic qualities shine forth because of our specific aims for the dwelling. What this means is that we each experience and understand the objective qualities of a dwelling *differently*, and so our relations with and in the dwelling become a subjective experience.

To return to the Right to Buy, what is germane here is the increased level of control experienced by the household. Their subjective experience of the dwelling has been altered because they are now able to exert a more fundamental influence over their dwelling environment, including even when to change it by moving to a new dwelling. The dwelling has therefore been privatised, in that it is no longer legitimate for the public to have an interest in it: it is now the sole responsibility of the resident household to maintain it, pay for it and to determine its use. Subjectively, then, *dwelling closes in on itself.*

It is this very private sense, of dwelling closing in on itself, that is at issue in these speculations. Our interest is where dwelling becomes and remains subjectively significant, free of objective and objectifying influences. What matters with dwelling is what we can do with it once we have *bracketed out* all external factors, such as design and physical structure, tenure, affordability, access and so on: what we should solely be concerned with is private use.[2] External factors are important, but they should not be allowed to crowd out the internalised private sense of dwelling.

It matters therefore how far, and indeed whether, we are able to bracket out the external. Thus how far do specific housing policies and their effects matter? Was the Right to Buy something fundamental, and are renters somehow incapacitated in their subjective experiences? Is what the Right to Buy gave a greater or even complete internalised sense of dwelling? The problem here is that the very thing we need in order to bracket out the external is the dwelling itself, and this presupposes we are able to see dwelling for what it is, free of these very external factors that get in the way! We are thus faced with something of a tautology: dwelling is the very thing we need to achieve dwelling.

This implies that we can never achieve a fully private experience and that external factors will always impose themselves. This may be true, but what matters here is the degree to which we are able to control our environment. The way out of the apparent impasse, I believe, is not to concentrate on ownership or on any specific housing policy, but to concentrate on what is at the core of the subjective experience, and which coincidentally made the Right to Buy such a success. This core element is that of privacy: the fact that dwelling can enclose us and coil us back onto ourselves, looking inwards and not outwards to what might threaten us. What the Right to Buy enhanced was the ability of the household to deflect unwanted intrusion. This suggests that what is important is the degree of privacy we can enjoy and not any specific housing policy. Policies can help or hinder, but it is the subjective relationship that really determines whether a dwelling environment is sustainable.

But what is the precise nature of privacy? How should we approach it? Presumably we should approach with caution, taking care not to destroy the delicacy of the fabric we use to protect us. To delve too deeply into privacy is to destroy it: we are seeking to explore that realm that ought not to be explored too deeply. But, taking a different tack, the question can be put as: why does it matter so much if intruders invade our privacy? By understanding just what privacy is we might also appreciate more fully the costs of intrusion. These, then, are the specific questions we should set about answering, and, on the way, we shall discover more about the nature of dwelling as a private entity.

Approaching privacy

The term 'privacy' simply means the state of being private and undisturbed. However, it can also refer to the right to be so. It is therefore something that we have or ought to have. Yet this is not a particularly helpful start, in that we have attempted to define one word – privacy – by using another – private – from the same root.[3] Thus, if we are to understand just what it is we have, we need to dig a little deeper. When we look at the word private we see that it is used mainly as an adjective – *private* property, *private* talks – or as an adverb, as in *privately*. This straight away informs us that the term is often used to qualify other concepts: 'private property' denotes the property as belonging to an individual. The use of the term demonstrates the condition in which the other concept operates or exists. When we have privacy, then, we take it with or for something else.

Yet, privacy is also something *we have*. It can be measured and quantified, even though the measurement may be all or nothing. It is a state we are *in*, or more properly, *within*, as in 'can I see you in private?'. Privacy encloses us and allows us to complete our business. Without being *within* privacy we could not do many of the things we consider important. But privacy can also act as a side constraint on others, where we are restrained from invading another's space. This means that privacy is also the state where others are *without*. So I can have my privacy without it infringing on yours, but you cannot have mine, because the attempt will destroy it. This is because privacy is always a subjective state. We cannot take the privacy of another and use it ourselves. Privacy is not a transferable commodity, even though we might only gain it at the expense of another (for example, we can have a room of our own because others share).

There is an implacability about domestic privacy. One just cannot penetrate – one cannot see in. Or rather we can only see through the filter provided by the show of dwelling itself: what we see is the public face presented to protect the very privacy of dwelling. Thus, in considering the nature of dwelling, we need to distinguish between the performative and the habitual: between dwelling as shown and dwelling as lived. We can only see how others live on their terms, when they accommodate us. Anything else is a violation that destroys dwelling. This is precisely because dwelling is *properly private*. So our presence would alter the rhythms of another's dwelling and we would not be seeing what they do, but what, in effect, we let them do (or rather, what they are prepared to let us see them do).

But we should not see a problem in the implacability of domestic privacy. This is entirely as it should be and we recognise it as such. Accordingly, it is those of us outside who use our reserve, as much as anyone pulling up the drawbridge or drawing the net curtains. We do not habitually force ourselves into the lives of others: to do so is to commit both a physical and a psychological violation.

With this in mind, we can explore the various meanings of the term. First, private can refer to that which is our own or personal to us. Second, it can be seen as denoting that which is confidential and to which knowledge is restricted. Third, it is something kept from general view or public knowledge. Fourth, private can refer to something not open to the public. Fifth, we may see it as referring to something secluded and inaccessible, either due to its particular location or because of the actions of the owner to make it so. Lastly, we might use the term to refer to services provided outside the state system and at the individual's own expense, such as private education or private rented housing.

There is a common thread that runs through these various meanings. When something is private it is a thing *kept apart*. Private property has a definitive ownership, which *separates* it from property owned by others and by the state. This keeping apart may mean that it remains secret and generally unknown. Because rights over the thing are restricted, we *exclude* unwanted attention and seek to regulate use according to our own interests. The thing, and to an extent ourselves, is *secluded* from others by its designation as private. In the case of dwelling, privacy helps us to separate and seclude ourselves from unwelcome attention and from that which we consider will prevent us from achieving our aims. The dwelling achieves this because it *encloses us*. It protects us from intrusion and unwanted attention.

Yet privacy also allows us to live in the dwelling how we wish to. Its seclusion provides us with the means to live how we see fit. This means that the dwelling itself is *animated* by our habitation of it.[4] The dwelling takes on a distinctly different form by virtue of a household living privately within it. This suggests a mutuality between dwelling and person. Gaston Bachelard (1969) sees the dwelling as providing a 'protected intimacy' (p. 3). The house is therefore 'a major zone of protection' (p. 31). It is the dwelling that secludes us from the unpredictability of the world and keeps us safe from danger. However, it is inhabitation that animates the dwelling and gives it its definition. Bachelard states 'the sheltered being gives perceptible limits to his shelter' (p. 5). Thus what gives a space the essence of home is that it is 'really inhabited' (p. 5). We give the dwelling its particular and especial meaning by our inhabitation. The space would lose much of its meaning if it were empty, but comes into its true significance through its full inhabitation. This is when the significance of housing shifts from its physicality into 'space that is supposed to condone and defend intimacy' (p. 48). The meaning of dwelling, as we have already seen, derives from its use.

The implication here is of a mutually supporting relationship. On one level, this is a banality: we cannot have the activity called dwelling without physical dwellings to inhabit. To state the obvious: dwelling needs dwellings. Yet there is a deeper resonance here, in that the physicality of the dwelling is not all that protects us. Rather what offers us security is the very relation between dwelling and inhabitant. It is the actual activity of dwelling itself that encloses us *and* the dwelling to create a new synergistic relation that unites the physical and the phenomenological together. It is the activity of dwelling that gives meaning to our relations with the physical space and allows us to reach out and grasp it for what it is.

Bachelard also shows us that dwelling allows for intimacy. In order to be intimate we need privacy, but, in this case, private does not mean solitary. It is where we are intimate *with another*. We still need seclusion and to be kept apart, so that we can act in an uninhibited and properly responsive manner with our intimates, yet we are not alone. Indeed in this sense we seek privacy precisely because we are not alone, and we would not seek the same sort of privacy were we alone.

This demonstrates an important quality of privacy: we seek it for a purpose. It is privacy *for* something. This will apply both when we seek privacy just to be alone, or to be intimate with another. But, of course, our purpose need not have a positive intent, in that we might want to get away from someone or something.

Privacy, therefore, can be shared, but need not be. In this sense it is like many other goods that we might seek at some times to share or at other times to keep entirely to ourselves. But, like lots of other goods we seek to hoard and treasure, do we ever seek privacy for its own sake? Do we ever just wish to be in private? Is it not the case that we wish to be private so we can achieve something better, even if this is just to think? Do we always wish to have privacy so we can do (or not do) something? Is saying 'I want to be alone' the same as 'give me privacy'? At the banal level the answer is yes, but this answer begs a question. We would seek to ask what it is that we want to be alone or private *for*. Now, of course, the person does not have to answer, but the clear implication is that they want it for something, even if it is to hide away from further questions!

But again might not the supposedly banal answer carry rather more significance than we have credited it with? Is not the precise virtue of privacy that it allows us to do what we want? It gets us away from those we feel would stop us doing what we want, how we want and where we want. So privacy is instrumental, but this is precisely one of its two virtues. The other is that it puts us in a position where we do not have to explain ourselves to anyone else and say what it is we want the privacy for. Privacy, therefore, carries with it its own defence mechanism. Once we proffer the right to privacy to somebody we henceforth deny ourselves any right to know what they wish to use it for. We might make conferring the right conditional – we might tell teenage children what they can and cannot do when left alone – but, once granted, we lose any practical means of policing the conditions (without breaching the grant of privacy).

What this suggests is that much privacy depends on trust. We do not enter some places, not because we physically cannot, but because we do not out of respect and mutuality. We want teenagers to act responsibly and know that they cannot if they are constantly policed and watched by adults. There has to be some mutual understanding between parent and teenager on the setting and respecting of limits. Likewise we refrain from saying certain things even though we might think them and believe that stating them would be good for the other person. We do not do so again out of respect so as not to be hurtful or personal. We consider it inappropriate to intrude so much on another's privacy. We have no right to say what we think – it is none of our business – just as others have no right to say what they might think about us. Without this mutuality there can be no privacy.

Yet problems can arise because we do not always know where the boundaries are, and so sometimes we find we have taken liberties without knowing why, or perhaps without even realising we have given offence. Part, but not all, of this fuzziness arises because of a fear of conflict, of not wanting to confront someone who has slighted or affronted us for fear of the consequences – of losing a friend and making an enemy, of making the affront public. But this means that someone might end up going even further beyond the pale than if we had dealt with them earlier. The difficulty is in balancing the as yet hypothetical reaction from the offending party with the current boundary crossing; typically, we choose the known to the unknown, even though it ends up hurting us more.

But this can also work to our advantage. In maintaining our privacy we hope others can be trusted, which allows us then to play on their natural reserve and fear of overstepping the boundaries of trust. We know most people we invite in will respect our home. Even when we tell them to 'feel at home' they still remain, as it were, on licence and we trust that this will remain the case. This is a self-imposed condition on the part of the visitor, which arises because the parameters of acceptable behaviour remain formally undrawn and thus they will be wary of appearing impolite or causing offence.[5] We rely on these self-policing actions of others to maintain our privacy. Strains develop if the restraint is forgotten and the guest really does feel at home, particularly if they refuse to leave.

We tend to respect the privacy of others even when we could reach out to them easily. This is the case when we conscientiously ignore people on trains or in lifts. We could easily start up a conversation, but often to do so would seem inappropriate and impertinent. But we do this all the more with our own dwelling. Whilst we wish to be civil to our neighbours and support them, we do not seek to force ourselves onto them. As an (admittedly banal) example of this, my neighbour's fence fell down and consequently we were able to see into each other's gardens. On one occasion we were both in our respective gardens enjoying the brief sun of the summer, yet we ignored each other, even though it was impossible not to be aware of each other's presence. But perhaps we could see this differently: rather than ignoring each other were we not respecting each other's privacy, exactly as we would have done if the six-foot fence were still there? I felt we could only have talked, or even acknowledged each other's existence, if we had happened to make eye contact and thus recognised each other's presence. Yet it would have been rude to stare at her in readiness of her looking across, and thus I deliberately looked away. It would certainly have seemed an intrusion to have gone up to the edge of her garden and begun a conversation. It would seem to me to have been rude, impertinent and intrusive (but, of course, she might consider me ignorant, arrogant, or aloof for not doing so. But then it would be rude to ask!). Is this merely a case of so-called 'English reserve', or is there something more fundamental about our not wanting to interfere in the space of others?[6] The spaces we were both in were not intended to be as public as they currently were and thus we maintained the fiction of privacy. But were both of us at the front of our houses, or meeting in the street we would certainly stop to talk. In this situation to ignore the other would itself be rude.

What this shows is that we see some parts of the dwelling as more private than others. Indeed only parts of the dwelling are in any way public. We use certain spaces to receive guests, but other places we reserve entirely for ourselves. We do not ordinarily give all our guests the freedom to roam, and nor do they expect it. We would not show our bedrooms to everyone.[7] What needs to develop here again is a sense of trust. We are more likely to treat family and close friends differently from those we hardly know. Yet, of course, some people, such as plumbers, electricians, heating engineers, etc., we will give as complete access as necessary even to these most private areas. And because they are there for a specific purpose – to repair the dwelling – we can accept this form of intrusion as being different from that of a relative stranger exploring our bedroom. But even with close friends and family, there are limits to how much we show to them, and how much they feel restrained. This form of reserve appears to be learnt. Children feel less inhibited about the differential privacy of space: for them a dwelling is something to use, and use to the full. All space is neutral, whether it is in their own dwelling or that of another. This feeling only alters if they feel threatened or frightened, and then they seek the security of what they know. Consequently children have to be taught to be insular and private. Or is it the case that a sense of privacy develops naturally with age? I am sure, using psychoanalytic theory, one could connect puberty with shame and a consequent desire to protect oneself from the gaze of others. Children are less conscious of their bodies until they become sexualised. They then feel the need to use space differently to protect their new sense of self. Paradoxically, they now seek to use space to exert their personality and hence decorate this space to demonstrate that new persona. An adult's bedroom, however, is not a public space, but one reserved for the most intimate and private encounters and where relaxation can be total. Whilst this too demonstrates a need to get away from the gaze of others, there is no necessity to exert one's personality through this space; for adults this is done elsewhere in the dwelling, in those areas designated for the receiving of guests.

Privacy operates differently according to the perspective of the subject and the observer: between the subjective assessment and the more objective one of someone looking on. My privacy can appear absolute to me, but is clearly relative to those looking at the situation (indeed the fact that someone can see me is significant of itself). For me, privacy is something I either have, or I do not: there are no half measures here. I cannot be almost, mostly or nearly private. Privacy as a condition is all or nothing: I feel I am undisturbed or disturbed, but I cannot be somewhere in between. But then we can be alone in a crowd. We can be lost in our private thoughts in the midst of a crowd, as if we are cocooned away. We achieve this cocooning through a variety of aids and strategies. We might use a variety of objects and strategies to build and sustain privacy, such as headphones, reading a book, avoiding eye contact or by giving only perfunctory replies to conversation. We use things to hide behind or block us off, or else we simply look away. But we can feel unbearably harassed by one person, such as a noisy neighbour, or, in the case of a stalker, by someone we might never see. On other occasions, we might like to be alone in one room in the knowledge that a family member is somewhere else in the house, and therefore is still with us in one sense at least. We might also enjoy a companionable silence, where we are each alone with our book, watching a film or listening to music. We are experiencing something personally (in the case of reading, it is also something different), but we gain solace and comfort from the proximity of someone we love and care for. It is important to us that we are doing something with or alongside this person.

This situation of being *together-yet-apart* is also seen with children, who, after a certain age, we can quite happily leave playing or in the bath whilst we work in the kitchen or upstairs. We feel they are safe, as do they, because we can hear them and reach each other almost instantly. Yet we would not countenance leaving them alone in the house for all but the shortest period of time. But are they really much safer? We are not actually able to observe them and thus prevent them from some forms of harm. My daughters, for instance, have only had accidents leading to a visit to casualty when we have been present and mere yards from them. Of course, no one can say what might have happened if they had been left completely alone. But what is important here is the *subjective* feeling of safety – and in this case, statistics really do not matter, subjectively every disaster affects the person 100 per cent. We can say therefore that children should only be *relatively alone*. They should be free from intrusion, but within easy reach of companionship, comfort and help. Importantly, both parties should know this fact. Thus we can be private in the sense of not facing intrusion and being able to act undisturbed, but this is related to a subjective expectation and the boundedness of these expectations. We are currently alone, but we also know, and need to know, that we can find companionship and comfort almost at once.

We can therefore put a boundary around ourselves. But if we extend out wider we are clearly sharing the dwelling and our lives with others: we are still capable of being looked over by others. An important part of parenthood is exactly that of managing the boundaries around children in such a manner that they are as unobtrusive to the child as possible, without creating a

In dwelling we seek our own insular place to pursue our chosen ends

dangerous vacuum. Relatedness to others can therefore be seen as a series of concentric circles radiating out from each person.[8] This relatedness is determined in part structurally by both the physical structures of the dwelling and the emotional and ontological structures of the activity of dwelling. Thus privacy is dependent on circumstance and the structures of interrelatedness within dwelling. What might appear to be absolute privacy to one is a form of sharing to another, and this can alter according to situation. Hence a parent will look in at a sleeping child who, within the fastness of sleep, is unaware of their parent's attention.

But whether privacy is absolute or relative, there is something special about our dwelling: being there has a different quality from any other form of solitude. We can lose ourselves in a book whilst on a train, but the space around us is not ours and we have little ability to control it. We try to cocoon ourselves but intrusions will still insinuate themselves into our consciousness: the ringing of a mobile phone, a crying child, someone moving in the aisle. Being within our own dwelling minimises these intrusions: it is space that we are more able to control and maintain in a condition of our choosing. We can isolate and insulate ourselves from the outside world. David Morley (2000) draws on Walter Benjamin's image of the domestic interior being like a box at the theatre, as 'a sanctuary from which the world can be safely observed' (p. 29). We can watch, but choose to withdraw and remain unseen.

As such, when the long journey home nears its completion the feeling that we can soon sink back into the comfortableness of our own dwelling is almost sensuous. We can soon fall back into it and it can gather us up without any complaints. Even if we are closer there to other human beings, it is noisier and demands from family press upon us, when we are home we still feel more private, simply *because* we are at home. This is the one place that we can control.

This control, given by this particular sense of privacy, is crucial to us. It is what David Morley (2000, p. 29) has called a 'psychic dependence'. We want the opportunity to change, but only when it suits us. We want to be able to move house, alter the dwelling, and so on, but on our terms, and for the reasons dear to us. We want to go out into the world, rather than have the world intruding in on us. We feel all these should properly be private decisions. Of course, we are constrained in what we can do, but this does not mean that the decision making is not private: second and third choices are still ours.

Private dwelling, as we have seen, does not mean living alone. We should concur with Gaston Bachelard when he emphasises the inhabited nature of dwelling as a place of protected intimacy: as a place we are within but with others. We need then to distinguish between solitariness and privacy: between the notion of aloneness as a thing in itself and the enhanced intimacy, comfort and control offered to us by privacy. The solitary individual is given to us in the writings and persona of Friedrich Nietzsche. In *Human, All Too Human* (1996) he demonstrates a distinctly different view on intimacy and trust from that we have played out here. Nietzsche tells us that, 'He who deliberately seeks to establish an intimacy with another person is usually in doubt as to whether he possesses his trust. He who is sure he is trusted sets little value on intimacy' (p. 137). But these are not the thoughts of someone seeking closeness with a loved one, of someone close to children or parents, but instead this is the caution one has towards a business partner. And Nietzsche shows an almost cynical view of personal relations in another of his aphorisms, where he states, 'People who give us their complete trust believe they have thus acquired a right to ours. This is a false conclusion; gifts procure no rights' (p. 137). If we accepted Nietzsche's view here, where there is no expectation of reciprocity and where we should keep our distance from others, we would have something like the perfectly self-interested maximiser of naïve classical economics. He is offering us nothing more than *homo economicus*.

The difference is that whilst the classical economists saw relations as basic stimulus and response, Nietzsche states his vision as of some higher culture of so-called 'free spirits'.

Nietzsche may have been both a great stylist and controversialist, who sought to offer us new insights into subjective experience, but then why are so many of the statements that he makes about our values, attitudes, motivations and actions so wrong? Is it his madness, or is it – paradox of all paradoxes – his very solitariness, his near complete lack of association with other human beings as equals? What Nietzsche demonstrates, not didactically, but through the very accumulation of his judgements, is that subjectivity has little to do with truth. He comes across – indeed he actively portrays himself – as an almost hermetically sealed individual, observing the world from outside, incapable of engaging with it. We can only presume this is because no sane person would accept his terms, a situation he mistakes as ignorance and a lack of culture. Perhaps, in Nietzsche's case, it is where one form of madness overcomes another. What held him together for so long was his tremendous ego that insulated him from any understanding of how others saw him; without that he would not have been able to write anything. He had such a tremendous sense of his own purpose that he could not see the reciprocal nature of private life. Instead his vision is one almost entirely lacking in intimacy and the sensibilities of closeness and comfort we have described as intrinsic to dwelling. Emile Cioran (1998) has stated that Nietzsche, singly amongst the great thinkers, lacked judgement. Cioran, who is commonly seen as one of the most able of thinkers in the Nietzschean style, describes his erstwhile master as 'too naïve', and goes on:

> I hold his enthusiasms, his fervours against him. He demolished so many idols only to replace them with others: a false iconoclast, with adolescent aspects and a certain virginity, a certain innocence inherent in his solitary's career. He observed men only from a distance. Had he come closer, he could have neither conceived nor promulgated the superman, that preposterous, laughable, even grotesque chimera, a crotchet which could occur only to a mind without time to age, to know the long serene disgust of detachment.
>
> (Cioran, 1998, p. 85)

For Cioran, the problem with Nietzsche was his disengagement. He had forgotten, or perhaps was never aware, that being alone and being in private were not one and the same. Cioran also reminds us that detachment and

Dwelling provides us with something to hide behind

disengagement involve a moving away and not absolute separation: the former implies a connection even though it is now broken, whilst the latter suggests a lack of any possibility of contact.

This offers an important lesson, namely, that privacy is not mere insularity. It is not about closing us off from the world entirely. But rather it is about the regulation of intrusion from the outside world and, importantly, *who* is acting as the regulator. The essence of private dwelling is not its solitariness, although we may crave this from time to time, but rather the manner in which we can control our surroundings, through our dwelling, and thus protect our intimacy. Unlike Nietzsche, we should not close ourselves off without any ability to reconnect with the world. We need to maintain some perspective about the world and the limitations it places upon us. This means finding a balance – perhaps an uneasy one – between being secure and preventing unwanted intrusion. To try to find such a balance we need to explore what happens when our privacy is invaded by those whom we would seek to avoid.

Invasion and intrusion

Privacy, necessarily, is a one-sided phenomenon. We quite like seeing into the lives of others, but we wish to restrict access into our own. We are interested in the glimpses of the famous and not-so-famous, to see how people whom we know from work, or in some other sphere, behave when 'at home'. Yet we would feel uncomfortable if others saw our private lives as some sort of spectacle. Most of us would not wish to see ourselves observed. We allow people into our dwelling because we trust them. Or, if we have no knowledge of them and have to let them in, because *we* can observe *them* and thus believe we can maintain control of the situation: we can delimit our privacy and show them as much (or as little) as we choose. We expect them to show respect, whereas, with those familiar to us, we *know* they will respect us.

And, of course, there are limits to privacy. If we share too much it becomes public. This is the dilemma of the celebrity, who sacrifices much of their privacy for fame. Indeed they may still crave privacy, but their status demands continual publicity. Hence, like Princess Diana or the Beckhams, they will decry the price of fame, whilst continually inflating the cost through acts of self-publicity. We could ask here: what are they faking, the need for privacy, or the anguish it supposedly brings?

But for most of us, our dilemmas are elsewhere. We need to share, if we seek intimacy, but privacy cannot be shared without it being diminished in some way: the very act of sharing publicises the private act. Through sharing, privacy inevitably loses some of its mystique and also its purpose, which is to hide us from others so we may act in a manner unbeholden to them. Now we may wish to diminish our privacy and share our lives with others. Clearly this is an essential part of our lives, and indeed it is what the very boundary of privacy itself allows. Yet we wish to share on our terms and only where the consequences of sharing are controllable or foreseeable. We need therefore to separate mutuality, which adds to our dwelling by bringing love, intimacy, comfort and a new generation, from intrusion and violation, which destroys privacy. What we wish to share are *those things we can share in private*. This is where two or more people pool their privacy within a physical space so that they can reinforce and be reinforced by those around them.

Yet there are many ways in which our privacy is intruded upon. Indeed, some of the very means we use to create privacy for ourselves in a public place can invade the privacy of others. The most common is the use of personal stereos, particularly in confined spaces such as trains and buses. Less common, but equally invasive, are those on a journey who insist on talking to us, regardless of any lack of encouragement they may get from us. Indeed the worst kind are those who do not actually even expect us to take any part in a conversation, but who want only to talk and not to listen. In this way they are, in a way, maintaining their privacy intact. They may be telling us personal details, but they are not allowing anything of us to penetrate. It is as if their story is being used to form a carapace around them: by retelling certain significant or comforting stories it is as if they are populating their immediate surroundings with meaningful artefacts, just as they might do in their own dwelling. Anything that we might say is an intrusion and to be resisted with a restatement of something of significance to them.

Perhaps the most annoying example of this form of intrusion is those who are able to twist any comment made by us into something substantive about themselves. So, to inform such a person that one has just ended a relationship leads not to the offer of sympathy or to enquiries about how it happened, but to complaints that someone else is burdening *them* with another problem! This may not be a case of arrogance, but rather an inability to connect properly with others: they see other people's comments merely as personal stimuli disassociated from their source. On one level this is sociopathic, albeit of a mild and relatively harmless kind. What it does show, however, is an inability to break out of one's private fantasies. The effect on others though is to denude them of any personal life themselves: they exist merely to feed the fantasies of the sociopath.

The virtue of private dwelling is that we can avoid public invasions. We are able to avoid the noise, the intrusive fellow traveller and the sociopath. But does our desire for privacy in our dwelling make us insensitive to others? For example, consider the manner in which we dismiss cold callers on the telephone or at the door. We tend to see these people as an intrusion on our private business, as an unwanted distraction. They always seem to call when we are in the middle of something else and then try to persuade us to do or buy something we have either never considered or did not know we needed. They might even insist that we cannot live without it. Their call, quite reasonably from our point of view, appears therefore as an intrusion that infringes on our privacy: we did not seek their advice, or request their product. We do not, at the moment at which we are disturbed, consider we need what they have to offer.

This lack of engagement is easily manifested in the way we receive the caller. When someone we do not know knocks on the front door, do we not often close the inner door so that the caller cannot see too far in behind us? Indeed, quite often when people open the door, they use it to hide behind and limit what can be seen, almost to the extent of peeping around the door.

They wish to control access until they know who is there. Only then will they open up the dwelling. This practice is intended to show that they are not expecting to welcome the person in, but rather seek to limit contact to a minimum and ensure that they can escape. By merely poking their head round the door they are giving the barest minimum of themselves. They seek to show that the caller is under sufferance and that they have not asked for the intrusion.

What effect does this have on the caller? Do they gauge the likelihood of a sale by the manner in which they are received, or are they immune to these cues, worn down by the indifference or hostility of those they seek to force themselves on? Are we now too sophisticated to be taken in by cold callers, and are they themselves so regulated and hemmed in by 'good practice' that we can easily escape them?

But are we ever right to dismiss them curtly or even rudely? Do we not rather have a duty (enforced by whom or what?) to be polite and at least hear them out?[9] Should we not be aware of the feelings of the canvasser, or is it fine to expect them to see the dismissal as just part of the job? After all, they are just doing their job and as it happens to interfere with us we can tell them (politely) to go away.

However, is such an intrusion always untimely? Presumably someone must say 'yes' to a caller selling double-glazing, or otherwise companies would not persist with it as a common sales technique. At some times they must be pushing at the proverbial open door. Indeed, perhaps there are some things we need to be told that we need. We need someone to tell us what we lack, even if this does involve intruding on our privacy to inform us of it. More likely though, we did not know we needed it because in truth we do not. We can just be *made to want it*, by a convincing sales patter, and then, when we have it, we naturally tend to insist that we need it.

Whilst the ethics of responding to canvassers might need reviewing at some point, my interest is elsewhere. The issue of intrusive canvassers raises the quite crucial but more general question: what are the limits of our privacy and what rights do they give us to dismiss the claims of others? Our claim to privacy might be seen as a claim to ignore any (or most, or the most inconvenient) claims made by others on us. But clearly our actions might detract from the ability of another to enjoy their privacy. We might be able to justify ignoring those who put their hand out to us because it infringes on our privacy, but does that act then make us responsible for what might happen to the beggar? Is it a matter for us that there are beggars on the street who have no privacy for themselves? Our own privacy can be used as a means to insulate us from the claims of others. We have a secure place that allows us to turn away from the outstretched hand. We can, should we wish, refuse to answer the door, take the phone off the hook, and leave the mail unopened. Beggars on the street, however, have no such option simply because they have no door to hide behind.

But of course, most of us do not use dwelling for the purpose of ignoring those in need around us. Yes, we may turn away the double-glazing salesperson, but this does not equate to selfishness as such. The salesperson is trying to sell us something we do not want and we have no time to waste in listening to any sales patter, however well rehearsed. Yet this does not mean we are insensitive to those in need: we have no duty to buy double-glazing just so that the salesperson can put meat and bread on the table. But merely because we *can* insulate ourselves from those we do not wish to engage with does not mean that we *will or do in every case*. We are capable of discriminating between the variety of situations placed in front of us. The question here is: is it better to be open to all, and thus then be able to see those we need to help, or should we rather treasure our privacy as the space that allows us to determine who we should help and when? The question turns on who considers or judges the actions we take: what appears to be selfish on the outside might be a justifiable moral position on the inside. In any case, we do not become moral persons through publicity – because of other people knowing what we do – nor are we immoral because of the myopia of those supposedly observing us.

If we see privacy as the protector of choice, and intrusion as where choice is denied or overridden, we begin to see why the limits of privacy are important. What matters here is just how effective we can be in protecting our privacy, and therefore what is allowed to intrude into our lives. We should not forget that, by definition, an intrusion is an unwanted interference in our private lives. So for us to choose to help another – to take them in, or to offer them comfort, money or support – cannot constitute an intrusion. Privacy begins where we are not prepared to turn intruders into friends.

So just what is selfish about dwelling? On one level, dwelling can be taken as the exclusion of intrusion, where we are able to set our own plans and lead the kind of life we see fit. On another level, it might be seen as turning our backs on our neighbours: as walling ourselves in to prevent the world from encroaching. One person's quiet enjoyment is another's selfish isolation. But what we have here, if one can stretch an analogy somewhat, is two straw men shaking their fists at each other. Dwelling is never completely private and insularity is never total. Likewise, even the most ardent collectivist closes the door at night.

We can illustrate the limits of intrusion and selflessness by the following hypothetical example. Suppose that we are members of some small community, say a church or a sports club. We meet with other members socially, after a service or after work, and we feel there is some sense of co-operation, of mutual support and fellow feeling between us: we are all people of the same type, we believe in similar things, share the same interests and generally have much in common. Now imagine that one member of that community was so desperately short of money that they were in danger of losing their home. Moreover this situation had arisen entirely as a result of their own actions – they had gambled away their money, or been dissolute in some other way. This person now approached several members of this community and expected them to help them: this dissolute individual expected their fellow members to use some of their wealth to support them. Would we see it as the responsibility of the members of this community to give up some of their income and property for the other person? Would they be seen as selfish if they did not? It might be that many in this community would respond positively if they were asked to make a small temporary loan, although it might create an embarrassing situation. However, something on a larger scale with no prospect of repayment would be seen as unreasonable. The fact that some people have more than enough wealth is not sufficient grounds to demand it from them. To ask for such support from one's family is one thing, but from a colleague or friend is another. We do not expect this level of support from people who are unrelated to us, even though they may have much in common with us. As a result it would be most unusual for any person to even ask.[10]

In this situation we would tend to see the request as unreasonable and, regardless of the views of the dissolute supplicant, we would not see a refusal, in others or ourselves, as selfish. More generally we do not expect even a particularly principled person, be they a Christian or a socialist,[11] to give away all their income to just anyone who asks for it, even if this person is particularly deserving of help. We may have admired Mother Teresa and others who devoted their lives entirely to helping other people, but this does not imply any criticism of those who restrict their benevolence to their family and the odd donation to a charity they approve of. Indeed, if we were all like Mother Teresa we would achieve very little: it would be the moral equivalent of taking in each other's washing, as well as being economically disastrous. People like Mother Teresa are valued, and are extremely effective, precisely because they are rare, and this has little or nothing to do with the accusation that, because she acts in her way, we are free to do as we please. They are admired as much for what they sacrifice, namely, a normal life that is centred round private actions. The sacrifice made by Mother Teresa was to lead her life in public. This is not a life most of us would or could lead. We might be encouraged to do more for others because of her example, but not to take her life as the model for us, any more than we are expected to give away our income merely because someone we know asks for it.

What this implies is that the normal life – the way in which we would and do live, if so allowed – is one where we are able to restrict our involvement with our surroundings and be private. And as such, this is not selfish. Living privately and giving part of our time and income to others are not mutually exclusive. For most of us this is a private decision. This is because the form of community we seek to be a part of is one that respects our privacy *and* allows us the responsibility to act as we see fit. This is the very form of community that both protects private dwelling and makes the request of the dissolute supplicant unreasonable.

But might not too much privacy still be a problem? Might we be unable to maintain a proper perspective, or sense of what is normal and acceptable if we lose sight of how others behave and act? We might be unable to socialise properly when the occasion demands. Privacy is like most good things: twice as much is not necessarily twice as good. This is shown wonderfully with an anecdote of an elderly couple who cleave to their dwelling almost at all costs, seeing it as anchor and armour. However, the couple were invited to a twenty-fifth anniversary party by longstanding friends. Their immediate response to this act of friendship was to say, 'Of course, we're not going!', as if it would be absurd to expect them to. For these people being put out (an interesting phrase in this context, for no one but them would do the 'putting') is an insult: just what are people thinking of, inviting them to go out for a party? It is an intrusion, and just too much trouble for them to be expected to accept. For this couple being 'at home' is central to their existence: insularity is an end in itself. Perhaps getting to the stage of the elderly couple is a process, beginning with wanting the home comforts and developing into a feeling of siege, in which even a party invitation is perceived as a threat to these comforts. And, of course, the very insularity that this process has engendered insulates them from any sense of the absurd or the anti-social. They are literally absorbed in their own little world.

We find this anecdote amusing, as a trite example of eccentricity in old age. Yet even if we do not go this far, is it not just a rather more extreme version of our own insularity, whereby we treasure our own comfort and security? There may be something of this couple in all of us: we cleave to what we know, and seek to maintain it and protect it from threats. These threats are often illusory and imaginary, of no substance other than our own insular fears. And, of course, most of us keep these fears in check. But we too use our dwelling – our privacy – as a carapace to protect us from what we perceive as threats, from those entities external to us which we cannot control. So we seek comfort in what we can control and cleave to it. It is external intervention that makes the dwelling contingent, in the sense that it makes the relation of dwelling to personal identity a conditional one, rather than simply one of simple referencing. This is because we find ourselves having to explain and justify ourselves: we find we need the reassurance of others. But our plans, which are central to our lives, are, of course, of merely passing interest to others, they being more focused on their own affairs. Is this a cause for concern or for rejoicing? Does it really matter that others are indifferent to us? This is clearly a question of degree. We want to be left alone, but not so much so that our pleas for help are unheeded or that our neighbours fail to notice us in distress.

Yet we do not expect, or want, strangers to take an active interest in our lives and how we live. We resent the 'nosey-parker' who appears to spy on us and judge us. We see it as none of their business and an unwarranted intrusion. We resent others using our front garden as a public thoroughfare, or as a play area. We expect others to keep off our property unless invited. We want to be able to make plans and not have them subverted by others. What we really expect therefore is a type of polite indifference, whereby we can formulate our plans, yet feel we will be listened to when we discuss them with others. We know that our neighbours are not very interested, and we would be suspicious were they to be enthusiastic, but we like to think that our plans matter sufficiently to at least be listened to. We do not want judgement, just politeness and then to be left to live privately.

Chapter 3
A brick box or a velvet case?

The unoccupied dwelling: an empty box?

Enclosing and enframing

Dwelling is both the performance of a technology – of things working to maintain us – and an act of forgetting. And what we seek to forget is the very technology that performs so much for us. Dwelling is where fantasy and reality intermingle. Dwelling is both the functioning of a series of prosaic entities and a series of aspirations and self-perceptions, which are disconnected from the real world by the very adequacy of the functioning dwelling. The insulation we achieve through dwelling allows us to dream. We may dream of a different dwelling, or that its aspects and relations might be altered in some way; we might dream of matters far beyond the quotidian level on which the dwelling stands.

The dwelling might be said to act as a receptacle. Walter Benjamin (1999) sees dwelling as 'age old' and 'eternal': as 'the image of that abode of the human being in the maternal womb' (p. 220). Particularly for the Victorian, the dwelling was a 'receptacle for a person, and it encased him with all his appurtenances so deeply in the dwelling's interior that one might be reminded of the inside of a compass case, where the instrument with all its accessories lies embedded in deep, usually violet folds of velvet' (p. 220). Despite harking back to the Victorian bourgeoisie, this image fully conveys the manner in which dwelling wraps us up within its padded folds.

Yet as a receptacle it operates in several ways. The dwelling is, of course, a physical entity, holding the activity of dwelling within it: it is the physical structure in which dwelling takes place. The dwelling also collects up important and significant artefacts and objects in our lives: it is where we place our most treasured possessions. And because these possessions are treasured, dwelling becomes a store of memories (Bachelard, 1969). This 'collecting' operates by bringing what would hitherto be disparate elements together, of collating the distinct, meaningful entities into a collective whole. The dwelling thus carries with it the idea of embeddedness, or of a proper fit, where the dwelling is the requisite holder of those things important to us: this is where the dwelling is the sufficient and necessary container for the activity of dwelling.

A key function of the dwelling is therefore to hold things in: to enclose those precious things and beings that we wish to protect. But we do not merely seek to hoard things. We wish to use them and live *with* them. Much of what we hold dear is not possessions, but relationships. What concerns us is whom we share our dwelling with as much as what we share it in.

The dwelling encloses us and our loved ones; it separates us from the world. Yet the dwelling itself is animated by its habitation: we, through our *in-dwelling* give it meaning. So habitation alters the dwelling, as the soul animates the body.[1] This suggests a mutuality between dwelling and person as a two-way dependency. The dwelling is given meaning by its inhabitation, and our lives are made meaningful within the space of the dwelling. What we should not forget then is that we cannot do much with anyone, without the wherewithal so to do. The box is important for what it encloses, but the enclosure itself is no less necessary for that. The dwelling is more than space and more than just an empty box. There is a symbiosis between the structure and activity of dwelling. We dare not ignore then the physicality of dwelling.

Yet there is an express danger in concentrating just on dwelling as a physical structure; this is where we concentrate on décor and amenity, on styles, on status and crucially on value. It is where the dwelling becomes commodified and is seen as an end in itself.[2] This is where, to use the jargon of Marxism, exchange value dominates over use value: where the dwelling as an asset and as a marker of status and success concerns us more than what we actually do in the dwelling we are now struggling to afford.

The problem here is one of control. Where the dwelling is an end in itself, even if we know the value of the dwelling and have used the dwelling as collateral, is where we are not in control. Rather we are beholden to forces external to our environment and have become dependent on a series of conditions – economic and social – over which we are unable to exert any pressure ourselves. In the rush for 'property' we have lost sight of our own needs. We have allowed the demand, and concerns of others to dominate us.[3]

Dwelling, when it is properly so called, is where we are in control. It is where we have a sense of why we dwell and thus what the dwelling does. However, this is what the dwelling does *with* us, as a party to the activity of dwelling, and not *to* us and certainly not merely *for* us. This form of control will not be outwardly manifested, but seen (if this is the right term) through habitual behaviour within the dwelling, through the actual use of the dwelling as a receptacle, base, nest and foundation for our ends and interests.

But important to this habitual use is respect for the dwelling itself: it is much more than just a brick box. Unlike the commodified version of dwelling, it is not a disposable entity, but one which of itself becomes a treasured possession, in which we can luxuriate and enjoy. Thus the structural integrity of the dwelling is honoured as part of the act of dwelling itself. The practice of dwelling respects its limits.

Yet despite this, it is habitation that makes dwelling and not the dwelling that makes habits. It is the physical aspect of the dwelling that we least recognise in its use. Of course, we know it bars certain acts and we know it is the parameter, or limit, of much of our actions. Yet this enframing becomes integrated into the habits of dwelling. It is only when non-physical issues impinge, such as the arrival of a new baby, a change of partner (or when one is left alone), when a family member can no longer cope on their own, or our expectations change, that we feel we need to change the physical aspects of the dwelling. The change in the physical aspects might be as fundamental as moving to another brick box, or might be altering or adding to what we have already. We might reshape it, getting rid of those now unwanted associations; or we might re-order the space to account for a new arrival. It is only then that we notice the physical limits and opportunities offered by the dwelling itself. Most of the time we just walk past and through these structures, having accepted them and integrated them into our perceptions of dwelling.

This is not to say that our experience of dwelling is not mediated by physical structures. For instance, and to state the obvious, we look out of windows and over walls. This opens up possibilities for us, but it also limits what we can see. We cannot look through walls and thus have to rely on the physical limitations imposed upon us by the dwelling. And, of course, we often put up barriers ourselves such as curtains, fences and walls. These are intended to prevent others from looking in, but they also limit us from seeing out. We consider this to be a price well worth paying for our privacy. We limit ourselves to what aspects we can see in order to maintain our privacy and sense of security. What is important here is that the dwelling modifies the view we have: our ability to be enclosed, to be private, and to exclude others, might also separate us from any proper sense of the threat that others might actually present. Thus a further price we pay for privacy might be misunderstanding. Yet we do not pay the full price because of the very efficiency of the dwelling in keeping us secure.

The dwelling orientates us in at least two different ways. First, it is a topographical system, consisting of places and spaces determined by their physicality: it conditions our sense of distance and proximity, through the separation of 'ours' and 'theirs', of what is possible and impossible, of what is legitimate and illegitimate. Thus the dwelling operates through a series of limits and foci: of preventing certain actions, whilst concentrating us on others. A determining, but not absolute, condition here is that of possession. What limits and focuses us is whether we do or do not possess an entity; whether our aspirations are realistic or naïve; and, whether we are selfish or capable of considering others before we act.

Second, dwelling orientates through a mesh of meanings. It is the space through which we traverse to gain an understanding of our predicament as social beings who demand the space to breathe. Dwelling, by these lights, is the very opposite of a system. The things which give our life meaning intertwine, contradict each other and subsist separately, becoming operational only according to a contingent context. We might thus see dwelling as a series of unconnected meanings, within a framework – the dwelling itself – that too carries meaning. Orientation can be an interior process as well as an external one. It should not be seen merely as axes and pathways into social space (Norberg-Schulz, 1985). When we consider the architectonics of interior space we see the dwelling as creating points of intensity, where we interact with others and develop relationships, and insularity, where we are able to operate without interference. In this regard, dwelling acts as a passive receptacle of interpreted and subjective meanings. Thus dwelling is as much emotional and ontological as it is physical. We need not see these ways of seeing – physical and ontological – as conflicting, but as connected through the use of the dwelling itself.

This might suggest a purely functionalist role for the dwelling, where its passive station merely serves as an orientating mechanism. But this is only the case if we see orientation in purely spatial terms and not equally as an ontological concept. Dwelling orientates our sense of being – our notion of ourselves as substantial beings in the world. In ontological terms, it is where our use of the dwelling signals its meaning and allows us to authenticate our passage through (Heidegger, 1971, but also see chapter 1). Thus we have a sense of place that goes beyond the physical, and dwelling operates beyond mere function to include the existential.

The most fundamental manner in which this orientating mechanism operates is by distinguishing between indoors and outdoors, as the effective boundary that separates us from the world. Indoors means one is *behind* something, which is itself substantial. As such it allows us to close off or put out those elements that disturb us and to make ourselves secure against them. But this image can also carry with it a sense of finality and decisiveness: we 'slam the door' on something to show without doubt our feelings. These phrases carry the idea that one cannot return to the *status quo ante*. We have 'ended a chapter' and put part of our life outside our normal orbit. But presumably, in ending something, we have also set up the possibility of beginning anew. Being indoors therefore suggests we have put something behind us, which now allows us the prospect of pursuing and attaining something without that interference. By closing off much of what is now external we place more onus on ourselves to attain what we seek. But the very act of closing off means not having to take so many risks. We are able to stick with the tried and trusted: with the known formula. We can opt out of those things we consider an imposition: we can slam the door on them. But, of course, all we might seek to attain is the exclusion of the external.

The contrast between indoors and outdoors throws some light on how we use dwelling. These two notions connect with ideas of space, place, boundaries and boundedness. They are suggestive of constraint and opportunity, of limits and possibilities. Going outdoors opens up possibilities and takes us beyond the particular boundary of our dwelling. We have gone beyond what is just ours into a less personally determined environment, where we become open to contingency, change and unpredictability. When we are indoors we can close ourselves off to many of these things. It is where we almost necessarily have to make the opportunities *ourselves* or, at least, it is where we would like to do so. When we are indoors contingency is less welcome. The essence of interior dwelling is its predictability: this is the nature of homeliness, where we can keep things how they are and should be, and I am what determines the *how* and the *should*.

Much of what we know about outdoors is conditioned by our internal environment, through the very act of 'looking out' from the dwelling. What we look out of determines how we view the external. This means that our dwelling literally *frames* the external. In many and frequent circumstances the external can affect the internal. It will do this on some occasions due to inclement or severe weather. On others it is more due to location – one lives on the coast or up a mountain and thus is more prone to the vicissitudes of climate. But more typically, our immediate external environment is so managed as to protect internal dwelling rather than the reverse. Hence the organisation of roads, shops, gardens, paths, and so on, all leading to our dwelling and helping to make dwelling comfortable and secure. The external environment here is managed to facilitate our dwelling.

Dwelling, being primarily subjective, is both fragmentary and elliptical. It has neither a consistent nor a singular form. This is an important understanding, but it is also one that needs immediate qualification. As we shall see, the essence of dwelling *for any one of us* is its regularity. Yet, in its totality, it cannot be understood with any completeness. What is consistent in its form for me, is eccentric to others. The subjectivity of dwelling leaves it

The structure of our dwelling frames the external world

opaque to the generalisations of science. We cannot find patterns beyond the habits within any one dwelling.

There is then an ambiguity, even obscurity to dwelling, going beyond any unclarity between verb and noun. Dwelling has an opaque quality that creates a disjuncture between the interior and the external environment. However, this is merely to state the necessity of dwelling to ensure privacy. Dwelling is also obscure in another, quite crucial sense. It is our very obscurity that protects us from scrutiny. That we are, so to speak, *nothing special*, is what allows us to live privately and pursue ends of our choosing. Hence the key problem of celebrity is that it makes the celebrity's way of life significantly more transparent: they cease to dwell distinctly as themselves, but take on a *lifestyle* that becomes distinctive of them as celebrated. Their dwelling, being publicised, becomes of a type: 'this is how these people live'.

The key benefit of obscurity is that it allows a sense of proportion in dwelling: we are able to use our dwelling as we wish, without the consequent fear of intrusion. Yet when the dwelling becomes transparent due to celebrity, the emphasis shifts away from authentic use purely to that of protection and security: hence the claim of celebrities that they cannot even open their curtains for fear of being photographed, let alone sit quietly in their garden. Celebrity means that one is forced into ostentatious displays of privacy. Paradoxically this merely makes the celebrity more apparent.

Physical structures have an implacability to use. They are formed as solid entities, within which we are forced to move. Hence we do not grasp the dwelling, but rather it grasps us. But the dwelling appears to differ according to the time of day, although not because of any changes it has made. Its apparent difference is due to us and how we perceive it. This apparent transformation is perhaps most noticeable at the extremes of the day: at first light or when it is dark.

The purest quiet is in the early morning. We hear the odd creak from the house and birdsong from outside, but little else, other than perhaps the gentle breathing of those closest to us. What marks this time is its clarity and optimism. It is a time of possibility. Consequently we are torn between savouring it and using it well. We are almost intoxicated by our clear-headedness. Yet, in the morning things appear different from how we felt them the night before. Much of the fantasy has gone with the daylight. We are more sober, rational and without illusion. Life seems somehow more quotidian. Is this because the world beyond what is ours is now more visible? We can now see all around us and it is much harder to continue with our dreams and illusions.

When all is black outside we feel more enclosed and isolated from the world. This may depress us, for instance, on the first early dark night after the end of British Summer Time. We feel the dark oppressing us and we cannot help feeling that the carefree days of the summer, which open out for us full of light and possibility, are now over for another year. From now there is just the slog of winter, and, of course, much more darkness, even when we awake.

Yet, there is also a warmth to be gained from this enclosure. The darkness outside contrasts with the fastness and comfort of the dwelling: it emphasises that dwelling encloses us and that we need such enclosing. Hence the great comfort we gain in shutting out the world by drawing the curtains: we can put it all outside of us in the knowledge we are missing nothing.

But it is not just in the extremes of light and dark that we gain this special sense of security. There is a wonderful complacency in being inside when it is raining: when it is possible to revel in the fastness of one's home, snug and secure and perfectly dry. There is nothing more pleasing than watching a torrential downpour – the spectacular violence of nature – but only so long as we are securely – and dryly – away from it. We prefer to watch the elemental forces of nature rather than be part of them – or rather we want the ability to withdraw from nature when we choose to. All this demonstrates one of the cardinal virtues of dwelling: *the necessary encouragement of complacency.*

Complacency

Part, perhaps even the main part, of the significance of dwelling is that it is an entity that needs no reflection for it to be operated. In that sense dwelling is properly *supportive*. It exists and operates prior to and without our reflection on it. Rather it is the space in which many, if not most, of our reflections take place. We do not need to know how the dwelling and its myriad amenities and functions work. Such knowledge would merely distract us from our main interests and ends. What we need the dwelling for then is to provide the background or the stage upon which we can play. This does indeed mean that we need dwelling to have the leisure to reflect, and that we can only think about the nature of dwelling whilst we have a dwelling in which to reflect. It is precisely the lack of any imperative that constitutes the major virtue we find in dwelling and, of course, this is precisely why it is an imperative that we have it.

The activity of dwelling should be seen as the compound of our individual experiences, which receive no explicit articulation except through the condition of dwelling itself: as the self-justifying aggregate of the very actions that it sustains. Dwelling is the process that comes out of, and is caused by, our experience, and when we look back, we review not dwelling itself, but the experiences themselves. Dwelling is thus a consequence of itself, where its maintenance is its rationality and its rationality is what we seek to maintain. Our actions constitute dwelling, as dwelling allows our actions to continue.

What this suggests is that, for the most part, our dwelling is used and not observed. We use it and this slowly alters the physicality of the dwelling. But seldom in a manner that we can separately quantify. The decorative state and condition of our dwelling matters less than our actions within it. We can, and do, carry on living in and with the dwelling, without noticing its objective condition. It is only when the use becomes impaired, or when others enter the dwelling, that we begin to look around and see it in a more dispassionate manner. This is because much of our relationship with the dwelling is unreflective.

When we do articulate our thoughts on our dwelling we tend to idealise it. This is partly because it is so central to us that it frames our perception on dwelling in a more general sense: to be without it is beyond our proper perceptions and thus we find it hard to articulate such a profound loss. But this idealisation occurs also because of the vocabulary we have to describe our dwelling. This vocabulary, naturally, is a shared convention. We discuss our dwelling in a conventional way in order to be understood. We do not have the vocabulary to describe our personal meanings, except in either banal or circular ways: 'the dwelling is good for me', 'it suits me', 'it's mine', and so on. This is because of the limits of conventions. Conventions, because they proscribe and prescribe in a manner understandable only to the initiated, are incapable of informing an outsider of how we live. They merely dictate the limits of actions and hence how we fit within understood and accepted bounds. Hence we tend to concentrate on décor, design, size, location and so on, as these are those things that have a common reference.

This suggests that there may be a distinction between the everyday linguistic conventions of dwelling and our actual experiences of it. Dwelling, as a private subjective experience, sits outside communicative discourse. It allows us to withdraw from social interaction, or rather, it allows us to limit the amount of interaction to a level we find acceptable. Hence, to challenge someone on how they live is likely to be seen as offensive.

But more fundamentally there is a distinction between the manner in which we discuss dwelling – the conventions of space, value, décor, etc. – and the way in which we actually use the dwelling. The latter is habitual and implicit, and in consequence unarticulated and perhaps incapable of full articulation. Dwelling has a *preverbal* quality: it lacks any positive articulation through any means other than its actual experience, in any way other than the acts themselves. When we discuss the components of dwelling we therefore lose something in the attempt to combine them into an understandable whole, or to standardise these experiences into socially coherent models. The shared language of dwelling is therefore something like a *highest common denominator*, under which sits the ubiquity of dwelling as a quotidian experience beyond the need for articulation.[4]

This lack of articulation derives from the generally imperceptible nature in which dwelling develops, both as a structure and as an activity. The dwelling changes only in tiny increments. We never see the crack forming, the paint peeling, yet, of course, after a certain point we cannot help but notice it. This is obviously related to our powers of sensory perception, but it is also a function of the unreflective nature of private dwelling. We do not scrutinise the dwelling in its common usage. It is only when the uncommon occurs that we notice any fault.

The distinction between the routine and the unexpected is therefore an important one. Because most minor problems (which if left unattended may become significant) have developed incrementally and imperceptibly, we do not get overly concerned about them. The state of decoration deteriorates slowly and imperceptibly, until at some point we begin to notice it. The problem, at some point, attains a certain critical mass that makes it a cause for concern. But it does not prevent us from living there and we can still choose to ignore the problem. Many of these things may be lived with almost indefinitely.

But our complacency breaks down when unexpected events occur, such as a major collapse, breakdown or system failure, or when a major change in relations occurs such as the gaining or loss of a partner or family member. What matters here is our sense of control. We can afford complacency because we consider ourselves to be in control of the situation. We might need to replace some fitting or redecorate, but we can choose to do so when it suits us without affecting the integrity of the dwelling and our enjoyment of it: the functioning of the dwelling is not seriously impaired should we delay these minor repairs and improvements. A calamity, however, makes it impossible to continue living in the dwelling as we would like, and we cannot retain our state of complacency until the problem is properly dealt with (and, of course, when it comes to the loss of a loved one, it may never be). In this situation, we have lost control and can only regain it with a considerable effort (physical, financial and emotional) from ourselves and perhaps not without outside help from an expert. Insuring the dwelling may give some financial peace of mind, but it still does not equate with the sense of complacent control we seek from the dwelling when it operates in such a way as to sustain our actions.

When the dwelling works properly we are complacent with and in it. It supports us and allows us to attend to our aims and interests without worrying about what buoys us up. Yet this very sense of safety can lead to a lack of any proper proportion, and this is precisely because of the very success that dwelling has in insulating us from risk. As a result we may not always be able to distinguish between the calamity and the minor problem, except in hindsight. Perhaps this is why minor faults in the dwelling – a small leak for instance – have such a disproportionate emotional effect and create a sense of anxiety within us. These faults make manifest the dwelling's complexity in terms of its function and just how much is really involved in securing the complacent background to our lives. As an example, consider the impact of something as trite as a broken door handle, which prevents us from gaining access to a room, or more worryingly traps us within. It can readily be fixed, but in the meantime it makes it clear to us how dependent we are even on simple mechanical devices: we are impotent in the face of a broken door handle.

What effect does this have on the fastness of the dwelling and our perception of it in terms of security? First, it tells us that security, such as locks, can also mean entrapment.[5] The mechanisms in the dwelling are blind and arbitrary in their operation. They do not work only for us or merely because we will them to do so. As equipment they would work equally well for anyone; what is more, they would work equally well against us as with us or for us. Dwelling, as a mechanism, is blind and implacable, with no purpose that can be dictated beyond its last or present use. Second, dealing with even such a trite mechanical fault might involve skills we do not have ourselves. Hence we would have to call on someone from outside the dwelling to fix the handle. So, what we consider private and personal can only be maintained and managed with the help of strangers. What we think of as uniquely ours depends upon the care of others. Third, it might only be possible to mend the fault by dismantling part of the dwelling itself. In this sense we not only see the internal workings of the dwelling, but also how readily the dwelling can be unmade. The dwelling is really a series of parts that fit together to form the whole. However, there is nothing inevitable in their current form and the components of dwelling can be readily understood as something else, namely, a series of disaggregated parts.

But fourth, we need to realise how quickly the sense of comfort and security returns once the fault is cured. And how we all too readily forget the insecurity and fears as the sense of comfort overwhelms them. As soon as dwelling begins to function as we wish it, we readily forget its disaggregated state. We lose sight of our dependency and it is precisely the renewed fastness of the dwelling that encourages us to do so. But, of course, we still know that our dwelling is linked with the outside, through a series of pipes, wires and cables. We know this because we use them and depend upon them. Yet, because we can close the door on the outside, we believe we have made this dependency invisible. We use the dwelling itself – its regularities and dependability – to block out what is beyond the threshold. Thus we tend to forget how much we are connected and how much we depend on the outside world merely to maintain our insularity.

We are able to do this so readily because many of the services we are dependent on in the dwelling are hidden and appear to operate automatically, such as water, sewerage, gas, electricity, etc. They are literally there at the click of a switch, or turn of a tap, as the most banal of domestic operations. They operate within the regularity of our habitual behaviour. Of course we notice them when we are billed, although this relates to affordability and not to functioning. This, however, is the limit of the relation, unless, of course, something goes wrong, at which point the nature of the dependence again becomes all too manifest. It is because we take so much for granted that the lack of function is so disturbing.

We need to consider, in the light of this, just how important is the need to hide the dependence on these external services? Is it not the case that if the complexity of the dwelling were made too manifest the whole complacency of dwelling would be lost? We need therefore to separate the maintenance of dwelling from our enjoyment of it, as the two do not subsist together. We cannot maintain the complacency that gives us comfort and an unthinking security, whilst continually being reminded of the dwelling's complexity and the relative ease of its disaggregation, which makes it clear that the dwelling, as an entity and potential jumble of disparate entities, is not beholden to us.

We do not know all parts of the dwelling equally well. There are parts of the dwelling that we do know very well, even intimately. We are extremely familiar with how certain rooms look and feel, with patterns on the bedroom ceiling, patterns on curtains and carpets, the décor of living rooms, and so on. We know these places so well we have to make the effort to notice them as distinct entities. These are the places we use frequently, either for work or leisure: they are the places that act as background to more major actions. However, other parts of the dwelling are hardly ever known to us or seen by us, such as the attic, the insides of machines such as boilers and water tanks, store cupboards, and so on. This relates, of course, to the amount of time we spend in them. In some places we choose not to linger, either because they are unpleasant, or because they have a purely functional role in the dwelling. Hence to go there implies dysfunction. Yet in some places function and a sense of embeddedness coalesce; for example, we might linger in a hot bath, or read while on the toilet. This is because we use these places frequently, even though their purpose, ostensibly at least, is entirely functional: the function is a usual one.[6] In this sense, particular functions and parts of the dwelling are taken for granted. When we go into other places – the loft, for instance – it is for a special and unusual purpose. An important distinction here is between usual (or regular!) and unusual or irregular activities.

How do we feel about those parts that are unfamiliar to us? They have a function, which is often quite a specific one, or as a place to store things we have no regular use for. But we can safely ignore their role, unless the functioning fails or we need to retrieve something. Getting to know these areas is frequently connected to problems or disruption, such as leaks, blockages, and breakdowns, or when the dwelling is being in some way transformed.

This suggests that we would, in normal circumstances, fully use only part of the physical space in the dwelling, and this applies even where all living rooms and bedrooms are used; for example, where there are four people in a four-person house. We fully use the major rooms and connecting passages, whilst other parts are only entered for more specific purposes and not generally lingered in. However, we still need these spaces, to ensure we can live intimately in those areas we are embedded in and know well. We need to store things away from these areas of intimacy and to hide the basic functions of the dwelling such as wiring, plumbing, etc. Most assuredly, there is an aesthetic element to this, but it is also due to the need to ensure that the dwelling appears as a place of comfort and leisure and not as an active machine.

This latter point is crucial. Le Corbusier (1927) may have referred to a house as 'a machine for living in' (p. 4), but this is a conceit shared by few if any who see their dwelling as a place of comfort and rest. It is the machinic quality of dwelling which we wish to hide. This is because, as Le Corbusier with his desire for standardisation knew only too well, this concept serves to objectify the dwelling as something impersonal and implacable.[7] But in doing so – standardisation, according to Le Corbusier, 'demands uniformity' (1929, p. 76) – the subjective level of dwelling is denuded and left subservient to the external gaze. We require the dwelling to operate and to do so consistently. However, the supporting mechanism should be discreet and unobtrusive: it should be hidden from view. What we seek is not a dwelling in which the functioning is obvious. Rather, in order to maintain our complacency, we seek a continuum: we seek *stability*.

Stability

The achievement and enjoyment of dwelling suggests a dichotomy between the active and passive levels of experience: that we are active at one level and passive at another. Dwelling is created actively, yet enjoyed passively, or the engagement with the external is active, whilst insularity has with it a certain passivity. This may lead us to suggest that judging the success of dwelling might be according to some measure of activity and passivity, with the more successful at the passive pole.

Yet is this the correct dichotomy? Might the proper distinction not be between conscious versus unconscious action? Is it not the case that we actively seek some purpose in the creation of dwelling that involves a direct relation with the external world, but once achieved we enjoy dwelling unconsciously, in a state that has no real purpose beyond its own continuance?

There is, of course, a link between these two dichotomies. The passive can readily relate to the unconscious, and the active to the conscious. The distinction might therefore more properly be between, on the one hand, our having a purpose or direction and, on the other hand, a relatively directionless enjoyment. We might also see the distinction as between striving for something and its achievement.

However, when looking at how we dwell, is there a real difference between active and passive? Is it not actually a matter of relative levels? What we seek to do is to maintain *the continuum of existence*, interspersed with peaks of activity, followed by troughs. These peaks and troughs might affect aspects of the continuum, but they do not destroy it. What this suggests is a purely qualitative distinction between dwelling in the immediate sense, which is largely active, albeit at a banal or mundane level, and the longer term, where dwelling is seen as passive. This is where it appears as a continuum in which we even out peaks and troughs within the banal meandering of everyday life. Thus the essence of successful dwelling, by which is meant dwelling that has been and can be sustained, is its stability.

Successful dwelling, therefore, is that which allows us to exist on a continuum: to be complacent and accepting of our situation. In short, it provides c*omfort*. Dwelling means that we do not have to make many decisions, and ideally to make any.[8] Dwelling is therefore where we are free of cares beyond ourselves and those intimate with us, or, to qualify this somewhat, where our cares are of our own making.

The operation of such a stable continuum means that dwelling, as an activity, loses any comparative sense. The comparative nature of dwelling, such as those matters that allow us to gauge economic value, status and stigma, relate primarily to external elements. Value is determined by standard features that can be compared such as size, shape and appearance. These give the property what might be called its *public value*. It may be these factors, along with location, that initially attract us to a dwelling. We have a limited budget and seek the best available opportunities for us at that level. We may have particular aspirations that manifest themselves in particular house types. We may be set against certain areas and certain locations because of how we, or others, perceive the area. These are all concerns that we may share with others.

But we would agree to purchase a dwelling only after having looked at the interior: when we have had the opportunity to gauge its potential to fit our own particular and peculiar dwelling needs. This is a subjective process and based on intuition, according to conditions which are not shared or necessarily public. Indeed we may not even be able to explain it ourselves, in that we do not fully know what we want unless and until we find it. Thus on some occasions we will know straight away that a property is unsuitable, without even having to articulate why. But then we may find a dwelling that appears to fit our idea of the dwelling we need, and we know we must have it; and again, we may only be able to articulate why later, once we have filled it and begun to use it. Of course, we need never articulate it at all: why we choose a particular dwelling is a matter for us and not for anyone else.

What this demonstrates is that the external features of dwelling are publicly competitive and open to comparison, whilst the internal, subjective condition tends not to be. This is principally because we can exclude access to others from the internal aspect, whilst the external is permanently on view. Viewed from the outside our dwelling sits next to or near others and can be compared: it is of a particular type, in an area with a known reputation. But viewed from within, it is not just of a type, but completely *ours and only ours*. At this level public comparisons are as irrelevant as they are inappropriate.

A sense of stability depends on how we relate to space. Typically we will move in it, use it, seek to explore it and then try to control it. But how we achieve this will differ significantly according to the meaning we attach to that space, for example, between our own dwelling, which is a space we know intimately, and a wild unknown environment. Actions in the dwelling, in a sense, are always in the past tense – we have moved, explored and controlled it – whilst a wilderness is still full of possibility and, of course, danger. What gives dwelling much of its meaning is the lack of danger and thus the overriding sense of complacency and well-being derived from the space we know best of all. We know what it does and we believe that there is nothing hidden there to threaten us.

It is fortunately rare that we have to create a new dwelling. The activity of dwelling is not often about the creation of a new environment, but about maintaining what we have already. This is even the case when we move from one dwelling to another. Much of what we have and want need not be newly made when we move: we take much with us. So, whilst dwelling is an ongoing process which leads to some development, it is always a development out of something, and not the creation of an entirely new entity. But then we would not, in most cases, want this sense of new creation as it would destroy much of what dwelling protects and allows. We seek to take our sense of stability and complacency with us – to fit the various elements back together.

This is even the case when we are living temporarily in a dwelling, for instance, on holiday. In such a temporary dwelling, with equipment we are unused to, and where not much is as we would like if we could choose, we still quickly slip into a routine, using the temporary dwelling in a regular and patterned way. We organise where to put things (groceries, clothes, etc.) and then do not change the arrangement for the duration of the holiday, even though the initial decision was entirely arbitrary. Part of this mirrors the normal patterns in our permanent dwelling, in that, so far as we can, we try and map our own spaces over the new area. But, of course this routinisation also depends on the nature of the temporary dwelling. Therefore what matters is the particular structure of the dwelling and what space it affords us to live in the manner to which we are accustomed. So we have no trouble adjusting to new structures and arrangements and quickly make our patterns around them. We are readily able to adapt to new situations as circumstances dictate.

But equally, once we come home we slip straight back into a routine as if we had not been away. And, importantly, we do not take much, if any, of the temporary routines back with us. These temporary routines quickly fade as we fall back into the ingrained habits and routes through our familiar dwelling. Perhaps this is what makes the temporary dwelling so bearable and unproblematic: we know that we will soon return to our regularities and habits and our sense of continuity will not be broken.

What is interesting is that, with some dwellings the length away seems to make no difference. We would still consider our parents' dwelling as *our home*, regardless of how long we have been away. The routinisation we have developed is here so ingrained that it has become part of our mental equipment, which can be readily reactivated.

The distinction between temporary and permanent dwelling is interesting in a further manner. We will tend to be more prepared to put up with discomfort and inconvenience in temporary accommodation than if it were permanent. Is it simply because we know it to be temporary and that our expectations of the function of the dwelling are different? On holiday we use the dwelling as a base that allows us to do other things, and hence we are prepared to put up with caravans, tents or shared space, knowing that we will only spend the minimum period of time there. Were we to live in these permanently we would quickly find them intolerable. Perhaps this explains why holiday dwellings are the dreariest of all when it rains and we cannot go out: their function is laid bare and their inadequacy for permanent dwelling becomes all too manifest. More than that, of course, it is not our responsibility – or place, as it were – to fix those things we do not like.

What this suggests is that our attitude towards a dwelling, and hence our tolerance and acceptance of it, are determined by the uses to which we are to put it. The purpose of the holiday flat is to focus us *outwards*, as a base allowing us to explore. However, our permanent home encourages insularity. The temporary dwelling pushes us out along new pathways and allows us sufficient respite when we have explored enough. It can be seen as a staging post assisting us as we explore. The permanent dwelling locates us or roots us in the environment and acts as a beacon for our return. The function of the permanent dwelling is not to push us out, but instead to *gather us in*. So if the dwelling exists, as Gaston Bachelard (1969) has it, to protect intimacy and to provide comfort and security, we would have different aspirations and expectations of it than if the dwelling were a temporary base allowing us to explore an area. What would be unbearable at home is merely amusing on holiday: instead of being unworkable and intolerable it is merely eccentric. In our permanent dwelling we eschew eccentricity, or rather, any eccentricity is of our own making and thus, of course, only seen as such by others.

Dwelling, even when it is considered eccentric, should be patterned and consist of regularities. These regularities develop with use and thus over time. Dwelling is rule-bound, and it is this that allows us to imagine and dream and to separate ourselves from the outside world. We can do this through the regularities of that structure we call dwelling. We can do this because the dwelling both encloses and enframes; we can do this because the dwelling gives us complacency; we can do this because of the stability dwelling offers.

Dwelling is then more than just a brick box. It is undoubtedly a structure, but a structure based not merely on bricks and mortar, but on emotional and ontological foundations: it is a subjective construction that builds on a physical structure to create something infinitely more useful, more meaningful and more creative. It is what enables us to withdraw and yet be part of a social world: what enables us to dream and desire, and what assuages, but also creates, many of our anxieties. It is a construction of sublime complexity, yet one that is always *ours*. Dwelling, then, is very much like a case, with us embedded in its deep folds of velvet.

Chapter 4
Talking about houses

Dwelling is full – it is cluttered up – with language. There is nothing apparently we enjoy talking about more than our house, particularly what it cost compared to what it is now worth, what we have done with it, and what we intend to do with it. Our housing, we are told, is the new symbol of the self: the badge of middle class membership, worn and polished with pride. Housing, it is said, is what makes the chattering classes chatter. And when we chatter we say so much about ourselves.

But within our dwellings, we also talk of things for certain ears only: secret whispers, hopes, aspirations and fears. Dwelling is the one place where it is safe to articulate our dreams. Dwelling is where we discuss the most banal and inconsequential things, which do not matter beyond the saying: dwelling is where language is as much about the saying as the said. Yet it is also the space where we state the most fundamental truths and make the firmest of commitments. Language is here the confirmation of companionship and togetherness: it is the very act of caring and sharing.

Dwelling also, as it were, speaks itself. Dwelling speaks in a way like nothing else we have or use. On the one hand, all dwellings everywhere and always are unique entities, in the particular sense of their specific habitation, their sense of meaning and the ends that they embody. Yet on the other hand, dwelling is ubiquitous: dwellings are after all 'everywhere and always'. Dwelling is thus particular *and* universal, special to each of us yet common to all. Our dwelling then can be seen as *an amplifier of values*. How we live demonstrates to others, and to ourselves, what is important in terms of the care of children, the importance of commodities and the insularity of the household. And like our values the dwelling will develop and change as our internal and external relations change. Our dwelling also confirms that we are like others. It may set us apart, but equally it demonstrates what we share with those around us. Therefore, in a certain sense, our dwellings speak for us about what we are, and about us to others; if we are candid, they also speak to us about who and what we want to be. The dwelling, then, can also be seen as a mirror that we hold up to ourselves. Much of dwelling is implicit and habitual, but it is also, perhaps inadvertently, expressive of our personality.

This articulation might not be a conscious process (and this is why it might be a dangerous thing to 'read' and then judge others – is it something *we* would readily accept?). We do not reflect and then act, but rather are led by convention, by accepted rules and norms that control, limit and direct us. These operate with and within language: language itself is based on conventions, which, in turn, are articulated by language. Thus we can fruitfully grapple with the conventionality of dwelling and how we use language conventionally to understand, discuss and dissimulate how we live. These entire speculations can be said to be concerned with how dwelling speaks to and of us; here I shall be concerned with some of the ways in which we talk about dwelling and the conventions within which this operates. As with all these speculations, my aim is not particularly to question, merely to understand better what place dwelling is, so that it can speak more clearly of and to us.

Housing discourse and ordinary language

But if my concern is with how dwelling speaks to us, should I not see this as a discourse? Ought I not, along with an increasing body of housing researchers, seek to develop a dwelling discourse? Could I not tap into this fertile area of research to help my argument along?

Discourse analysis has indeed been used in a most interesting manner by a number of housing researchers since the mid 1990s.[1] Discourse can be seen as a method of analysis that attributes significance to language as the signifier of substantive entities. This involves using techniques that analyse the use of language and show how certain actions can be attributed with significance by the labels attached to them.

Fairclough (1992) therefore suggests that discourse can be seen as both textual analysis, in the sense of the structure of language, and as specific to particular situations. Thus there is marketing discourse, counselling discourse and perhaps even a housing discourse. Thus there are special discourses aimed at exclusion and inclusion depending on our facility with that language. Hence the very use of a term, say 'problem estate', can help to 'create' the entity itself. A good recent example in the housing literature is where Franklin (2001) uses discourse analysis to question notions of quality and design standards.

But does this allow us to develop a dwelling discourse? I have tried to suggest that dwelling is exclusive at the household level – we seek to exclude all others from our household – but that it is inclusive in the sense of enclosing all those who use a dwelling. We all place the label 'keep out' in front of our dwelling, but this is a sign of a common language with few exceptions. The very ubiquity of dwelling might therefore militate against the development of a dwelling discourse.

Yet discourse theory goes further than merely an analysis of language, and has been developed into a thorough critique of ideology. As Jacob Torfing (1999) has suggested, discourse is now used in a wider sense than mere texts and language. Following Jacques Derrida (1978) and Ernesto Laclau (1993), Torfing defines discourse as 'a decentred structure in which meaning is constantly negotiated and constructed' (1999, p. 40). The structure is seen as 'an ensemble of signifying sequences' (p. 40) and allows for the inclusion of both physical and non-physical objects.

Torfing (1999) argues that discourse theory offers an anti-essentialist view of the individual subject as constantly constructed and reconstructed socially:

> In sharp contrast to the essentialist conception of identity, discourse analysis emphasises the construction of social identity in and through hegemonic practices of articulation, which partially fixes the meaning of social identities by inscribing them in the differential system of a certain discourse.
>
> (Torfing, 1999, p. 41)

What this means is that the subject is created by discourse – their identity is constructed through discourse – as much as discourse is created by individual subjects in speech acts. One might therefore suggest that a social housing discourse is not merely a label or a description of practices. Rather, in addition to these policies and practices, it is made up of the dwellings, the tenants, those organisations representing tenants, landlords, the surrounding environment, and the perceptions of the wider society. What is important to note here is that this discourse is not static, but is decentred, contingent and shifting. The discourse alters as the context changes, but the discourse also helps to change the context. An example of this is the manner in which the National Housing Federation (NHF), the lobby group for English housing associations, has sought to 'rebrand' its members' activities. In response to survey evidence that social housing was for 'losers' and that working in the sector was not seen to be of high status, the NHF employed branding consultants to try to remodel the image of housing associations as being 'iN [sic] business for neighbourhoods' (NHF, 2003). The clear aim here is to try to assert a new identity for social housing providers in the face of structural, political and ideological obstacles. Social housing was seen, rightly or wrongly, to be failing, so, it is suggested, its role should appear to change. The underlying assumptions here are that there is no given role for housing associations, but that it has to respond to changing political and ideological conditions, and hence recreate a new discourse for itself.

We could develop these insights further and seek to develop a dwelling discourse using the work of Derrida, Laclau and others. However, I have chosen not to do so for several reasons. First, I wish to remain true to my starting principles for this project, which are to steer clear of overt theorising in favour of description and the appreciation of the correct questions (Wittgenstein, 1953). What I wish to do is to open up, if only in some small way, the manner in which we discuss private dwelling, and to do so without trying to fit these insights into some overarching (and possibly, overreaching) theory. Second, my aim in this chapter is somewhat less ambitious than that of those who use discourse analysis. I just want to consider some of the ways in which we discuss our dwelling, and how we use certain terms and phrases to enhance and even create meanings. But I do not want to try to systemise this into anything too significant as yet. My aim in this book is to cover a broad range of topics that seem to me to be germane to the private use of housing, and consequently I cannot afford to progress all themes to their fullest extent. Perhaps, therefore, this chapter might be seen as a step towards developing a dwelling discourse that might be added to existing work and serve as the basis for future analysis. Third, as I have already intimated, this whole project might be seen as a dwelling discourse. It seeks to investigate the manner in which dwelling helps to construct meanings for us, but also how we construct dwelling as a meaningful set of practices. Now this may be so, but it would still need to be fully worked out and explicitly stated, and I have not space for it here.

But if this book can be seen as a dwelling discourse, this does raise one of the main doubts about using discourse analysis in housing (and indeed more generally). When we begin to consider what a dwelling discourse might be, we soon find that it encloses a huge range of activities and interests including the key issues looked at in this book; it also includes issues not fully covered such as child care, property rights, gender, technology, architectural styles, employment patterns, mobility, and so on. Now this might seem to be a key benefit of any theorisation – if a theory can enclose much that is significant it might be useful. But might we not also argue that a theory that excludes nothing offers us little room for analysis. As an example, we can compare discourse with theories of power. Most theories of power, be they Marxist, liberal or Foucauldian, are based around a dichotomy or dialectic of inclusion and exclusion. They involve the theorising of mechanisms for discriminating between individuals and groups: they are means by which we can state the relations between these individuals and groups, *and seek to explain them*. However, it seems to me, that with discourse all we can do is list what discourse includes or state what we mean by the term, and then come to some generalities about its pervasiveness. What we are left with then is to say that 'discourse is everywhere and everything is discourse', which perhaps does not take us terribly far!

But it is not my intention to develop this argument, any more than I have sought to expound discourse itself: a fuller rehearsal of these arguments will have to be left to another time and place. What I want to do for most of this chapter is to use ordinary language philosophy to consider certain ways in which we talk about housing. What I am seeking to do here is to address certain key phrases as exemplars of the manner in which we refer to housing, and how these implicate the notions of intimacy and privacy within our own housing. I would suggest that there is much to be gained from considering how the tradition of ordinary language philosophy might tackle the manner in which certain words and phrases are used in housing discourse. To my mind though, the advantage of ordinary language philosophy is that it takes a more piecemeal approach, which allows us to take concrete examples and examine these within particular contexts. This approach, albeit in a non-programmatic manner, looks at how words are used in context. What it attempts to do is establish what we mean when we say certain things in certain places. In this way, it is hoped, an added dimension can be given to the burgeoning number of studies that consider the force of discourse in housing and dwelling.

What do we mean when we say ... dwelling?

Some of the language used to discuss dwelling is fascinating: certain phrases have a particular meaning and resonance to us. Perhaps, in exploring these, we could make use of J. L. Austin's stock phrase of '*what do we mean when we say ...?*' (Austin, 1962). Of course, we may never fully understand what we mean, and we may not really mean it when we say it (let alone really know how it is received ... but this is beginning to get all too Derridean). Yet when anyone says anything, they do it with some intention and we can legitimately seek out what these intentions are.

So, for example, just what is meant when someone tells us to '*make yourself at home*'? Do they really mean that it is up to us to create a sense of home – *make yourself* – even though the phrase implies that something is being offered or given to us? Is the host suggesting that what we should do is create our own sense of home *here*? Are we supposed to do the things we would actually do at home, or are we not to defer to our host's sense of the acceptable? Unless we know these people well we will not be aware of what their terms are, and thus risk offending them. If I habitually lie on a settee with my feet up, whilst smoking a cigarette, is the host saying 'do this here'? If it is my habit to make myself a light snack when I feel like it, should I do that too?

But also consider what is meant by 'make'. We are being asked, or even told, to do something: the phrase is an imperative, albeit a polite and gracious one. Nonetheless we have been told to do something by our host, who ordinarily would be at our service. Is the host really relieving themselves of their responsibilities? Is what they mean, 'you make yourself comfortable, because I'm not going to do it'? This is probably not what is meant, but what if we took their command as such, particularly if one imagines this being said by a host whilst they gesture expansively and sit down complacently? What if we said, 'OK, I'll do it then!' and promptly poured ourselves a beer and raided the fridge? We would not be making ourselves at home, but simply being rude.

What is meant by this phrase is not 'do as you like', or 'do as you would at home', but rather it is an attempt to make one feel comfortable and at ease: that one can dispense with a certain formality – but not with all formality. We should see this simply as an example of some common set of values: some common sense of what it means to be at home. We are not being given any licence, but merely told that we should not be anxious and that nothing is actually being expected of us. The meaning is therefore the reverse of the actual statement: one is to do nothing particular, but relax and enjoy the hospitality one is being offered. Yet we are clearly still bound by an unspoken commitment not to overstep our welcome or to act in a manner that the host finds uncongenial. This means we can never fully relax, as we have no accurate means of gauging where the limit is, except, of course, through an understanding of what we would deem as unacceptable in our own home. Thus, what we are being asked to respect is a limit and not a licence, and we are left to 'make' that judgement on the basis of what we would do 'at home'.

Perhaps one of the most annoying of all phrases used by schoolteachers is the question asked of the misbehaving pupil: '*Would you do that at home?*' This is related to the above discussion in that it too presupposes some judgement of behaviour based on what we do 'at home'. The implication here is that one should respect the school environment, as one would treat one's own home. Yet is this really an appropriate thing to suggest? When one is at home one can quite readily sit around naked or partially dressed, eat with a spoon or pick one's nose – all things deemed to be impolite in public. The essence of dwelling is its informality, where we live with those who are prepared to forgive our faults even as they try to reform us. How we act at home is, in many ways, exactly how we should not, and would not, act in public. It is where we are not held accountable for every action and where we are free from judgement. So the answer to the first question is that one is in fact more likely to 'do it' at home.

But it may be that the aim of this phrase is actually to connect up notions of dwelling, such as respect and care for others, within the public sphere. It is as if 'at home' is where it is deemed we act properly and that we should seek to emulate this in public. Therefore the phrase, however inaccurate it may be with regard to actual practice, shows the elemental significance of dwelling as a mechanism for social stability. It is in the privacy of dwelling that we are socialised and 'made ready' for social life. It is our parents who teach us to behave socially. What the phrase 'would you do this at home?' is drawing attention to then is the sense in which dwelling shapes us as social beings. It is this sphere that sets the standards by which we are judged when we venture out into the social world.[2]

The key point here is that, whilst we can be informal 'at home', we also treat this space with great respect as our secure and trusted base. We want it to be special, and so it is expected that we behave in a manner that is respectful. It is in public where we might be less inclined to show this respect, as we are using things which are not ours and to which we have no great attachment.[3] Thus, in a perverse way, to act in an anti-social manner is to behave in a way we would not do 'at home'. Now of course, this says nothing about how we actually do behave – otherwise we would not be asked 'whether we would do this at home' – but rather signifies the expectations by which we maintain our sense of dwelling and its relationship to public space.

But we also have a distinctly different sense of dwelling as dishevelled and unkempt: as a place that is well used. This is seen in the expression '*lived-in*'. We use it to refer to dwellings, but also human features: for example, W. H. Auden's *lived-in* face, with its creases and apparent similarity to a walnut. What is interesting when it is used in this manner is that it suggests that the person has experienced a varied and diverse life, having taken risks and been battered as a result. It is a phrase used to describe soldiers, or those who have spent a life at sea, or a lifetime drinking. The suggestion of this phrase is that of having been well used: of not being new, but rather showing the signs of wear and tear.

But there is also the connotation of comfort. Auden's face is still a kindly one, for all its folds and creases. He appears as a gentle and compassionate man: one who has suffered, but whom suffering has not made bitter. There is a certain sensitivity in his expression that makes one feel he understands the complexities and difficulties of life. He does not look out at us in judgement, but with a resigned and vulnerable expression that makes us think that he can share our sufferings, because he has had enough of his own.

This is the aspect of dwelling that we also take comfort from. Dwelling receives us and accepts us. As we saw in chapter 3, Walter Benjamin (1999) said dwelling is as if we are lying embedded in deep, usually violet folds of velvet. It is plush, and like old velvet, it bears our imprint. It too is 'lived-in' and bears the marks of that continued engagement. And what is crucial here is that dwelling accepts us unconditionally: it too is sympathetic to our cares, and absorbs them as part of the routines and habits that appear like well-worn tracks on our familiar path. Dwelling becomes home when it is, to restate the phrase of Gaston Bachelard (1969), 'really inhabited' (p. 5). It is when it is used and occupied in a committed manner that we can say it is a home: this is precisely when it is 'lived-in'. And like a home, we can say that what identifies the face of Auden, or indeed the old Samuel Beckett, is that sense of being really inhabited, of the active mind behind the persona that is continually questing and searching to live more and to the full.

In the quest to live our lives as fully as we can, do we stop to consider what we mean by our language and whether the manner in which we use it determines what we experience? Or put another way, just how much of our sense of dwelling is dependent on the language we use? So, for instance, the housing and building professions, as well as politicians, now commonly use 'home' instead of 'house' when they refer to physical structures: social landlords manage and build homes and not dwellings or houses. The reason for this is clearly that home is a warmer, more emotive concept, which converts a brick box into something with a much stronger resonance. Accordingly, when we discuss those lacking a dwelling, we call them 'homeless' to emphasise the full import of what they are suffering, and the full possibility of its redemption. 'House' is a cold and empty phrase, which becomes inhabited and warm when translated into 'home'.

Speaking only of homes adds a greater significance to what housing and building professionals are doing: they are not building or managing brick

Homes, we are told, are now made for us by professionals

boxes, but creating something warm and welcoming to residents. But in doing so, are we taking something away from the concept of home itself? It is no longer what Bachelard terms 'really inhabited space', but just a physical structure. Thus the misuse of the word diminishes what it hitherto signified. The aim of adding significance to the quotidian tasks of managing and building reduces the idea of 'home' to something empty and cold.

The misuse is significant in another sense, namely, that it implies that homes are 'made' by those other than the household. Homes, we are now led to believe, are made by professionals ready-made for people to live in. The household no longer has to create or make the home: the work has been done for them. This situation has several consequences. First, because home is ostensibly created by professionals, this implies that no effort is needed on the part of the household. The suggestion is that homemaking is easy to achieve and can be readily made *for us*. Second, this view carries the apparent belief that home is transient. Building homes implies that we move from home to home and do not take it with us. A home is made for us to move into and we should be grateful. Third, this idea implies the standardisation of homes according to professionals' understanding of their clients' needs and aspirations. The result is the provision of identikit homes, based on standard design briefs and models. This creates an increasing homogeneity of styles aimed to fulfil standardised purposes. We need only think of terms such as 'starter home' and 'executive home' to see this process of standardisation. Fourth, this will tend to impersonalise the notion of home and dwelling more generally: it becomes a commodity that is bought and sold and treated as such. Housing is commodified according to economic rather than human values (King, 1996; Turner, 1976). Lastly, but implicit to all the above, this notion of home assumes the professionalisation of the role of homemaking: homes can only be made by others, by 'the experts'. Professionals tell us what we need or, in other words, they actually deem to tell us what home is.

But this externalisation of the values attached to home and dwelling means that economics and status dominate over the ontological and emotional values that we ourselves invest in dwelling. This relates to another set of common terms used when discussing our dwelling. These terms relate dwelling to a sense of possession. This relates not just to the obvious terms, such as *ours, mine* and *my,* but the use of the term *property.* We talk of housing, collectively and individually, as property, and whilst this has a different association from the generic sense of a right to something, there is a clear echo of that when it is used in the sense of *domestic property.* The importance of language here is to stress the exclusivity in the relations between *our property and ourselves*: it being ours, we can prevent others from accessing it. Our dwelling, then, is the most common form of *private property.* What is interesting here is how the one word – private – affects and alters the meaning of the other. The word 'private' effectively gives meaning to 'property': it gives a sense of exclusivity and particular ownership. Private means the property is not shared but ring-fenced for the exclusive use of certain persons: the term 'private' qualifies our understanding of property to the particular.

Associated with a sense of possessiveness is the frequent reference to the dwelling as an *asset,* where it is seen, and where we expect to use it, as a form of personal wealth. Dwelling is here seen as a means for personal gain and security that can be used as a form of collateral. This gives further credence to the sense where dwelling takes on a more publicly defined use, conditioned by legal and economic formalities. For something to be an asset it must conform to some recognisable and generally accepted standard. In particular, it must be a transferable commodity. This demonstrates not only the connection with property, but it also shows the import of the association of dwelling with personal wealth creation. Seeing dwelling as an asset depersonalises and objectifies it into something determined by a common measure, rather than the means of enclosing subjective and personal experience. This particular use, or abuse, of language, then, alters the significance we place on housing by destroying that which is its most personal function, namely, as a store of personal values. The irony, of course, is that this occurs through an attempt to emphasise one form of value – the economic – that the dwelling has to us and us alone: it is *our* asset.

There are also fascinating terms that derive from the legal field, and in particular the term *quiet enjoyment*. Just what does this term imply? Is it a statement of rights – what we can or ought to have – or of responsibilities – of what we should ensure others have – or is it a combination of both? And how does 'quiet' modify 'enjoyment'? Is there a suggestion that 'loud enjoyment' is not to be sanctioned? The phrase is then suggestive of privacy and of being left alone to use our dwelling as we wish. This is subject, of course, to our not disturbing others: a quite considerable restriction. Thus quiet enjoyment is not an absolute condition but a relative one. What is questionable, however, is who is to determine whether the enjoyment is sufficiently quiet? Presumably this would be, and has been, done by the courts, on the basis that someone has been accused of not being 'quiet' enough, or of not being allowed such an enjoyment. Or perhaps it has developed from the other direction, in terms of what level of enjoyment is deemed by the courts to be reasonable.

Dwelling, home and meaning

Where this discussion on particular terms leads us is to comment on the use of the term *dwelling* itself, rather than using *house*, *housing* or *home*. The importance of dwelling is that of range. As Christian Norberg-Schulz (1985) has suggested, dwelling in its fullest sense is human settlement on the earth. This is the sense in which Martin Heidegger uses the term in his essay, 'Building, Dwelling, Thinking' (1971). As we saw in chapter 1, dwelling, for Heidegger, is that which we do to give our environment meaning. But dwelling also encloses the smaller scale of the domestication of nature; the urban settlement, with its political and communicative functions; and, of course, the private enclosure we refer to as our dwelling or home. Thus dwelling equates to more than just personal accommodation. But this makes it clear that this personal accommodation is not separate from the wider environment it sits within. One way of viewing this is to see a series of concentric circles emanating out of each individual. These circles ripple out and widen as they leave an individual. Yet, they quickly overlap and sometimes almost appear to merge with the circles of others to form larger waves. As we have seen already, this relates to Edmund Husserl's notion of the *lifeworld* (Husserl, 1970).

This begins with the *homeworld*, but extends out to other worlds further and further away from us, some of which are completely alien to us. Husserl saw these worlds as intersecting or overlapping to create the lifeworld in its totality, as a combination of the familiar and the foreign, the close and the distant. Dwelling, therefore, is a concept that allows us to connect an individual's quiet enjoyment with the noise and swirl of the community and the complex otherness of the wider world.

These phrases and words are all means by which we communicate the meaning of our dwelling to others. But this also serves to show what we hold in common: the use of certain phrases such as 'home' resonates with others who also have or want the very same. There is then a common understanding. This understanding is common because we have common mental processes and mental acts. We generalise, through the use of language and hence thought, about how we use the dwelling.

Ludwig Wittgenstein's argument against the possibility of a private language shows how, despite subjectivity, we have much in common, and this allows us to make some general statements (Wittgenstein, 1953). Self-consciousness might lead to what Wittgenstein saw as the 'first-person illusion', where because we know only our own mental states (pain, ecstasy, etc.) directly, we see them as unique. They are the things I, and only I, am experiencing. We know that others report feelings of pain and ecstasy, but we can only know the mental states of others indirectly, through their descriptions of them. Hence they may appear different from those mental states we have. And, of course, we have no external means of determining how the states of others compare with ours: when someone says 'I am in pain' is this the same as the way I feel when I stub my toe?

But language is more than just a series of arbitrary signs without any reference points. When we say 'pain' it refers to something that is, and must be, beyond us. As Gottlob Frege (1997) has described it, language denotes both sense (what we understand when we grasp the expression of being in pain) and reference (what the expression stands for, in this case the description of a pain), and for a language to be meaningful the references have to be commonly held. We must have a shared description of what it is to be in pain. Accordingly, we cannot have a private sense of pain known only to me and a public reference of what pain is, or else we could not communicate in a manner that could be understood either by ourselves or others. So what we do then is to refer to things we have in common through a public language describing our mental states, which themselves have a public reference. This suggests that what we are referring to are common entities. They have a sense and a reference due to the public language we use in describing them.

And so when we refer to *comfort* or *privacy* or *security* these are references to mental states we have and know that others also have. We know this precisely because of the common reference. We therefore know that when we share common references while discussing dwelling we also know there is something in dwelling itself – as a description of certain mental states – that is in common with others. This is surely the most significant of arguments for the commonality of dwelling: that, no matter how subjectively we enjoy dwelling, we have this sense of subjective enjoyment in common with others.

But should we properly be concerned with meaning at all, when we are considering housing and dwelling? Might it not be more useful for us to forget meanings, common or singular, and just live there? As I have suggested, we can quite readily enjoy dwelling without reflecting on what it means. Amos Rapoport (1995) is quite rightly critical of 'the meaning of home' literature, on the grounds that it is a circular argument, where the fact we see the home as meaningful is seen as constitutive of the meaningfulness of home! Perhaps, therefore, it would be more useful to concentrate on concepts such as 'use' and 'significance'.

However, is there not a substantive difference in considering the meaning of housing compared with the much more nebulous concept of home? The distinction here is that housing is a readily identifiable concrete entity, which is understood conceptually and materially – we can lean against it, stub our toe on it, feel it and touch it – whilst home is not. Home is a vaguer concept that denotes psychological and emotional states, and we recognise it precisely because these particular states are so important, and hence, we feel, meaningful. There is not the same problem of circularity when dealing with housing, in that the very notion is not defined by its meaning as tends to be the case with home. We can rely on its physicality and structural integrity as a means to define it (however partial this might prove to be).

But does this argument apply to dwelling? Dwelling is not merely a concrete physical entity, but one intended to encapsulate both home and housing. Therefore can we not see dwelling as having a *meta-meaning*, where it consolidates all we seek from housing as a concrete entity *as well as* the more nebulous associations we have toward home? Dwelling is so significant because it can take in any number of levels from solidarity to security; from fastness against the elements onto an emotional sense gained through intimacy and insularity. Dwelling allows us to accept distinct, but interlocking, levels of meaning ranging from our shared habitation on the earth through to our most private sense of belonging within a certain physical space.

But in any case, what is to be gained from unpicking meaning, particularly at the acutely subjective level we have been discussing? Is not the fact that something is meaningful *for me* enough? It is precisely that we seek to attribute meaning to the home, as *my home*, that makes it so important to us. Once we understand that we need go no further. In academic terms this is indeed banal, but we do not dwell merely to give academics something to dissect: haven't these academics got homes to go to?

Is not then the great paradox about dwelling precisely this: that we use dwelling primarily as an escape *from* meaning, as a way of cutting off significance, particularly shared significance? Speaking more properly, dwelling allows us to segment meanings and to pick and choose those convenient or needful to us. Dwelling provides us with a semi-porous boundary by which we may limit our involvement with the various layers of the lifeworld beyond our own particular homeworld. Or rather, the significance, and therefore the meanings, that we do share are hidden from us by the fact of the dwelling's privacy. Thus the 'meaning' of dwelling is that it filters us from social meanings. This is not to suggest, of course, that the connections are not there, or that they are not of significance themselves, but rather that dwelling allows us to state the meanings as personal. We share them with others, but we experience them ourselves singly.

An idealised view of our dwelling might be: '*The place where we do as we please, make as we please and with whom we want; where all our views, interests, hopes, beliefs and desires are legitimate, and where there is no means of gainsaying this legitimacy*'. But this is an ideal that we might never attain. Perhaps we might never even try to realise it. This is because our dwelling is usually shared with others, and if acted upon, this idealised claim would be reduced merely to power relations. It would no longer be a statement of subjectivity, but one of subjection: one where either I am able to impose my ideal on others, or be coerced by the ideal of the more powerful other.

Most dwellings are shared by several people, who come from different generations, who have differing views, interests, hopes and opinions. We might think that the resolution of differences between these individuals is the main purpose of familial dwelling. Yet we would need to consider how and on what (or whose) terms a resolution could be achieved: what sacrifices, what conflicts and how many suppressions of hopes, desires and interests are we to permit in order to resolve our differences? Might not these relations be merely arbitrary and unjust to some or most of the household? This might be so, but we ought not to lose sight of the fact that this form of living is the most likely to successfully marry (!) individual privacy with social interaction. It is the place where responsibility gets intertwined with autonomy: where we realise the costs and benefits of our privacy. And just what are the alternatives? There would appear to be merely two options: the complete isolation of total separation, or external direction by some communal authority. The apparent choice is between atomism and being ruled over by the dictat of strangers: neither option would appeal. So we would have to moderate our ideal statement by clarifying what we mean, as it were, by *we*. Only then would *we* agree that these views, interests, hopes, beliefs and desires are legitimate.

Or perhaps we should forget ideals, and just live together and speak about our ends and not of the means by which we achieve them. We should obey those conventions that have grown amongst us, and not lose much of what is significant in dwelling in the striving for something we cannot achieve without hurting those we love.

Convention

What affects the way we perceive and relate to our dwelling? Do we perceive it as it actually is, in eidetic terms, or are we constrained by the environment that we exist as part of? Our perceptions will depend on whether we work in the home, in the sense that our work is homemaking; on gender; on age, and thus on how we use and experience our dwelling; on key life events such as divorce and separation, birth or death of a child; on whom the dwelling is shared with; on reasons we moved in (for example, is it our 'dream home' or just an investment?). Can we ever bracket out this *natural attitude* given us by gender, age and the other specificities of the extended material world, and see a dwelling as it really is? Would it still appear as a dwelling if stripped of all our notions of what a dwelling should be? Indeed would it be recognisable as a dwelling at all? Thus, is it not our expectations that make the dwelling what it is? This applies to our dwelling, but also, of course, to the dwellings of others. What differs here is the level, type and intensity of the expectations we have of ourselves compared to those we have of others. We can forgive something in ourselves that we could never forgive in others. The questioning of taste always takes place away from home.

What matters are the conventions within which we operate. Much of what we do, including the use and meaning of language, is based on convention (Lewis, 2002). Language is based on a series of conventions that become rigid once they are adopted. These are the way in which we speak and the way in which we intend and receive meaning in what we speak. But how, beyond language itself, might one relate convention to dwelling?

The manner in which we use a dwelling can be properly said to be conventional. It has a particular purpose and this is determined by a common understanding of how we do and should live. This means that convention serves (at least) two functions. First, convention dictates how we understand the significance and importance of dwelling. It tells us what the dwelling is for. It shows us how it interacts with us to create something sustainable and understandable. Second, convention informs us as to how we should use the dwelling. It sets the limits of acceptability: the effective means by which the activity of dwelling is socialised and how subjective experience connects with the objectivity of social relations. The conventional nature of our ordinary lives allows us to communicate with others, to co-operate with them, and to arrive at a mutual understanding based on some common principles. Dwelling is therefore grounded in a conventional life. Yet our dwelling, no matter how determined by convention, remains a full *individual* system. One is still a separate individual, within a separate household, and this applies whether one acts eccentrically or entirely conventionally. What conventions permit, because of their connection into the social, is a means of understanding the basis for our actions and those of others.

We can see eccentricity as where we break with convention. But it is precisely through the operation of convention that we are able to understand an action as eccentric. In this sense the convention carries with it its own breach. Any convention carries with it some, probably imprecise, sense of what it would be to break out of its limits. Moreover a convention is often understood by its breaches. We are able to see how important the convention is by reactions to those who breach it. It is therefore tempting to suggest that eccentricity is still determined by convention: it is a reaction to, and therefore conditioned and limited by, convention. In consequence, eccentricity is not really a rejection of convention at all. We might breach a convention not because it is irrelevant, but precisely because it matters: it gives consequence to our actions, even if those actions are little more than puerile.

That something is determined by convention implies that things need not be as stated. It is taken for granted and exists as it does because of some general acceptance. It is the normal state of affairs, and hence eccentricity is that which appears to differ greatly from it.

But conventions are still, in a sense, contingent entities. We could change them if we were so minded. A convention then is not immutable. Rather conventions are forms of precedent, in which we accept a way of doing things as normal and natural; yet an acceptance of apparent naturalness should not be seen as actually denoting that conventions are laws of nature. So convention in terms of dwelling is not an absolute. We are provided with boundaries, not rigid fixed positions. Conventional dwelling is ruled by proscription, not prescription. There are limits that one may not go beyond, but there is latitude within these limits. This gives some scope for variation and for choice. This relates to John Turner's argument about limits (proscription) and not lines (prescription) of action.[4]

But if this is really the case, why do conventions not change? Why do we feel that we cannot do something because of convention, even though we believe that the sanctions for doing so may be small? Might it not be that we know that change is always consequential? Once we have chosen one route we cannot reverse back to our starting point. Thus once we have established a convention we bring forward a series of consequences, the responsibility for which we cannot shirk, and this applies just as much when the convention is broken as when it is kept. We cannot break with convention without some consequence, and perhaps we can never be really sure of its true extent in advance.

But also conventions, being truly implicit and related to received wisdom, present an epistemological limitation. Once we have a convention it is no longer possible to conceive of that part of our life being organised in any fundamentally different way. There are other possible worlds, *but only until we create our own*. Having done this all other possibilities shrink away and we find it hard to conceive of an alternative. Or perhaps there are those who do not appreciate that limits exist and thus walk over them in blissful ignorance. The eccentric is one who either can conceive of an alternative, or is just ignorant of the conventional limits in the first place. Perhaps some, if not many, eccentrics are blissfully unaware of their difference.

But how does this relate to dwelling? In particular, how does our understanding of dwelling relate to common sense and received wisdom? And here I have to cry *mea culpa* and admit to an error in my earlier thinking on dwelling. Is not the situation the very opposite of my argument in *The Limits of Housing Policy* (King, 1996), where I opposed received wisdom with the vernacular? But instead of vernacular dwelling being in opposition to common sense, might it not in fact represent it? Should we not see common sense as being exemplified in how we ordinarily live? Ivan Illich's use of common sense was akin to the notion of hegemony, or of a dominant ideology (Illich, 1992). It was not just a commonly held view so much as one that was imposed. Yet this is a rather tendentious usage of the notion of common sense, particularly as the essence of the vernacular is precisely that it is held in common, and is defining of a particular community.[5] Hence any vernacular entity is formed through social relations: it has a *sense* because of what is held in *common*. What is needed, then, is to reclaim the notions of common sense and received wisdom as concepts akin to the vernacular and not opposed to it. This is because vernacular practices are taken for granted and generally accepted, and it is these qualities that give them their particular resonance for us. If we had to think constantly about the vernacular it could not operate for us. The vernacular, being made up of a series of conventional attitudes, works precisely because we do not have to think.

And so too, dwelling works because it excuses us from reflection, instead allowing us to rely on received wisdom and a common sense of our selves and our environment. We need not be aware of a convention for it to apply fully and consistently. We do not need to have tested its limits and to have borne the costs of transgression in order to operate according to its strictures. Like people who find mountains irresistible, we obey a convention 'because it's there'. But then, unlike any mountain, a convention is only there because we have obeyed it!

But would one need to be aware of the absence of conventions? One might suggest that we could fail to be so aware, because of the very lack of limits of acceptability: if there are no limits there is no transgression and, presumably, no knowledge that we have done wrong. But if this situation were ever to pertain, what would be absent would not be the convention, but those things that conventions allow, namely, the ability to communicate with others, to co-operate with them, to be civil and respectful of their autonomy and needs, and so on. Without convention we could not live in anything other than the proverbial state of nature. In this sense, we truly live conventionally and we cannot live without convention, and indeed never have. To understand we need only look at the common criticism of social contract theories.[6] The social contract is where we agree to limit our own freedoms and actions to ensure mutual protection, which guarantees a peaceful life for us all and brings us out of the brutish state of nature where we have only our wits and naked power to protect us. Yet, on what grounds could we expect other citizens to keep their part of the contract: how could we trust them and enforce their obligations? To do this we would already need some mechanism to ensure the enforcement of the contract before we could enter into it. We would already need a sense of who 'we' are in order to determine who to contract with: a sense of community precedes contract. Thus the contract is already a necessary prerequisite for itself. Convention operates similarly. Without conventions we have no need for them and cannot be aware of what we lack. If we are aware it is because we have already experienced the convention. This means that the only entities that can judge the necessity of conventions are, properly speaking, the conventions themselves.

So dwelling speaks to us and we speak about dwelling. But it speaks and we speak in a patterned and rule-bound way. We dwell conventionally and so we are able to understand how we and others live, just as we use a common language, with common meanings in order to express our aims, hopes and aspirations on dwelling. And inasmuch as we all speak with our own accent and speak our own thoughts, so too our dwelling speaks differently of us – all in a language that is common and entirely conventional.

Chapter 5
Ripples
Sharing, learning, reaching out

Children place themselves at the centre and everything dwells around them

We have already made good use of Edmund Husserl's analogy of the lifeworld as a series of ripples, moving out from the homeworld (Husserl, 1970). These ripples come into contact with those emanating from other individuals where they clash, causing eddies and agitations. But Husserl also suggests that some ripples merge together to create larger and more significant formations. This analogy is useful with reference to social interaction, which may lead to conflict, but equally it may create solidarity and concord. It also demonstrates that even though we may live privately, and seek to keep ourselves to ourselves, our action will influence others, and our aims and ends will be affected by the actions of others.

So we need to appreciate how we interact and how this interaction affects dwelling. Most assuredly this is a huge topic and to cover it fully is beyond the scope of this project. I have therefore limited myself to some thoughts on how we come to accommodate others, to see what are the conditions that create agitation and those that make for concord. Having done this, I then wish to address how our dwelling is plugged into the wider world. I shall concentrate here on the purported and real effects of television and the Internet. These are both means by which we connect our dwelling to webs of influence beyond our control. It can also be seen as the main way in which our dwelling is invaded by global forces.

But what I also want to show is that, whilst ripples may disturb the equilibrium on the surface, they may be unnoticed below the surface. At this level there is both a resilience and an equanimity to surface agitation, so that there is much below that remains unaffected. We should not then overstate on the basis of surface effects. But we can be even more positive, in that on occasions we learn from adversity and through challenge. When we sail out in a boat we hope it has been tested, and that these tests have not all been in calm waters. It is by putting entities, and beings, under stress that we learn how they cope, what their limits are. We will also find that through stress we extend ourselves to a higher level than we had previously enjoyed.

So whilst dwelling is about control and the ability to maintain an equilibrium, we also know that we have to face elements that we may not be able to control. As children we must operate according to rules made by others. As adults we are freer, and may be able to make rules that others must live by. But adults must still respect boundaries and may not operate independently of the world around them. These constraints may complicate our life and agitate us, but without them there can be no concord. We all make ripples – this is what we do when we dwell – and we must try to flow with them as best we can. We must share what we have, seek to learn from those around us, and reach out to others as we bob along on the ebbs and flows of dwelling.

Accommodating others

If dwelling is subjective, and it most assuredly is, then how can we make common, or even universal, statements about how we live? If we see our dwelling as so personal to us, as our world drawn close around us, then should we even try? I can demonstrate this problem with a trite, but hopefully revealing example. On the door of my study I have a wonderful drawing done by my eldest daughter when she was five. It is of herself, her sister and her parents standing together looking out of the picture with our first names above the figures and with arrows pointing to each one. What is fascinating about the picture is the scale of the figures. Her younger sister (three at the time), her mother and father are all roughly the same size. However, she has drawn herself half a head taller and as more substantial than the other figures. As a result she dominates the picture.

This says much about how children's lives are very much centred round the self. The boundaries of a child's world are drawn very close to themselves. They are at the centre of a very small circle and the universe centres around them. Of course, this is a result of a lack of awareness and knowledge of the extent of their lifeworld, rather than anything calculated. However, the difference between children and adults is here one of degree. An adult's circle may be considerably larger and it will interlink with others' circles, yet the person is still at its centre. And what we centre on are those little habits, foibles and pursuits important to us.

But if our little ways are just so different, and if we are so self-centred, then in what sense can the meaning of dwelling be said to be social? Of course, there is the obvious point that nearly all of us live in dwellings. We consider, quite rightly, those who do not have a dwelling have a serious problem. Moreover, they need not just any dwelling, but one that is of a certain standard and is sustainable. Clearly, then, we have common notions of what constitutes dwelling. It is not a purely subjective psychological condition that is merely interior to me. But we know that what actually constitutes sustainability and the right standard changes over time and according to culture. More particularly, how we each use and relate to our dwelling is different and possibly unique. There is a degree of relativism involved in considering what dwelling is, has been and ought to be.

The answer to this conundrum is that we *share much of what we do in private*. Dwelling is indeed something that is personal and private: it is a space where sharing is very limited, in that we would only wish to have a select few intimates with us. The essence of dwelling, as we have seen, is security and privacy. Yet, if we consider this for a moment, we see that many of the things we use the dwelling to ensure, such as security and privacy, are held in common, even though they might be exhibited differently. It is just that, in each case, what matters is *my* security and *my* privacy. Much of what we do is shared, in the sense of being the same as in other households – the manner in which we decorate the dwelling, and prepare and eat similar food; the things we watch and read; the worries and concerns – yet we do these things separately and in private. We would not wish to share our worries beyond the dwelling or invite strangers to share a meal or choose a book from our shelves. But despite this, we share much.

But our yearning for privacy is not a problem. It is how we want and expect our dwelling to be. Privacy is not arbitrary, but a necessary prerequisite for shared living. What permits us to share is privacy itself, and the sense of security it brings. We can share precisely because the dwelling offers a boundary around us. This allows us the freedom for intimate relations with family and loved ones: indeed, to show and share our worries and anxieties. This boundary unifies and creates the whole through inclusion. Through separation from the external we become bound together. It is how we get close enough to know and care for our loved ones. Without privacy we could not share in those things we consider the most important in our social lives.

One of the most important ways in which we share is in the upbringing of children. It is in and through the shared space of dwelling that children learn, and as they learn we can protect and preserve them. David Morley (2000) suggests that the home is seen by the child as a series of rules by which they learn to emulate their parents' standards of behaviour. He suggests that 'children, through learning to live in the rooms which their parents have furnished, learn the remembered values of their parents' memories – of the rooms which they grew up in. Thus is habitus transmitted through generations' (p. 20). We cannot understand dwelling fully without appreciating the role of this private socialisation, of how children learn and develop in the relationship with their parents. It is through security within the dwelling that children receive socialisation.

Yet the dwelling for children represents both a more total and a more subjective experience than is the case for adults. For children, especially the very young, the dwelling is the virtually complete range of their experience: the world comes to them, and they venture out only in a managed and controlled manner. But they also lack the range of experience of different types of dwelling, in terms of the physical organisation of space and the household arrangements within that structure. For them, their dwelling is simply how dwelling is. It is only as they venture out, visit friends and perhaps move from one place to another that their horizon broadens to include a comparative sense. Learning in the dwelling, therefore, is as much about understanding the limits of their subjectivity, so that they appreciate how much is shared by others and how much – or little – is unique to them. They learn that what *I do* is not a single and unique list, but a series of interlinked, yet discrete circles of influence, containing different and distinct groups with their own habits, norms and expectations.

Most dwellings are shared and this means that what is mine is also somebody else's. More than one person can legitimately say 'mine' when referring to the same space, the same artefacts and the same experiences. Strangers in the dwelling make it less familiar: family, naturally, makes it more so, and that which is familiar to us is incorporated into dwelling. There develops a unity, if not of purpose, then of existence. The deepest level at which we can share is the quotidian, for it is here that we forget to compete, to bargain and to chase. The strength of shared dwelling is its very banality, its everydayness.

But just because we share we do not all agree about the importance of different aspects of our dwelling. We have different priorities, likes and dislikes, interests and purposes to fulfil. We might, in practice, subsume some of these for the greater good of the whole, but there is no hard and fast way that this might be achieved, other than by compromise and resistance. So part of dwelling – and perhaps a considerable part at that – is conflict. What is important for us is the manner in which we accommodate and moderate this conflict in order to sustain ourselves and those we love, who, of course, are often the very ones we collide with.

Just what impact does conflict have on our sense of place, on our sense of belonging, and the meanings we attach to dwelling? This will doubtless differ according to who we are. Children do not have the same expectations in terms of control and ownership over the dwelling. Also they might not have experienced any other dwelling. This perhaps means that they have a different sense of belonging from that of adults. Belonging for them is related to their ability to use space and is not connected to ideas of ownership, control and maintenance.

But why should we expect to have a sense of belonging in common? Surely it is enough that we share and feel we belong *on our terms*. Why should it matter that what one person gets from the dwelling is different from that of others who share it? By way of answer, we need to be aware of others, because they can be affected by our actions. We share what they see as their space, and they are quite right in seeing it as theirs. Successful dwelling is where we can accommodate the sense of belonging that our partners feel: where we can share the dwelling and not feel it is being taken from us, or where it is given on terms we find hard to accept, but have no choice but to accept.

Some places grow in significance precisely because they are shared. That, after all, is precisely why the marital or parental home is seen as so important:

it is not what size it was, where it was, but whom we shared it with. The place where we grew up is of elemental importance to us and grounds our future experiences of dwelling. These foundations are only challenged once we set up a new home (which may in time, and should we choose, become a parental home for others). What challenges our childhood foundation is the very act of sharing with another who has a different set of roots, grounded in their childhood home: it is this compromise through sharing that challenges us to create something new. And this dwelling will always retain some particular special significance because it is a shared place. So, for example, we might not want to stay there alone after the death of a spouse or child. The dwelling is now always in some way empty. But others, however, might take this as a reason never to leave. In this case they turn the dwelling into a shrine and feel they have a responsibility to maintain it. Queen Victoria had Prince Albert's clothes laid out every morning for years after his death, as if by holding on to these routines she were still retaining something of that person. Loved ones can still be present, even if, physically, they have left.[1]

Yet there are times when we want to be alone in the dwelling. This naturally occurs in certain parts of the dwelling, the toilet or bathroom, for instance. But it also occurs when we are sleeping, reading, doing homework, playing a good game, and so on. Yet even when we are, technically, alone, we enjoy knowing that others are around: that they, like us, can be there if and when we need them. What matters is the familiarity of their presence, not that they necessarily do anything with us: to be around is enough. Hence we can undertake some activities together, such as reading, whilst being totally silent and, of course, reading different things. Just being in the same room together makes it a shared activity. The closeness of the other person comforts us, and affirms and validates our action. Likewise, watching a film together is often more enjoyable than watching alone. That someone else shares the experience and lives through it with us expands the moment, and somehow vivifies it, confirming it with a wholeness it otherwise would not have. Importantly, the essence of sharing is wholeness and not mimesis: we are not copying, but doing one thing together.

It is often difficult to accept a new person into the dwelling, and that new person may find it hard to establish themselves. There is a feeling of not wanting to be taken over by the new person, yet perhaps seeking to 'take over' them, so that they behave 'properly' and respect the norms and culture of the dwelling. The issue is one of establishing rules and limits. But it is also something of a battle, of trying to impose our rules and limits, and resist those of the other. Crucially, this is not a conscious or a malicious process,

We can feel secure because we know others are near

but one of *accommodation in confinement*. The process of acceptance is one of mutual accommodation: of finding areas of commonality and acceptable difference, where we can give and take to create something we can see as sustainable. This process of accommodation is a continuous one, even if it is at its most extreme and definitive at the beginning. The continuous nature of this accommodation is, of course, most pronounced with children, where the relationship develops from nurture to conflict and, hopefully, onto mutuality.

Much of our mutual confinement is chosen: we choose to live with others, to have children, to take in a lodger, and so on. Many of the situations that arise from confinement are therefore instrumental to circumstance, and do not form an imperative, if only because these situations are literally of our own choosing. But power relations are clearly involved here. Some confinements are not chosen: children cannot normally choose with whom they live, but find themselves as part of a family. Thus what are free choices for some (parents) are merely confining for others (children). But, of course, having once chosen to have children we are stuck with them! Like most decisions that really matter, choices within dwelling are one-way only. Of course, some confinements, such as prison, are precisely about reducing choice. In this case the prisoner is forced to accommodate according to terms set by others.

Would there be such a difficulty in accommodation in confinement if the dwelling were merely a physical space? What creates the conflict is the relational nature of dwelling: the different interests, aims, hopes and aspirations that seek to bloom whilst coexisting within a confined space. This conflict reaches its most extreme when normal interests come into contact with, and get overridden by, an imperative. Consider the disproportionate impact caused by the arrival of a new baby. The dwelling appears to contract as a result of bringing home a human bundle barely twenty inches long. This is partly because of the mass of artefacts now deemed necessary to care for a baby. However, more germane is the fact that we now not only share the dwelling with an extra person, but with one who cannot be held responsible for their actions, or manage them themselves. Newborn children are implacable in their needs. They cannot be reasoned with, nor sensibly ignored. They exist on an entirely elemental level consisting only of short-term needs. So the function of the dwelling alters, and routines are redrawn to suit the rhythm of the child. The space is no longer our own but has been invaded by someone who insists on taking, yet cannot give anything concrete in return.[2] This is perhaps the most extreme example of a tyranny induced by choice. It is a tyranny from which we can expect no respite because it is entirely of our own making. Moreover, we do it willingly.

This amply demonstrates that the sense of responsibility that comes with dwelling is not so much attached to the physical entity, but to what it envelops: to state the point again, a dwelling is a means and not an end in itself. The duty is to ourselves and to our family. This is perhaps felt most acutely when we bring our first child home. We close the door and then realise that we are now primarily responsible for the care of this helpless and entirely dependent child. There are no longer midwives and doctors mere yards away who can respond immediately to our call. We cannot help thinking, 'how quickly could someone get here if we needed them?'. This feeling quickly goes away, and almost certainly will not occur as much or at all with a second child. Children quickly become embedded in the dwelling environment, and the routines of the dwelling centre on their needs. As a result it is impossible to remember what the dwelling felt like before the children arrived. Of course, we would not want to live without them, but we find it hard to remember how we actually did.

There is an important category difference, then, between *being-with* and *being-in* or *having*. Being-with takes the understanding of dwelling to a higher level. Whom we share a dwelling with determines the manner in which we view it, both currently and in hindsight. If relationships fall apart no dwelling can be sustained, and this pertains regardless of amenity and ownership. Comfort struggles to coexist with antagonism.

The nature of *sharing-in-privacy* comes more clearly into focus when strangers appear. An important change comes over the dwelling when we have visitors. The presence of outsiders, welcome or otherwise, retards certain aspects of the private use of our dwelling and sometimes prevents it altogether. The problem here is that it makes us aware of the dwelling as an entity rather than as a site, that we need to clean it, repaint it, tidy it, and so on, in order to conform to some generally held norms. We cannot use the dwelling entirely as we would like, because we are beholden to others as their host. We can no longer merely use the dwelling and its contents, but rather we now feel we have to justify them: we find ourselves explaining why the dwelling is as it is, and how we would change it. We start to see the dwelling more as the stranger does. Much of this derives from the dutiful interest taken in it by the visitor, even though they are likely to forget this piece of inconsequential knowledge as soon as they leave. Social relations within someone's home are bound by an etiquette that emphasises the material at the expense of the existential. This is precisely because the visitor cannot breach the private boundaries. Thus, in order to communicate cordially – and to ensure we keep our distance – we discuss the dwelling with the outsider's eye.

Looking at it, as it were, from outside, the dwelling of another is always alien, until we are accepted and accept it. Perhaps the latter is the most important – the point at which we feel it is part of us, and thus we can properly become a part of it. Yet some dwellings, even though we have not lived in them for a while, such as our parents', for instance, we would immediately feel a part of again as soon as we entered. It is not regularity that creates acceptance, but the precise conditions of relation between dwelling and us. Once gained these relations will stay with us, often unto death.

Plugging in

Some of the ways in which we share are more anonymous and seemingly less amenable to our personal control. These ways of sharing, or rather coming into contact, with the wider community are via television and the Internet: technologies we are now comfortable and conversant with, but which we may not fully understand. The first is a one-way means of communication in which images, (relatively) uncontrolled by us, enter our dwelling; the second is by definition interactive, yet, as we shall see, also has issues about control.

The media, and in particular television, being controlled increasingly by a small number of transnational corporations, is implicated in the debate over globalisation and the collapse of locality as a focus for solidarity. Television can be portrayed as the means by which our dwelling is invaded by the impersonal and homogenising interests of Disney, McDonalds and the Murdoch media empire.

Nearly all of us watch television, often to the extent that it dominates our living spaces. Many families are now owners of multiple television sets with families spread about the house watching different things on their own personal sets. The television is then inevitably an important influence over what and how we share. But it also casts a shadow over our notions of privacy and necessitates a subtler notion of what it is to be secure and fast in our dwelling.

Likewise, the Internet is becoming a normal part of our lives. We are now as likely to email family and friends as speak to them. It has allowed many to work at home, and it has opened us up to vast amounts of information, images and opinions. Yet the very uncontrolled and diffuse nature of the World Wide Web has created concerns over who is using the Internet and how one can ascertain motives. We can get tangled in the web, precisely because we cannot control it, or understand its complexity. What might be a useful tool for most of us, allowing us access to information and entertainment, can equally be used to prey on the vulnerable. Hence in 2003 Microsoft closed down their Internet chat rooms as a means of preventing paedophiles from grooming children. This too, then, is significant for our speculations on dwelling. The idea that children, through using their computers in their own room, as their parents watch television downstairs, might be being groomed by a paedophile clearly compromises the ideas of privacy and security that are at the heart of our ideas of dwelling. We need therefore to appreciate that there are occasions when we – by that I mean 'society' – will need to police certain aspects of private dwelling.

I have suggested that I can only give a partial picture of these issues. There is a huge and quickly expanding literature on the implications of television and cyberspace. I cannot hope to do it justice here (at least not without seriously unbalancing my project), and so I shall engage with only one writer whom I consider to be one of the most interesting commentators on the effects of television in the home. David Morley, particularly in his book *Home Territories* (2000), has brought together insights on the home (both personal and national), belonging and gender with his research on the use of television. His work therefore offers the basis to explore the effects of television and then to assess just how serious these are. In particular, I wish to consider two points he makes amongst what is a detailed and wide-reaching analysis of how the media create images of home and nation.

First, Morley suggests that technologies such as television can:

> be analysed in terms of how they come to be embedded within pre-existing domestic routines, [but] they are, simultaneously, technologies which also have a disembedding effect – in so far as they potentially function to connect individuals within the home to others, geographically elsewhere.
>
> (Morley, 2000, pp. 86–7)

So just as the television can become seen as part of our normal habits, it can also detract from that protected intimacy by broadcasting violence, wars and cruelty into our living rooms. The television set can be seen as 'at the junction of the inside and the outside, the channel through which the news of the public world enters the domestic world' (p. 87). It transgresses the boundary that protects the privacy and solidarity of the home. It allows the impersonal world to enter into our dwelling. This world is unaware of us and we, on our own, cannot mitigate its effects. It has an implacability, which means we must either join it or hope we can ignore it. But if we wish to connect we must do so on terms set by others.

Second, Morley discusses the impact of what might be termed 'privatising technologies', where the integrity and solidarity of households is threatened. Devices such as the freezer and the microwave have allowed for individualised meals consumed at different times, and this has diminished our sense of home as a collective good where we interact and exchange as a family unit. Instead the home has been individualised by these technologies. Likewise, multiple television ownership and the Internet, along with mobile phones, Playstations, Gameboys, etc., have merely exacerbated this. These privatising technologies have caused people to withdraw further within the home to their own separate domestic spaces, leading to the fragmentation of the family as they all use their own personal devices. Morley's point here is that these devices have fragmented family life and the sense of home as a collective entity in which burdens are shared and gifts offered.

For Morley then, there is a double effect created by the use of technology. On the one hand, it has a disembedding effect, connecting us to an increasingly globalised culture. It helps to homogenise our lives around a series of global brands which we all recognise. But, on the other hand, we use technology that separates us from those around us, that helps us create our own world away from those we live with. What we have, then, is the creation of atomistic units based on the consumption of globalised products.

Yet just how sinister are these developments? Morley discusses the idea of control as central to the home, but in what sense do these technologies remove this control from us? Those individuals sitting in the same house doing separate things can still be said to be in control. Are they deluding themselves when they consider they retain this control? These devices must, we can assume, have entered the dwelling as the result of a conscious act. They were all purchased with the aim of enhancing the experience of dwelling within private space; they are means of getting away from others. Likewise, I would suggest that Morley overstates the disembedding effects of television. Despite his emphasis on globalisation, Morley points to 'the continued geographical sedentarism on the part of the majority of the population' (2000, p. 14). He argues that most people still have a horizon that is very local. Indeed he acknowledges early in his book that the concerns for globalisation, migrancy and flux that concern him are in fact those of an intellectual elite. The sort of mobility and constant change he discusses are experienced by a small group of bourgeois intellectuals and others in the media and commerce, but this is not shared by the majority.

Morley mentions this, but then tends to operate as if it is unimportant. The rest of his work, interesting as it is, asks us to suspend this insight and concern ourselves with the concerns of this intellectual elite. Yet our horizons do remain local, and this is shown even in the type of television that dominates the schedules. The most popular programmes are on house design and renovation, gardening, and soap operas specifically about distinct localities (*Eastenders, Coronation Sreet, Neighbours*) and/or tightly-knit groups of friends offering each other solidarity and support (*Sex in the City, Friends*). The focus here is very much on the domestic and personal. Much of *Eastenders* and *Coronation Street* takes place in the local pub, and *Neighbours* consists of a series of conversations in the houses of the various characters. Even if we are watching Australians and Americans having these relations in parts of the world we are unfamiliar with, their concerns are recognisably domestic and local. In this sense, the globalised media, for all their terrors, are merely showing us how ubiquitous dwelling is.

What these programmes show us, *should we choose to watch them*, is that we have common notions of what constitutes a dwelling and a comfortable life. It is not a purely subjective psychological condition, in that notions of security, well-being, even privacy, are commonly held, even though they might be exhibited differently. Despite the private nature of dwelling, much of how we live is conditioned socially, and this may be achieved partially through the virtual ubiquity of the television (especially relevant here are home and garden programmes), as well as ideas of 'culture' gleaned from lifestyle magazines and newspapers. We live in rather similar ways to each other. This, of course, is not surprising, but it does not mean that we have not chosen to do so.

I wish, therefore, to propose a different view of television from that expressed by Morley. We do not literally have to watch television all night; we no longer even need to get up and walk over to the set to turn it off. Likewise, there is nothing to prevent a family sharing a meal together every day, talking over the day's events as they do so. All one has to do is arrange it and not allow other things to encroach. We have much more control over the dwelling than we pretend we have. We are not forced to live in a particular way. It is we who allow the television in. So why have we become its prisoners? What do we lack within ourselves that prevents us from controlling an inanimate glass tube?

Perhaps the problem is that we are too separate already and cling to the television for comfort, as our only window into the world. Much of the common ground concerning how we live comes through the media (television, radio, etc.) that *we have installed in our private dwellings expressly for our private use*. Frequent references in everyday conversation to the latest scandal, *Coronation Street* or the *National Lottery* take for granted a set of common and shared reference points. This should not necessarily be seen as limited only to certain social classes. *The Archers* fulfils the same purpose for the middle class, as did series such as *Twin Peaks* in the early 1990s.

This may suggest that much of what we take to be private to us is conditioned by the social. *We have private experiences in common*. Yet, importantly these are still private experiences. It is what *I* choose to watch in *my* own home. One is not, properly speaking, forced to play the *National Lottery*, watch *Coronation Street* or listen to *The Archers*. We can and do, in this sense, make our own entertainment. However, it so happens that others choose to do the same thing. In so doing, it gives people something in common – something to share – even though they may not wish to participate in that activity with anyone else. We might all watch or listen on our own, and the thought of communal *Coronation Street* watching or *Archers* listening might be anathema. We want to watch and listen on our own, making sure we do not miss any of the programme, and then discuss it in the appropriate (public) place: the discussion takes place, as it were, on neutral ground. Indeed, we enjoy discussing these programmes and feel disappointed when others are not able to participate.[3] Likewise, we can be excluded if we do not watch or listen, and hence cannot participate in this communal activity.

Therefore, we still have as much in common with others as our ancestors did with their contemporaries: we just experience it privately. Put another way, we view public affairs privately. What is different from Robert Putnam's nostalgic vision of 1950s America is that our new communal activities have developed spontaneously and without co-ordination (Putnam, 2000). One is viewing in private, but television images are public or communal, and thus shared. TV is a voluntary act both in terms of viewing and broadcasting and thus poses no moral dilemma (so long as there is an 'off' switch): it is not really an attack on our autonomy. We should not forget that we relate to popular culture individually, as if it is ours. Indeed, it *is* ours.

There are, however, clear social limits to what we can do in our own dwelling, no matter how private we seek to be. There are certain things that can never be acceptable. But how are these limits justified? For example, one can be imprisoned for downloading and storing pornographic images of children. Yet one is not specifically harming anyone else here.[4] The damage has already been done to the child, and is not lessened by any one person not looking at the pictures or being prosecuted for doing so. We rightly punish those who are caught abusing children in this despicable manner, but why for the mere act of storing the resultant picture? We do not punish those who just look at the pictures *without* downloading, largely, of course, because we would find it too difficult to trace them, short of a chance discovery (this, after all, is the way in which most of these cases come to light). Is it merely therefore a case of being *able* to punish those who store material, rather than those who just look and do not keep? Yet if we had a sure-fire and practical means of finding those just viewing child pornography, we would surely take the opportunity to punish them.[5]

The issue is that we view something as wrong and take action when and if we can do so against those actions. Yet this can only happen when the public and private come together.[6] Hence, in a famous recent case, Gary

Glitter was only caught when he took his *personal* computer (PC) to be repaired. If his PC had not malfunctioned he would not have been found out. The police, in conjunction with Internet service providers (ISPs) can trace particular usage and this has been used to break paedophile rings, but presumably this again has only been done because of some well-founded suspicion.

In cases such as that of Gary Glitter, is there an element of being punitive – of making an example of an individual with a high profile – precisely because we know we can only catch a tiny percentage of perpetrators of these crimes? We therefore make a great show of those we can catch as a deterrent to others. We try to control private actions through very public sanctioning, even though we all know that a huge element of chance is involved in finding those involved in these activities. What this demonstrates is that many of the acts which society wishes to prevent us from doing in private cannot be actively policed. Instead it must rely on a general prohibition and exhortation backed up by 'lucky breaks' allowing for high-profile prosecutions. In practice, therefore, these social limits on our private actions tend to be self-imposed. We ourselves do not use the Internet in this way, even though we know we can, and would have an excellent chance of avoiding detection. Hence, speaking more generally, we can understand why many Arab states and China are so determined to ban or heavily regulate Internet use and access to PCs, precisely because they know that once in use these machines simply cannot be controlled.

As we have seen, the importance of private dwelling is that it allows us to behave as we wish without having to explain or justify it to anyone. What we like to think is that we neither need nor seek the approval of others for our hobbies and habits. Others may not approve, as they, quite legitimately, do things differently, but this merely legitimises our own interests and actions: we have a duty to protect the freedom of others, and often the best way of achieving this is through indifference. Moreover, it is not the role of anyone else to give an opinion of how we choose to live. How others live is therefore simply not a matter for us.

But again as we know, this is really just an ideal. We know, whether we are prepared to state it explicitly or not, that there are limits to what we can and should do. The difficulty comes in stating where the limits should be. For example, a landlord will want to safeguard their property, and therefore how their tenants behave is not a matter of indifference. Most tenants will appreciate this and respect that the property is not theirs. Some will act like this because they know that there are sanctions available to the landlords. But most will behave without the need for sanctions, on the basis of an unarticulated reciprocity.

These limits, though, are not simply where the effects are public (although this may frequently be the case), as is shown by the Internet porn example. What we do in the privacy of our own home matters and, in these cases at least, should be regulated. Is what matters here the sheer seriousness of the case? Some things are just not acceptable for any reason, and there is no possible mitigation when it comes to the sexual exploitation of children. This is the case, but it is question begging: *why* is this totally unacceptable? The answer here is in the fact that what is being damaged is the sense of the inviolate individual. Is it not the very sense of private life, with its explicit sense of control of, and over, the self, with its concomitant ideas of personal autonomy, freedom and the integrity of the person, that is being shattered here? This is especially the case with children who depend on others to protect their still developing sense of self. What is happening is that the integrity of a person is being violated through *publicity* – by the private self being made public – even when, as in this case, the images are being viewed privately.

This relates back to, and in this case turns around, the point about the communal element in private television viewing. We are viewing in private, but the television images are public or communal, and therefore shared. Television watching is a voluntary act both in terms of viewing and broadcasting, and thus poses no moral dilemma (at least in the sense discussed here). But with the Internet example, the problem is not the private viewing so much as the violation caused by making images *public* beyond the control of the violated individual. It breaks down the private/public dichotomy by reversing the intentions of broadcasting, which is public, *but where viewing is private*. In this case, the viewing makes public *what should be private*. Thus, whilst the user of the Internet may claim rights to privacy, this can only be achieved, in this case, at the expense of another, whose rights are more *fundamentally* violated. This point is not intended as an alternative to strong arguments against Internet porn, such as the degradation involved, or the encouragement it gives to further violation. The point here is to show where the limits of private activity within the dwelling might lie, and that private actions have consequences beyond the dwelling which influence and limit the legitimacy of certain actions within the private realm. This particular private act is illegitimate because it improperly publicises what should be kept private. Thus, even if an act of child abuse never occurred again, the viewing of (historical) images would still be illegitimate and rightfully punished.

These are not the only social relations that matter. For instance, how do legal relations alter the experience of dwelling? Do they alter it at all in its fundamentals, or is the relationship between person and dwelling relative to particular individual circumstance, and not contingent on issues such as tenure? One would have thought that issues of permanence and control, which are determined, in part at least, by tenure relations, would have some impact. Alternatively, along with Peter Saunders (1990), we might see some important aspects that contribute to dwelling as innate, such as the apparent desire to own property, which we might see as a natural expression of territoriality or possessiveness. But then much of the criticism subsequently attracted by Saunders was precisely because he tried to associate the innate with particular and temporally bound legal and financial advantages. There were huge financial, political and social incentives towards owner-occupation in the UK throughout the 1980s, which gave this tenure considerable advantages over all forms of renting. But if housing subsidies and tenure law are contingent relations, much of the 'innate argument' is lost, just like much of the paper wealth Saunders discusses in the preface to *A Nation of Home Owners*.

But, ignoring any sense of the innate, ownership does affect how we relate to dwelling. As an example, living in a place owned by others, such as a holiday flat, raises some interesting ontological issues. We are fully aware our stay is temporary, and we are thus less committed to it. We know that we can walk away from it, and that we soon will, and thus we are prepared to be more flexible for the time we are there.[7] *We take it precisely because we can leave it.*

Yet this very temporary nature shows the contingent nature of dwelling. This is due to the grey area of where the boundaries fall between 'theirs' and 'mine'. We have rented the dwelling for the duration of a holiday and we treat it as ours for this period. We move things around; use them in ways that might not be prescribed (an ashtray doubles as a soap dish, a casserole as fruit bowl); we stretch out and relax. We adjust the dwelling to suit our routines. And the owner has to take on trust that we will respect their property. Yet we know there are limits to what we can and should do. In particular, we know that the owner has a right of entry. More practically, they have a key and can access the dwelling at any time they like. So we must trust them to respect our privacy and to leave our belongings as they are. There is, then, an uncomfortable balance between possession and ownership here. This is only made more so when we are owner-occupiers who are used to controlling access to our dwelling on our terms. We are used to using the dwelling as we choose, without being beholden to others. Much of the temporary dwelling is in a state, in terms of its décor and organisation, that we would not have chosen or seek to retain if it were permanent. There are, then, continual reminders that our stay is temporary and that we have only limited rights over this dwelling. What makes this bearable is the specific use we make of temporary dwellings.

The very process of dwelling is social: it is a shared process. We have latitude in the process of creating our dwelling environment. Conventions limit us, but they do not prevent us from creating dwelling as we wish. But dwelling should not be seen as about the absolute or total creation of environments. We do not usually start at 'year zero', or with the bare earth. We do not often wish to build the dwelling, but accept the completed structure and work within its constraints. Likewise, we do not create the relationships between ourselves from scratch. What we do is maintain and develop what we have received or inherited. Many of the memories we have are shared with others – our brothers and sisters as children, or our parents. We re-embed those memories into a new space and link them with other thoughts and feelings that we share with others with whom we now seek to share our adult lives. We live in space that has been made by others, and that has usually been lived in by others. It has traces which are alien, but which we might not seek to eradicate immediately, or at all. We might choose to keep parts of the decoration, or accept someone else's adaptations. We might see the process of creating *our* space as an incremental process. Or, indeed, we might see that what we do within the dwelling overrides any trace of a previous occupation without the need for any physical changes. What constitutes the creation of *our space* – of 'real habitation' – is as subjective as taste itself. Yet regardless of this subjective nature, the creation of dwelling is a development *out of* an already existing entity, and not the creation of something new. We draw from a social pool, we mould and we model to create something that is ours, and then we pass it on to someone else. What we have, then, we share. This allows us to protect those we love and teach them that when dwelling is shared it is at its most sublime.

Chapter 6
Want it, have it!

The paradox of dwelling

The public obsession with housing, as expressed in the media, dwells on two things: house prices and décor. The news is filled with speculation about the direction of house prices and the consequences of any change. Experts speculate on the effects for the national economy of any changes, and comment on what this means for personal and aggregate wealth. The question deemed to matter is: is housing still a good investment? In other words, what can we expect of the future? Second, in recent years, we have become inundated with television programmes and magazines on décor and domestic design. We, or some of us, avidly watch other experts pontificating on colour schemes, soft furnishings and fixtures and fittings. We watch the tastes of others being excoriated by style gurus and then we are advised on how to do it 'properly'; we can now have no excuse for not living well, so long, that is, as our house is sufficiently valuable to make the future something worth planning for! We are now, it appears, a nation of neurotic snobs, sneering at the tastes of others, whilst worrying about our investments. We watch programmes advising us on 'good taste' and the proper use of space, and wonder if we too are not guilty of 'style crime'.

What we have done is to move away from machines for living in and towards machines for desiring. We are no longer merely content to live in our house, it must now provide so much more. It must provide financial security for ourselves and our children, and it must say something about the persons we are. Our dwelling is our own advertisement as well as our pension and our children's future. What it is no longer, if it ever was, is simply our home – the place where we dwell.

Of course, the above is both a caricature and an overstatement. Whilst we watch these programmes or read the financial pages, we are sitting in our own dwelling, benefiting from the privacy, security and intimacy it brings with it. We are still dwelling in the ontological sense, even when we are focusing on house prices and colour co-ordinated fabrics. But because we are dwelling,

Our dwelling displays both our affluence and our conformity

we are able to take its very facility for granted. We can safely ignore those facets of our lives that bring privacy, security and intimacy precisely because we have ... privacy, security and intimacy. We can take these things for granted and are then free to look elsewhere. And what we look for is to fulfil our desires.

But what is it we desire? Is it something within our dwelling? Or is it driving us to look outside the dwelling for something beyond our current horizon? The short answer is, both: we seek something more than what we have and exercise this both in terms of using what we currently have, and also in striving for what we might have. Yet, as we have already seen, the situation is more complex than this, and this is because it is the dwelling, with its horizons fixed, that allows us to desire at all. The horizon that encloses us – the dwelling that grasps us – enables us to desire more of what we have and something we currently do not have. Dwelling is the stability that opens up the possibility of transformation and makes it tenable to desire. It must also be said that this very stability given by dwelling makes it *safe* to desire: it means we can seek for more without risking what we currently have. Dwelling takes much of the gambling out of the actions of desire, and for this paradox we should be grateful.

What are the limits of desire?

What does it mean to say we desire something? The word is one we constantly use and use in different ways. A desire is something we have, but it is also something we do: it can be a wish and the act of wishing for; a longing and to long for; a request and to request; and, of course, it is both the appetite and the thing we wish to consume. We use the word to refer to a range of feelings from quite liking something to a feeling of desperate craving for something. It can be used to refer to some vague notion of what we might like sometime in the future right through to our basest animal urges. Desire is therefore a word with a considerable range of uses.

But the word 'desire' now comes with a considerable baggage: it is one of the totems of post-structuralist thought and thus when we discuss desire we must also give some consideration to how the word has become imbued with some theoretical significance. Much of this theoretical thrust in post-structuralism is borrowed from psychoanalysis, where the notion of repression plays a key part.

We have desires precisely because we do not have the things we want. So, in order to have the desires we must be lacking in something. Hence to say 'I have my heart's desire' is to suggest that any craving has ceased; this is the very epitome of complacency. So perhaps complacency should be seen as the opposite of desire. This is important because of the manner in which post-structuralists use the notion of desire, as something transgressive and potentially transformative. It is in this sense that their discussion of desire is different from that of traditional psychoanalysis. Anthony Elliott (2000) suggests that both Freud's and Lacan's psychoanalysis 'personalises' desire by relating it to the sexual realm of the nuclear family. Lacan (1977) sees desire in terms of prohibition of the 'Law', this being something akin to paternal diktat. It can therefore be seen, suggests Elliott, as 'reactionary', presumably because it takes the traditional role of the family as a given. In contrast to this 'reactionary' notion of desire, Elliott describes Deleuze and Guattari's critique of 'capitalist' desire as channelled only along prescribed pathways. They seek to open up this reactionary state through impersonal flows of 'schizoid' desire, which can apparently herald a radical transformation of society (Deleuze and Guattari, 1983).

What this suggests is desire without boundaries, or to argue that, if there are boundaries, they are there to be broken. Desire, then, in this post-structural sense, is seen as being a disruption and a breach of stability. This may be portrayed as being absolutely democratic – all desires have an equal right of expression – but one wonders what the effect of the resultant state of continual flux might actually amount to, especially when we apply it to dwelling. On one level, dwelling allows for transgression. It can do this precisely because of the privacy it allows. Dwelling can thus provide for non-conventional lifestyles and personal experimentation. Yet this can only occur where there is a definitive boundary, as provided by the dwelling itself. It is because the dwelling encloses and restricts others from viewing that so-called transgressive acts can occur. Without these boundaries – which prevent others from transgressing – these acts would be difficult and would lose the sanctuary given by privacy.

However, the boundary makes the transgressive act invisible. It is therefore only transformative for the individuals concerned. But these individuals are presumably already amenable to such changes – they already wish to have their desires met – and thus what is actually being transformed? One might therefore suggest that these acts are not transgressive, at least according to the 'depersonalised' rubric of post-structuralism. This is of course true, but it merely shows the limited nature of post-structuralist conceptions. Once we attempt to 'depersonalise' desire, what do we have? We can discuss so-called impersonal flows of desire but only through ciphers such as expressed wants and needs. The problem for post-structuralists is that, in attempting to depersonalise desire, they only succeed in collectivising it into generalised constructs. The result is that desires are only described as consisting of actions that these theorists approve of. Hence so-called 'capitalist' desires are disapproved of, and are to be replaced with the rather indeterminate notion of 'schizoid' desire.

Just how can we collectivise desire and leave anything there intact? If desire becomes depersonalised, if we seek to uncouple it from the subjectivity out of which it grows, we are left merely with a new form of collective political notation: the replacement of rights or need with desire. But what this creates is a form of political stasis, precisely because there is no way in which desires can be expressed collectively. The whole essence of desire, as a psychoanalytic concept or when used more generally, is that it is subjective and personal. This does not mean, however, that it is reactionary *per se*. Indeed, applying the term 'reactionary' to desire in this general sense is meaningless. Merely because desires are personal does not mean they cannot be homoerotic or transcend the traditional family unit. What it does suggest is that one cannot take particular senses of desire to be transformative of themselves. Rather desire, once it is integrated into the lifeworld of an individual, loses any sense of being transgressive. Desire, when it is *mine and mine alone*, is always normal. Transgressions are absolute stages and not continua. Thus any transgression leads to a new sense of normality. Dressing up desire in collectivist garb hides this obvious fact, but only by denuding the concept of desire of any of its import.

Therefore one can see desire as being transgressive, but only when it is seen as something we already have. Yet the act of achieving that desire returns us to a condition of stability. This is precisely how desire operates within dwelling, where we move from a state of longing to one of complacency, or rather, to speak more exactly, to a condition whereby we can crave whilst being within the cocoon of complacency that is dwelling.

But it is also because desire is mine and mine alone that we should seek to limit and bind it. Without limits desire can spill into exploitation and becomes not 'schizoid', 'capitalist', 'decentred', or whatever notion post-structuralists wish to place on it. What desire without limits becomes is a question of power, of relative abilities to impose our will on reluctant others. It is only through limits and boundaries that we can be assured of consent and compliance, because these act as means of prevention, or as brakes on the desires of others. What post-structuralists forget or ignore is the competitive nature of desire. Because they collectivise desire they assume all desires are, or can be, shared and equal. But when desires are untrammelled, we lose the ability, collectively and individually, to protect the weak. This is, we must suppose, not the form of transgression sought by post-structuralists such as Deleuze and Guattari, but its very opposite. Perversely then, what they caricature as 'capitalist' desire, with its inherent reaction and oppression, is just what they would create by releasing desire from its bounds.

Limiting desire to where it can be safely applied is, to use Robert Nozick's jargon, effectively a side-constraint (Nozick, 1974), which limits what others may do to us, thus preventing coercion and allowing us to pursue our own ends free from unwanted interference. This side-constraint is, of course, a considerable impediment to the exercise of our own ends – we are limited only to the use of what is ours and what we can persuade others to give freely – but without this constraint we would have no surety of attaining anything other than by naked power. Therefore seeing dwelling as a boundary which we respect and honour is a means of legitimating the desires of others, but in a way that does not impose these desires either on us or on any unwilling individual or group. Dwelling therefore offers both the limits of desire, and also the space in which desires can be both fed and longed for.

Desiring dwelling and dwelling in desire

So, bearing in mind the theoretical baggage that desire has to carry, what are the links between dwelling and desire? We have already seen the paradoxical quality of dwelling and desire: that boundaries give us the freedom to express our desires, but in doing so they must be limited to ensure that others have a like freedom. Yet this does not adequately express what it is we desire in and from dwelling.

The most obvious thing we desire is a dwelling itself. We seek a dwelling of a particular type, with certain characteristics, of a particular size and location, and for a particular purpose. This latter point is important and starts to point to a more nuanced position. We do not just desire a thing for its own sake. Instead we desire a dwelling for what it can let us do, and that has enough space, is in the right place, has the right level of amenity, is sustainable and affordable, and so on.

This description is fine as far as it goes, but it appears to relate to a desire at a fairly low level. It sees desire as about calculation, or cost/benefit analysis, where we can weigh the pros and cons and the various options open to us. This is what we might, rather facetiously, term the theory of *rational desire*, the state in which desire is little more than choosing from available options.

But the essence of desire is that we want to choose without constraints. There is little that is really rational about this type of choice. Indeed we might suggest that desire comes into play precisely when we go beyond the rational: beyond that which is within bounds and that follows on from our last move. Desire is where we seek to go beyond ourselves into a new realm. If this is the case, does the question of desire only arise when what we want is beyond our reach? By definition what we desire is not the normal, the everyday, or that which we can just reach out and touch. For something to be an object of desire, does it not have to appear to be currently unobtainable or only attainable with a great effort?

Desire is for that which we do not yet have, for that which is just out of reach.[1] To be particularly excruciating, the object of desiring must appear to be attainable: it is tantalisingly close in front of us, but with one last push, one greater effort, or if things were only slightly different, we could attain it. We need some incentive to carry on and so for desire to exist there must be something to which we can attach ourselves, but which we can currently only long for: something which is yet just out of reach. As we have seen, to attain our heart's desire is to stop desiring.

This raises the obvious question, and one central to any theorisation of desire, namely what is the more important – the desire or its object? Are we, as human beings, born to crave and long for what we currently do not have – is it something hardwired into us – or is it just a consequence of our acquisitiveness? Clearly we all desire things, and what we desire is not a constant either for each of us or for any of us over time. What I desire most now may be different from what I desired most last year, and it may well differ from what others may most desire. Perhaps then, when someone has attained their heart's desire, we should not expect this to be a permanent state. Once they have assimilated this most-wished-for object into their lifeworld, they might start to crave for something new, something that did not register previously because it was subsumed by the earlier desire, or because it was not possible until the first object had been attained. So one craving may follow on from another, or it may simply replace the void left by the attainment of what we now hold. We have our heart's desire, but then …

Is what is important in desire the seeking and not the attainment? Might it not in fact be crucial for us not to attain what we desire, for then what would we do? We may see that what we have craved so much for, and made so many sacrifices for, is flawed, foolish and unfulfilling. We find that our dream home is still just a brick box like all the others. It must still perform the same basic functions as the one we had previously. The new gadget or piece of furniture may look just right, but it still has a purpose to serve regardless of its aesthetic appeal. As we live with these items and use them, we quickly find their faults and limitations – those small things that annoy us because they are not quite right, and those things that could be made better. What occurs here is that the object of desire has become normal and so ceases to be anything special. We then latch onto something else that we do not have and can just see tantalisingly out of reach. We have to keep aspiring in order to feel that we are progressing and achieving something: we need to feel that there is something still ahead of us, and not just a flawed and sometimes regretted past and a lacklustre present.

The fear generated by desire, therefore, might not be in failing to attain our heart's desire, but in actually fulfilling it and then finding that there is still a void. What we thought was 'the very thing', was not really particularly special, or rather, we have not been transformed very much by achieving that thing. This appreciation, which amounts to finally accepting that dwelling is really a means and not an end in itself, may be traumatic. Why have we sought it so earnestly if we are still empty and unfulfilled? What else could or should we have done? Would it have made any difference if we had not done anything at all? Who indeed has noticed what we have achieved? We have our dream home, filled with all the appliances we could wish for; we have found the partner we have so deeply desired and earnestly wished for. Yet the earth still orbits around the sun and not us, other people still maintain their interests and take no more notice of us. We come to realise that the longings we have sought to fulfil are subjective entities that may erupt inside us, but leave the world as indifferent to us as it ever was. What the fulfilment of desire makes clear is that my desires are not shared by others, and that others are left unmoved by my achievement of them. My desires may well be thoroughly incomprehensible to others. For some people this object I have desired has been available to them all the time: they could simply grasp it at a time of their choosing, and it is in consequence an object of little regard and unexceptional. For them it is trite and banal to desire what is such a common object. For other people this object is so far away as to make meaningless any effort towards it: they cannot possibly ever attain it, and so it does not register on their senses as an object of desire. In both these cases, there is the question of why we have bothered to expend so much energy. What has our desiring amounted to, but a futile, pointless and perhaps even perverse quest for an inconsequential item?

What might account for the discrepancy between one individual's subjective desires and those of another? Why are the desires of some seen as absurd or preposterous, whilst others are seen as conventional or banal? Might it not be that there is some matching up between what we desire and the possibility of its attainment? We fantasise for that which is just above us, that is for those things just out of reach, and which therefore may be achievable. We may want the proverbial 'untold riches', and the palace of our dreams, but we strive instead for what we can reasonably achieve. We desire comfort and security for our children and ourselves: a bigger house, a better area to live in, a paved drive, and so on. We seek something that equates with a fantasy or image that informs others and ourselves what we think we are, or should be, or even could be.

Yet what do we do when we attain it? We start to reach for the next notch up: we aim for a higher level or indicator of success. We embark on a journey over a series of peaks, the size of which depends on status, expectations, and so on. So for some council tenants owning their current dwelling through the Right to Buy might be the apex of their desires, whilst for other more affluent households it might be a walled detached house in an exclusive area.

All this might suggest that the desire for the 'right dwelling' might create anxiety and problems for us, and that this is leading to the conclusion that desires are entirely negative. Yet we can return to our initial paradox and so turn this around to see dwelling as having a protective function, where it is the very thing to shield us from the trauma of unfulfilled desire. Dwelling helps us by harbouring our fantasies. It is where we can dream away from others, without the cruelty of another's gaze, without the opinions of others knocking down our dreams. In the privacy of dwelling there is no commentary on our desire.[2] Dwelling gives us a safe environment in which we can formulate and implement our plans. It is the place that gives us comfort and security. Dwelling wraps us up in its warmth and care. In this environment we have sufficient freedom from care in which to wonder wistfully about the future and seek to achieve new horizons. Dwelling is the safe harbour out of which we can sail, in the knowledge of a safe return and security once we are again safely gathered in. In this sense dwelling makes desire safe.

This suggests a further role for dwelling, as the 'home' or site of desire. It is the place where desire is licensed. Dwelling is where we can fantasise: where it is safe to imagine the end of constraints and thus what happens if our fantasies are realised. But dwelling is also where it is safe, to an extent, to experiment with the limits of constraint. For most of us these limits to desire are when we share our privacy with our partner. In dwelling desire is linked with intimacy, and the dwelling becomes the place where we can fulfil and refill our desire for those we love. This is another way in which desire is made safe by dwelling.

But we should not forget that it is also a place where desires are forced on others: privacy can create coercion where there are no effective limits on the desires of one and these are fulfilled at the expense of another. We like to see dwelling as an intimate space in which consensus and consent rule. Yet high walls that allow for intimacy and shared desire can also cast a long shadow over the vulnerable who are unable to escape these walls. For them intimacy and desire are a prison and a hell. Hence, as we have seen in the discussion on invasive technologies in chapter 5, there must always be limits to privacy. Certain conditions of privacy, when one is isolated but not alone, can offer no constraints to desires and the sense of power that can come with the fulfilment of the craving. Dwelling, then, can be the space where desires (as well as basic wants and needs) can be suppressed for the benefit of others. We should not forget that most child abuse occurs within the family home and is committed by someone whom the child knows well. Similarly, the dwelling can be the site of domestic violence, where the desires of one partner, usually the male, override the objections of the other party.

There is no necessary equality in desire, and this relates not to imagination or the very subjective sense of our desiring. Rather inequality of desire, like any political relation, is defined by the possibility of fulfilment. Hence, for some and perhaps even for many, desiring must remain just that: a longing or a wish that just cannot be fulfilled. It is not entirely flippant to state that psychoanalysis is the ideology of the leisured classes!

Consumed by desire

The everyday transformation of dwelling is made manifest through consumption. However, this process is in no way transgressive. Instead it conserves, by reinforcing the centrality of dwelling for the creation of personal desire. We depend on the habitual and the known, but this does not inspire us. So we try to take dwelling out of the habitual and into the fantastical. We seek to make the dwelling into a special arena, by adding items and replacing old features. To achieve this transformation we look outside the dwelling to seek our pleasure. We look instead to the media to inform us of how our dwelling can be transformed. We want (or convince ourselves that we want) what is outside ourselves, to have our sense of self confirmed by others, according to standard modes of reference, rather than by ourselves alone through our everyday, habitual activities. What we are seeking here is a form of confirmation: we desire not to be alone, not to be different, but to be part of a homogeneous community with common references. This is no less of a subjective process, but what is lost is a sense of authenticity, a sense in which we can confirm our belonging in our own vocabulary, rather than in an entirely conventional one.[3] In essence, then, we subsume our authentic selves into a common understanding of what dwelling is and what our dwelling means. This, as we have seen, is apparent in the concern for house prices and public taste as determined by the popular media. As Martin Heidegger (1962) demonstrated, this collapsing of our independent being into inauthenticity – the herd mentality – is linked to anxiety. We are anxious about our condition in the world, and this is manifested in the way in which we conform to popular norms without considering their specific import for us. We gain security in the herd rather than through exercising our autonomy. Because dwelling forms the background to our lives and, in consequence, is transparent to us in its ready functioning – and hence is a common process – we find ourselves focusing on what externalises the dwelling in an attempt to demonstrate our acceptance of popular norms. In other words, we consume so as to exhibit our acceptance of common tastes.

But how much of the construction of dwelling is based on illusion and how much is authenticity? And, related to this (although to be dealt with more fully in chapter 7), how much is anxiety part of dwelling? By way of opening this issue up, imagine the questioning of a DIY enthusiast as follows:

Q: 'Do you like where you live?'
A: 'Yes, of course. I love it'.
Q: 'Then why are you so intent on changing it?'

What would be an appropriate answer here? Or is the questioner really just missing the point? What is demonstrated by the act of transforming the dwelling? What does this show about our cravings? Is the dwelling underperforming, is it letting us down? Or do we have some new purpose in mind for the dwelling? Are we re-creating the dwelling to fit our self-image or some other image of what, or where, we would like to be? Are we doing it because we can or because we ought to? Might we not legitimately extract from this just one point: does the DIY enthusiast see their dwelling as a place for living in or as something from which they can fulfil their desires?

Perhaps for the DIY enthusiast it is not a matter of not liking their dwelling, but that they are trapped within a circuit of desire. They simply

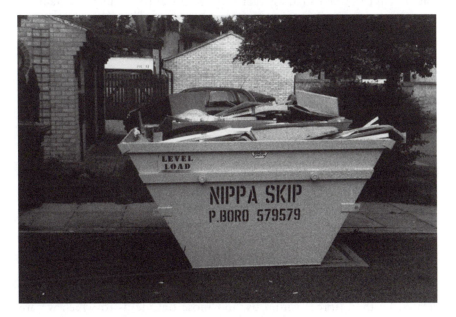

If you like it so much why do you keep changing it?

cannot refrain from seeking more, be it space, amenity, fittings, shelves or whatever. Their belief – what drives them – is that further improvements will allow them to reach what they think of as a higher standard of living. They believe that by improving the dwelling they can fulfil themselves more completely. But, of course, this attempted movement up is continuous. When they have done enough, or as much as they want, to their current 'dream house', it is then onto the next: to a new dream with more amenities and, crucially, a new challenge. Indeed, even before completing one project they are looking to the next.

This relates back to the anxiety of achievement, whereby we fear a void if we ever completely fulfil our fantasies. What may well be occurring here then is the 'desire' to continuously miss our desired goal. We manage our dwelling so that we just fall short and so we have to go on again, always with the hope of fulfilment, but, subliminally at least, always seeking just to fail. Once we reach one apparent summit we see the hill still stretching out further above us and so we start out for the next summit, secretly hoping that this one is not the real summit. But what we cannot face is staying still, of saying 'here and no more', of actually fulfilling our fantasies. We thus face both the anxiety of failure and the anxiety of success.

But the dwelling again has a role of its own to play here. Dwelling might help to sustain a fantasy that keeps reality at bay. It might sustain the Sisyphean process of continuous improvement. The very fastness of dwelling – the privacy, security and intimacy of dwelling – might keep us open to desire by making the untenable appear attainable, because we do not have to face up to the objectivity of our situation. We can collude together against the world. We can ignore reality and plan to fulfil our desires free from interference from outside. In the sanctity of our privacy we are not forced to face up to the possible consequences of our actions: like all fantasies, they are consequence-free – but only as long as they remain fantasy. Once they come within reach they become consequential.

This is the purpose of a refuge in the fullest sense, as a place where we can be hidden from what seeks us and would destroy our fantasies. By closing the door on the world we can refuse to accept the reality of our condition: we have, as it were, closed the door on reality. We can instead continue the pretence and accept only those parts of the outside world that we wish to. We thus create our own reality – what Slavoj Žižek (2001) refers to as the 'Real'. This concept refers not to reality *as it actually is*, but to reality as we would have it, created by those forces within us, and those outside us to which we are susceptible, such as the media, ideology, and so on. The Real is where we can maintain our fantasies and continue with the escalating circuits of desire. The Real, then, sustains our notion of dwelling as consumption.

Yet, on the other hand, we can escape the Real by dwelling. This gives us the space that allows us to live differently, creating a space outside the Real by throwing off the external and false notions of what we desire.[4] Of course, we can always be accused of merely creating an alternative fantasy, but if this is all we can do then it is no less sustaining: one person's authentic life, after all, is another person's self-delusion. This only becomes apparent when we seek to implement our plans and we face the prospect that the Real – our integration of fantasy with our current predicament – must contend with the indifference of the world.

From desire to anxiety

Yet, contrary to all the above, is not dwelling that place where we also have no alternatives but to face 'reality'? Is dwelling not that place where we cannot hide from ourselves: where we need not – perhaps even, should not – put on a mask (a persona), but instead where we must face the brutality of the unobtainable? Is the condition of dwelling not one of desire, nor one of possibility, but of limits and boundaries? Might not the side effect of locating ourselves in a space we can call 'ours' be the limitation of other possibilities? What, then, if the opportunity cost of dwelling is the breach of fantasy?

And so our dwelling might be a place where desire is absent, or rather, what we desire is a lack of longing, where we desire to place custom over craving, habit over longing for what we do not have. Are not there some, or even many, people who already have attained their ideal? If these people do exist, and many would boast of it, how can we account for this? Perhaps they appreciate the nature of their desire and so, to return to the jargon of psychoanalysis, they have sublimated their desires and have allowed the dwelling to merge with their own authentic self. Or the supposed attainment of their desire might be due to complacency and the habit-forming quality of dwelling itself. Friedrich Nietzsche (1996) says that habits are pleasurable. We find pleasure in what we have, but this is a type of complacency based on habitual and implicit relations. The pleasure is in the regularity, the very lack of transformation. According to Nietzsche, we try to impose these customs on others, as we believe them to have the greatest utility. We will cleave to them even when they become hard to sustain, in the belief that these customs can uniquely maintain us as we should and ought to be. This might be described as a form of *negative desire*: a desire to maintain what we have, to impose it on others and to cleave to it at all costs. We might suggest that this negative desire is better described as *anxiety*. We wish that a certain type of dwelling, and the concomitant lifestyle, could be free of anxiety. We want to be free of insecurity, free of discomfort. We want to ensure that we have what we think we should have. We want ourselves and those we love to be safe and secure. These are things we have, and insofar as we desire, it is a desire to keep them. All these, then, can become the very sources of anxiety.

We can see then that negative desire has a dark side: the very fear of unwanted change. What if the dwelling goes wrong: if our heart's desire is destroyed? What if there is some disaster which makes the dwelling unfast and jeopardises our security? What if our dwelling is violated when we are away and left damaged and our belongings taken or ruined? What if all we have striven for – all we have achieved – is destroyed by an unknown and uncaring other? And might this anxiety not grow with the more we own? So, as we accumulate the things we desire we become more anxious about an attack on them.

So we are anxious if we do not attain what we desire, but we remain anxious because we might lose it when we have attained it. This is why we try, as Nietzsche says, to impose our habits and customs onto others. It is an attempt to protect what we have. We begin to fear those different from us: those we perceive as 'below' us who would seek to supplant us and take what we have for themselves. We fear those who do not live as we do and who do not wish to: what we might call the embourgeoisment of fear!

But these are all things that can be relieved by dwelling itself. This need not be related to ownership, but rather to the need for privacy, security and intimacy. It is this that allows us the freedom to do what we would like – to play discordant music, to read subversive books, to watch films of dubious taste, to indulge in sexual activities with other consenting adults, and so on. The purpose of dwelling is to permit this, and that is why we so earnestly desire this place of our own. Dwelling, therefore, is where we can fulfil our desires. And this is why we so earnestly fear its loss. Dwelling cannot cure us of our desires, nor, as we shall see in the next chapter, can it take away our anxieties. It does, however, provide us with the best protection on offer.

Chapter 7
Fear and the comfort of the mundane

Dwelling matters so much, we can say, because it ensures that nothing much else matters. What dwelling gives us is an anchor, something secure with which to give us confidence and a sense of safety. At least that is what we suppose it does. But clearly, and for a number of reasons, dwelling is not so much the anchor we use to secure us, as the anchor that is tied fast around our necks to ensure we sink. Dwelling, despite all its virtues – and we would not want to be without it! – causes us anxiety. As we have already seen, this anxiety might derive from desire: from a sense of unfulfilment, or perhaps even the fear that having it all will not amount to much after all.

But surely, we might argue, any anxiety we have over our dwelling is contained. And this is, of course, literally true. However, it is the very container causing us to be anxious: what hides the anxiety, causes the anxiety! Indeed it might be that containment is precisely the problem. The four walls that surround us protect us, but also prevent us from releasing the tensions and worries of our lives. If privacy has a problem it is that it cannot be partial: it is an all-or-nothing situation. We cannot pick and choose what we wish to show and expect that to be respected. If we open up, then, we risk showing everything, and that does not alleviate our anxiety but merely extends it. And this is made worse by the sharing of privacy, as what one person wishes to publicise might be the very thing another is ashamed of and wants to remain private.

Yet, because of dwelling, we do not go naked into the world, and this is surely a source of comfort. Dwelling does help, and it may be the sense of privacy that greatly assists here. If the source of our anxiety is outside the dwelling, then clearly our boundary can also ward off this sense of dread: for many, therefore, being safe and secure and private is a comfort, even if it does mean that we are alone (or perhaps, it is precisely because we are alone).

So there are two sides to this problem of dwelling and anxiety – the unfulfilled wish to escape to something different, and the need to crawl back under the stone away from the madness of the big, unfriendly world outside. So like privacy, and much else besides, anxiety is something we have because of something else. There is an instrumentality to anxiety and one of the causes can be dwelling itself. But then one of the instruments we use to assuage anxiety is our dwelling.

There is then a circularity here, and with it the danger of confusion and obfuscation. How can dwelling be a cause and a cure for anxiety? Are we not making too much of dwelling, by placing too great an emphasis on this rather nebulous and ambiguous term? There is, undoubtedly, this risk, but we should not forget that it is the very opacity of dwelling that is its chief virtue. Hence we should neither be surprised nor disappointed by the apparently changeable character of dwelling. Accordingly, in the first part of this discussion on anxiety, I wish to indulge in a discussion of popular culture, in particular a recent film, David Fincher's *Panic Room*, which, I believe, opens up many of the key issues around anxiety and dwelling. From this examination of an admittedly fictional – and rather extreme – case we will be able to show some examples of general anxiety within dwelling, and point to the ways in which dwelling is both cause and potential cure for the more mundane stresses and strains under which we live.

Room to panic

Stephen Mulhall (2002) considers the possibility of discussing films philosophically (and hence taking them seriously as things in themselves). Can it, he begins, be justified to discuss conceptually what is intended as popular entertainment? Is there not a danger of reading things into a film that are just not there? Mulhall recognises this dilemma, but argues that this is based on 'a rather impoverished conception of the intellectual powers of film and of the pervasiveness of matters of philosophical interest to human life' (p. 8). What he appears to be saying is that the view that films are not serious enough for philosophy is either to denigrate filmmaking, or any form of popular entertainment, or to say that 'proper' philosophy has no place amongst the everyday and what interests the common herd. It is then a form of elitism that relegates philosophy to its redundant ivory tower. We can, of course, use these exact same arguments in defending a philosophical study of housing which, after all, is the very place where the common herd grazes.

Mulhall's argument is, I believe, a strong one (even though we should beware of overinterpretation) and indeed one that could be used more widely to justify a philosophical approach to housing issues. If philosophy is to be of any use it has to engage with how humans actually live and think. This need not involve any loss of rigour: it is rather more likely to increase the status of philosophy as a set of procedures that are actually engaged with the everyday.

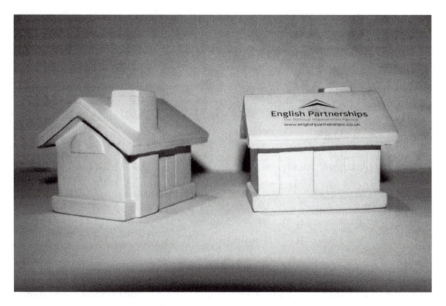

Housing as a symbol of stress

Mulhall's approach is also a useful one in that his analysis of film is not coloured by any particular preconceptions. Taking his lead from Stanley Cavell (1979), he argues that those who do study film according to some particular theory 'exhibit a strong tendency to treat the films they discuss as objects to which specific theoretical edifices (originating elsewhere, in such domains as psychoanalysis or political theory) could be applied' (p. 7). The film is seen merely 'as a cultural product whose specific features served to illustrate the truth of that theory – as one more phenomenon the theory rendered comprehensible' (p. 7). What Mulhall seeks instead is an approach where 'films can philosophize' (p. 7): where the film is seen as being capable of saying something substantial for itself and is not just an opportunity to extend an already well-rehearsed theory. As we saw in the Introduction, this point is also made by Jerome Bruner (2002) in his discussion of stories and their importance to us. Bruner suggests that a fictional narrative gives 'shape to things in the real world and often bestows on them a title to reality' (p. 8). Fictions can give 'experiential shape' (p. 8), a way of referencing, categorising and understanding people and situations in which we may find ourselves. Fictions, we can almost say, validate our experiences by giving them a reference.

Therefore what follows is a study of a particular film, David Fincher's *Panic Room*, and what it might tell us about the significance of our housing.

This film pulls out several important factors relating to housing, all of which can be said to centre on anxiety. It demonstrates the need for security from real threats, but also that this security can itself threaten us and make us impotent. *Panic Room* also demonstrates the double-sided nature of technology, of how it can protect, but also how we become so dependent we are unable to survive without it. It shows the implacability of our dwelling, that it can quite as well work against us as for us. It also tells us something about the nature of choice and how it is always bounded, and about the nurturing quality of our dwelling. In short, we can learn much from a study of this film. So, whilst one can see the following discussion as exemplary of a possible approach to housing analysis, there are also specific insights we can glean.

I have suggested that *Panic Room* says many interesting things about how we live and the anxieties that derive therefrom. We should not, of course, take the film literally, and so I am not suggesting this is actually what commonly occurs. There are some important ways in which this film is out of kilter with dwelling in its generality. First, *Panic Room* is violent and action-packed, and this is the very opposite of what we want of dwelling. Of course, violence in the home is not unknown, and its extent and effects are not to be diminished. However, the violence of this film is not in any sense what we want from 'home'. Second, it is certainly not typical to move into a dwelling where there are $22 million of bearer bonds hidden, of which only a small number of rather crooked people are aware. Third, a four-storey luxury Manhattan townhouse, with its own elevator and panic room is not typical of how most of us live. All of these can be seen as reasons to detract from the film's relevance.

Yet I would suggest that the film does offer a useful way into an examination of the anxiety that goes along with housing, and it is precisely the exaggerated and overblown manner in which this anxiety is depicted – the extremity of the violence, the extent of the violation and desecration of family and property – that makes it such a useful vehicle for analogy. Of course this is not how most people live, or what most can experience (although again we should not diminish the impact that the violent invasion of our dwelling might have).[1] What is important here is not the particular story of a mother and daughter being trapped in their dwelling by three violent invaders, but how it shows the vulnerability that goes with dwelling. The fact that this story is overly dramatic does not diminish its import. The very exaggeration within the film manifests much about the anxieties of modern dwelling.

All but the opening and closing scenes of the film take place over one wet and windy night. A recently divorced woman, Meg (played by Jodie Foster), and her diabetic daughter, Sarah (played by Kristen Stewart), have moved into a huge Manhattan townhouse. One of the peculiarities of the house is that it has an impregnable panic room off the master bedroom: a concrete and steel-encased room with its own power supply and phone lines, with banks of television screens linked to CCTV cameras around the house. Meg's initial reaction to this room is, inappropriately, to panic and show signs of claustrophobia, especially when the estate agent locks them in. Her fear is of the technology, of what it might do to them if they misuse it. She is not apparently interested in how it might protect them. She does not expect intrusion – this is not the foremost consideration when viewing a potential home. Accordingly, the last thing we see her doing before going to bed is to attempt to close down the panic room, presumably to ensure that there is no risk of being trapped in there. However, all she succeeds in doing (conveniently, of course) is to disable the main house alarm system and to turn on the CCTV system in the panic room. In the early hours three burglars effect an entry to the property with the aim of stealing some, as yet unspecified, items. They are under the impression that the house is still unoccupied: this is the first of many demonstrations of their incompetence. When Meg awakes and finds the house invaded she successfully gets her daughter and herself into the panic room. It is then we find that what the burglars want is actually in that room.

The rest of the film consists of more or less improbable, but really quite gripping, attempts to get Meg and Sarah out of the room and for the two of them to be rescued. They manage a snatched phone call to Meg's ex-husband, who eventually turns up just as one of the invaders is murdered by one of his accomplices. However, the ex-husband merely becomes a hostage and a further means to get them out of the panic room. He is thus unable to offer his ex-wife and child much in the way of assistance. Towards the end of the film Meg finds herself outside the room (having gone to get her daughter's medication) with the two remaining invaders and her daughter inside. At this point two policemen arrive, having been called by the ex-husband, but Meg is forced to dissemble because the burglars have her daughter. She thus sets about making the burglars' escape as difficult as possible once they have recovered the $22 million from the safe in the panic room. She does this by destroying the CCTV cameras, blocking doors and so on. The film ends violently, but with mother and daughter unharmed. The final scene shows them browsing the property pages for another dwelling.

The film has, perhaps rightly, been criticised for stretching out what is a rather thin concept. However, Fincher does this skilfully, making good use of imaginative camera work and hinting at complexities within various relationships, such as the situation of Sarah, the daughter of two recently separated parents who finds her loyalties split. Once safe, who should she go to, her injured father or her mother who has effectively saved her? We also see something of the motivations of the burglars, particularly Burnham (played by Forest Whitaker), an employee of the company that installed the panic room, who has become involved in the crime because of problems in paying custody payments to his estranged wife. In consequence our sympathies lie as much with Burnham – who, we should remember, is actively destroying the domestic harmony of one family to try and create some stability for his own – as with the mother and daughter under attack. But whatever the weaknesses and subtleties of the film, the main point here is to consider what relevance this story has for dwelling as an activity which we are continually engaged in.

First we can look at how the film starts. It begins with mother and daughter viewing a possible new home. We see the anxiety over whether it is right for them in terms of location, size and price. They are made to feel anxious and to come to a quick decision for fear that it will be taken by someone else. But perhaps most important is the fact that the move to this new home is enforced, in this case, by a divorce. They have to move not out of choice, but because of a huge disruption to their lives. They can choose where they go (and being affluent helps), but it is clear from their behaviour in the early part of the film that they would have preferred not to have moved at all. There is an initial tension between mother and daughter about moving into the new house. The daughter, Sarah, complains that her mother did not ask for her opinion on the house. Her mother replies that she did not ask her because she did not want Sarah to say she did not like it. The daughter appears ambivalent: she has not settled and is unsure that she will settle and says that she had a perfectly good house before. Likewise Meg shows her anxiety, but through tears and a reliance on alcohol.

These scenes remind us that much of the anxiety and angst about dwelling comes when we move. Even when we move for positive reasons we still have to deal with the possibility of things going wrong, and we may have doubts as to whether we have done the right thing. But these worries are much worse when the move is enforced due to some major change in our lives. As with the case of Meg and her daughter, we are often forced to move because of some significant, and perhaps unwanted, situation – in this case it is a divorce, but it might also be caused by the loss of a job. But whatever the cause, we have moved when we did not really want to. How does this reluctance affect the new dwelling and our approach to it? Can we use it fully? Are we properly committed to it when we did not want to move into it in the first place? Whatever virtues the new dwelling has, these are merely incidental to the reasons for the move. As we shall see, the film also ends with another enforced move. What this suggests is that all choices are bounded. We do not make choices for their own sake, but because of some specific event or change. Moreover, there are some choices we would prefer not to make at all, as all the options are worse than what came before (King, 2003).

But these relatively minor and perhaps expected worries are soon overshadowed by a much more immediate and serious anxiety when Meg finds the house occupied by three obviously hostile and dangerous intruders. Prior to this event, all Meg's actions in the film had been banal and internal to the family – unpacking, eating, bathing, and putting her daughter to bed. The action, such as it is, has been concerned with homemaking. But when the house is invaded, the concern moves to the violation of that home. The horror of it is by no means lessened by it being their first night in residence – the threat is as palpable.

Meg's initial reaction is disbelief and only then is she galvanised into action, rushing to gather up her daughter from her room on the floor above and hurrying to the panic room. Of course, it is this room, and what it offers and forbids, allows and prevents, that is at the centre of the film's interest for us here.

The panic room offers the epitome of isolated seclusion, of freedom from intrusion, the ability to watch and address one's adversaries, and the resources to survive. Yet it is also its nemesis: complete dependence and loss of autonomy. As we have seen, the very thought of this room brings on an attack of claustrophobia in Meg. The room indeed fits its billing: it induces panic. It is therefore, as well as a means of offering apparently total security, a *site of anxiety*. Of course, this anxiety arises partly as a result of the intrusion that has caused mother and daughter to enter the room. But it goes further than this. In the room there is a great reliance on technology. This is what allows anyone to see out and to communicate with the outside world. More fundamentally it is technology that supports life within the room. But this very technology also limits the amount of control the inhabitants have, even whilst it defends them. Security comes at the cost of imprisonment, because once the occupiers are inside they cannot leave without great risk. They are completely dependent on the intruders not staying too long, or on external help from police. This dependence on technology becomes more obvious when they realise that the telephone is not connected. Their only form of communication beyond the house is now by shining a flashlight through the air vent. Once the technology fails, they have only a very basic range of options open to them.

There is a resonance here with Martin Heidegger's discussion of technology (Heidegger, 1993). He sees the essence of technology as reductionist, of reducing nature and beings, including humans, to a standing reserve or stockpile to be used for technological purposes. All nature and being is reduced to a resource for technological expansion. Consequently Heidegger calls this enclosing by technology *enframing*. This notion is particularly apposite here, where the very technology of the panic room completely surrounds and threatens to overwhelm Meg and her daughter. They are enframed by the steel and concrete of the panic room: it is a technology that is limiting and reduces them to the basics of human life, to elemental survival.[2]

What the enclosing technology of the panic room further demonstrates is that we cannot have complete security without impotence. In the face of attack the mother and child can only respond by withdrawing, like a snail into its shell. In the panic room they might be invulnerable, yet only by becoming entirely inactive and ineffectual. They are safe there, but they can do nothing to prevent the house from being violated. This level of invulnerability can only be achieved by closing ourselves off entirely from the world around us. We may be safe, after a fashion, but we are no longer able to influence anything around us. We sit idly by, out of fear, whilst murder and mayhem occur beyond our shelter. We fear to go out because we risk assault ourselves, and so we stay cooped up and ignore the violence being done to others, just as Meg and Sarah hold on to each other inside the panic room whilst the ex-husband (and father) is being savagely beaten.

Complete security, therefore, means isolation and ineffectuality in the face of threats to us and others. We wring our hands and say 'what can I do? I have my family to protect'. So the natural urge we have to protect those closest to us can itself be used as a shield, as a means to keep away risky and unpleasant tasks that might come before us. We could have helped, we could have sacrificed ourselves, were it to be futile or otherwise. But we have a ready excuse. We can justify looking the other way because we are protecting our family.

The panic room can then be seen as a metaphor for the manner in which we commonly react to a threat: our first reaction is to withdraw, instead of facing the aggressor. This is, of course, an entirely natural and life-preserving instinct. We fear a confrontation and so we step away or retreat further into our shell. Accordingly, when the dwelling is threatened, because of harassment, intrusion or whatever, we do not fight those harassing or entering, but move back further into the dwelling to seek what protection we can from it. We do this even though we know it has already been violated and that we are not safe from intrusion, attack or harassment (our hiding places are seldom as secure as those in the film, and in any case the sense of security is psychological and not physical). But this withdrawal does not help us to escape; it merely makes us more vulnerable. Yet if we do give up the dwelling, what have we left? What have we to cling onto? What security is there? The dwelling is all that we have to protect ourselves. If we give it up we will be both threatened *and* bereft.

The panic room also shows that we have layers of security. The doors and windows are locked throughout the house, but we still need somewhere safer. We still seek a further layer, just in case. We want a further bolthole that will protect us, in case the first line of defence is breached. Likewise, our dwelling shows this layering of security, but of course on a different level. There are places within the dwelling that are never public. These are places we can withdraw to if we feel under threat, or if we seek to be properly alone. We might skulk off to the study, garage or garden shed, or children might go to their room. Just like the panic room, some places in our dwelling are seen as more secure than others, and this security derives from the knowledge that we can keep others out.

But there is an important difference, and this is shown by the anxiety of the couple even after they are safely in the panic room. The room is unfamiliar; it does not welcome them unlike those special places that we have made ourselves. So, security comes from familiarity as much as the physical bars and bolts. This relates back to the anxiety and indifference shown by the pair earlier in the evening. The dwelling is still unfamiliar and they have not settled into it as yet. Therefore there is no place in this dwelling from which they can seek comfort other than relying on the implacability of technology.

Indeed the film shows the mutual implacability that can arise between our dwelling and ourselves. Meg is so desperate to protect her daughter and herself that she thinks nothing of destroying the dwelling in doing so. Their new dwelling, in the face of this threat, is shown to be entirely instrumental. First we see it as their new home, then as a refuge, then a prison and a constraint, and, when Sarah goes hypo, as a threat to their lives. Thus if the dwelling hinders them – the CCTV cameras allowing the burglars to see Meg throughout the house – she will break it. As a result Meg treats the dwelling in just the same rather cavalier manner as the intruders do. The technology of the dwelling moves from being friend to foe and back again. It has an implacability to the vicissitudes of our lives. It does not react to our fears and anxieties as we do, and so it stops, properly speaking, being home and becomes an obstacle.

Another facet of anxiety is the very sense of violation itself. Once the dwelling has been entered it ceases, in a sense, to be ours. So when Meg runs out of the panic room to get her mobile phone and her daughter's syringe, it is as if the dwelling is no longer hers. She is now 'intruding' on the claimed space of others. She is only there under the sufferance of intruders. What has occurred is that she no longer has control over the dwelling. What dwelling gives us above all else is this sense of control over our environment. We can prevent others from entering; we can use it as we like; it is ours to do with as we please. Yet, with these intruders in the house, this is no longer the case. Meg and Sarah no longer have control over the dwelling, but have given this up as the cost of their immediate safety. They no longer *possess* the dwelling. Indeed it is the dwelling (or part of it) that possesses them. This very lack of control is highlighted, somewhat ironically, when Meg is called to the door by the two policemen. She uses her rights as the property owner to refuse them entry and sends them away. But she is forced into doing this precisely because she has lost control of the dwelling, with the burglars holding her daughter within the panic room.

In some ways we can see the panic room as the very opposite – a perversion – of the maternal womb,[3] a place that should be warm and comforting, offering succour and support. But instead it is claustrophobic and a site of anxiety. It is a place that we want to leave – nothing could be more desirable than to leave this place – yet to do so would be to submit to violation and violence. To use Martin Heidegger's phrase we would truly be *thrown into the world* (Heidegger, 1962). This sense of the violation of the maternal is one that features in several of Fincher's films, particularly in *Alien3*, where Ripley finds that she has been impregnated by an alien when she is asleep and therefore unable to defend herself, and in *Seven*, where the serial killer murders Officer Mills' pregnant wife.

But if the mother and daughter are to be saved – if they are to develop their situation and create new possibilities – then they must leave the panic room. Just so, we too must leave the womb if we are to develop and become a person as such. Staying in the panic room diminishes the two women and prevents them from engaging in any life other than one of dependency. So too a child, if it is to become fully part of the human community, must leave the womb with all the vulnerability and possibility of violence that might ensue as a result. Indeed the very leaving of the womb itself is a traumatic departure from warmth and seclusion. Yet if we are to continue with our mortal journey it is a necessity.

A constant theme in Fincher's films is the inadequacy of the domestic to cope with extreme situations. The heroes of films such as *Alien3*, *Seven* and *Panic Room* are driven to destroy domestic intimacy and security. In *Panic Room* it is the weakness of the ex-husband when he appears that is significant as a pointer to the otherworldly nature of the domestic. Like the ex-husband, we are so unprepared for violence that we can be of no real use to those we love. He is extraneous to the survival of his ex-wife and child, as shown by the fact that it is Burnham who takes the gun from the ex-husband to kill his last remaining accomplice. Likewise, the doctor, Clemens, in *Alien3* offers medical comfort and intimacy to Ripley, but is almost immediately killed by the alien. Thus Ripley is to be denied any intimacy in her fight against the aliens. In *Seven*, Mills is never at home with his wife, concentrating instead on building his career and proving himself to his colleague. In consequence, he is not around when the serial killer, John Doe, calls. Later when John Doe is telling Mills what he has done, he mocks the fact that Mills did not even know that his wife was pregnant. Ultimately she could not trust his reaction to tell him: he could not see her anxieties or share her worries because of his own preoccupations. This destruction of the domestic is also a theme in *Fight Club*, which begins with a parody of the designer home, with all the designer labels shown to us. But we later see it being blown up as the anonymous hero (played by Edward Norton) rebels against consumerism and takes on a neo-Nietzschean macho übermensch mentality.

In all these films what is being destroyed is the domestic. For Fincher, it is not possible to enjoy a normal private life without it being violated, and this violation is caused by the very intensity of the characters in these films. All the characters are striving for something: a new independent life (*Panic Room*), the urge to destroy the aliens (*Alien3*), a rejection of consumerism (*Fight Club*), and a need to prove oneself (*Seven*). Thus Fincher paints intimacy as doomed, as vulnerable and open to threat. This threat is due to a lack of complacency, an inability to find tranquillity in a key character. Instead their striving for something becomes all-consuming. What he is showing are the limits to domesticity, and how it survives only within a cocoon of apparent normality. Dwelling is not built to deal with the extreme situation, but is rather conditioned for complacency and regularity. We base our lives on the tacit and habitual – we run on well-worn tracks – but then find it hard to respond once under threat from the unknown and the unquantifiable. And, quite often, like Mills and Ripley, it is our characters, and our own choices, in terms of career, indeed of where we live, that open us up to this unpredictability. In *Panic Room* this destruction of domesticity is only enhanced by the use of computer-aided camera techniques, whereby the camera appears to follow cables and to go through walls and floors. This serves to demonstrate the porous nature of domesticity. It shows how dwelling is open and vulnerable, and how privacy is so easily breached. The camera, like the three intruders, has no difficulty in penetrating the dwelling.

But after the mayhem and the violence there is a long pause, and for several seconds the screen is blank. We think that the film has now ended, but instead we move to a final scene. Sarah is lying on her mother's lap as she sits on a park bench. She is reading out property details to her mother. They are again house-hunting, and so the film ends as it began, with mother and daughter looking for somewhere suitable to live. The story therefore ends with a calmness and a sense of normality. Sarah and Meg are getting on with their own lives. The trauma of the burglary has not brought husband and wife together again – that would be too pat an ending. Rather mother and daughter are doing what they must do in order to continue living. But, importantly too, the film ends as it *has to*: with the mother and daughter house-hunting. What other response could they make? Clearly they could not remain where they were: they need to make a fresh start and can do so. But it makes it fundamentally clear that what we all need first and foremost when we lose our dwelling is to find another one. And, of course, the move is enforced and their choices are restricted to what is available – and to what is different from what they thought they wanted at the start of the film!

So, despite the extremity of David Fincher's portrayal of domestic violation, there is much that we can take from it, and the detailed discussion of this piece of popular culture has been worthwhile. In the discussion that follows nothing is so extreme, but anxiety is still there. We still have the impotence that comes with security, the unpreparedness to change that dwelling brings with it, and the general sense in which we respond to the extraordinary by panic and anxiety. So, back to the everyday!

Anxiety and the mundane

Friedrich Nietzsche (1996) boldly states that 'One will seldom go wrong if one attributes extreme actions to vanity, moderate ones to habit and petty ones to fear' (p. 46). But is he right here? Should we really compare fear with pettiness? Might it not be the case, as shown by our discussion of Fincher's work, that we should link extremity with fear? Indeed the reactions shown by the threatened mother and daughter were as far from vanity as we could wish.[4] Rather the basis of their reactions was quite properly fear. Likewise we might be able to see a link between pettiness and vanity: why else does one see the small slights and little affronts unless one has a particular opinion of oneself? Isn't Nietzsche here arguing like an old bourgeois grumbler moaning about the little niggles of life?

But what if he were correct in this one little phrase, and that pettiness *as well as* extremity is a result of fear? Might we not see many of our actions – the reactions to small slights, the recoiling from unwanted attention – as fear, or more properly anxiety? If this is the case we have a way into looking at the everyday activity of our dwelling, both for ourselves and with others. Hence there is no real discrepancy in linking fear both to the petty and the extreme. It is merely that we need to distinguish between extreme fear and petty anxieties. Nietzsche's search for the epigram has led to an oversight about the nature of anxiety, namely, that it is not a fruit of the event but the expression of an internal state: anxiety and fear move from the inside outwards and do not come from beyond us.[5] The fear and anxiety belong to us and not to the event.

It is the anxiety that derives from the petty things that interest me here. But, first, a caveat is due. Something may look petty from the outside, when observed dispassionately and free of context. However, for the person undertaking the act, there may be a sound reason for that act and it may feel to them as something substantial. Thus one person's pettiness is another's considered and justified action. What we need to remember is that what is at issue in these speculations is the subjective aspects of dwelling. Hence, we should not be judgemental, but aim to understand, even when we do not approve. This is important because, to reiterate, much of what constitutes dwelling is banal, being based around the everyday. But this does not detract from its meaningfulness to those involved.

Perhaps there is little that is more mundane than decoration, or the concern for how the dwelling appears. When we go into another's dwelling we can privately deplore their choice of décor, yet we will state otherwise. We will refrain from commenting for fear of giving offence, because we treasure the relationship with the host, and we are unsure of how comments might be received. How can such a comment ever be seen as constructive? We are not, after all, trying to improve someone, but to comment on their taste. A host may deprecate their dwelling, in terms of décor or tidiness, but one will ritually contest their view, and the host will almost certainly hope or even expect to be contested. We would need to be a close friend or family member to agree with the host's deprecation and say the house is indeed untidy or shabby. We would here be challenging something that is very personal. We would need in essence to be a part of that household, or to have shared many common experiences. Hence siblings and parents might say what they like and have it accepted (although the motivation and meaning would differ between parents and siblings). Most others need to watch what they say, and this is a condition that is largely self-policing, so that we might suggest the maxim, 'do to the ornaments of others as you would have done to yours'.

Yet is the standard self-deprecation of the host not merely a means of seeking reassurance? Perhaps they really are unsure whether the house is as tidy as it should be, or that the décor really is tasteful. What they want, therefore, is to be reassured, and they seek to achieve this by presenting the dilemma in as off-hand a manner as they can manage. Thus the very last thing they want is for anyone to concur with their view. This suggests that we need to have confidence in the host, and they in us, to be honest with each other. Yet it is precisely when such a relationship has developed that such issues cease to matter. Discussing dusty shelves then becomes a conspiracy rather than an affront.

But who do we decorate and ornament the dwelling for? Do we do it merely for ourselves? We, after all, are properly held responsible for our tastes, even if the comments are mainly behind our backs. Or do we decorate for those who may visit us? Do we have some person in mind when we clean and decorate ('What would so-and-so say if they saw the place looking like a tip?'), or do we only run around with the duster when someone is coming? Is not this one way in which we show anxiety about our dwelling? We wonder what people think about how we live: is it tidy enough, do they approve of the decorating or the carpets, have we dusted the shelves and is the lawn mown? Or do we just keep the house tidy for own benefit, so much so that it just becomes a habit?[6]

Finding answers to these questions, however, is difficult, at least beyond asking them of ourselves.[7] They are questions we would find difficult to ask of others. It would be seen as an impertinence or, at best, none of our business to question how somebody chooses to live. Accordingly, we would, and perhaps should, keep our questions and our opinions, to ourselves. We would only express our feelings when we were safely out of earshot. Yet is it important or significant that this is one question that we would never seem to ask? If we cannot ask it, why then do we put such an effort into the internal decoration and ornament of our dwellings? What is hidden here beneath our scruples?

There might be a link here with the notion of respectability. We do things because it is the respectable thing to do: it is what others expect of us, and thus we are seen as acting responsibly. It might be said that we are conforming to a social norm. A norm is a sanction (or the threat of a sanction) which precludes us from taking a particular course of action (Elster, 1989). Norms reinforce a particular position, or in Foucauldian terms, they discipline us (Foucault, 1977). We act in a particular (responsible) manner because our behaviour is affected by the threat of sanction. After a while this behaviour becomes habitual and thus we take it as normal and the threat of sanction recedes, even as the behaviour becomes a habit.

But just how does this process of norm setting and sanctions work in practice? Who is there to judge us? Doubtless one could respond, again following Michel Foucault, that we discipline ourselves, and thus rely on what is essentially a modified notion of false consciousness. We behave in a particular way because we believe it is in our interests to do so. Yet is not the problem here that we are doing something precisely because we wish to? All we are doing is making the dwelling look as we wish it to look. As such, this makes it a rather benign form of discipline. Of course, it might be really as simple as doing something because we like it or want to. We decorate and ornament the dwelling to make it look 'nice'. In this sense, we can leave the theoreticians to argue over our motives whilst we sink into the cushions and turn up the volume to cut out the noise of their babble. The important issue here is precisely that we feel that we do not have to account for our actions: would not we say if challenged, 'It is mine and I can do what I like. You may not approve, but what has it got to do with you?' Theoreticians may patronise this perspective and see it as naïve, but how do they live? Foucault, by all accounts, lived the life of a successful bourgeois and apparently did not feel the need for assurance that he was doing the right thing (Macey, 1994).

Yet the position is more complicated than it would outwardly appear. We actually tend to hold two apparently contradictory views concurrently. Thus, we might say of our dwelling that, 'It is mine to do with as I please'. Yet this can and does operate alongside, 'I must keep it tidy and tasteful'. On the one hand, we appear to suggest that we can do what we like, but, on the other, we have an imperative sense that we must look after the dwelling. But these two statements can be brought together satisfactorily as, 'What right have you to criticise my taste?' This perhaps need not be as trenchant as it sounds, but is merely a more assertive statement of the host's desire for approval: another way of saying, 'Do you like it?', but with the answer already presented for us.

Perhaps one of the reasons we get anxious about the state of our dwelling is that we are forced to see it as others do (or how we think they do, which amounts to the same thing). On these occasions we might look at the dwelling as they do, and we see the dust, the cracks and the places that need touching up. But usually, of course, we are too occupied with use. Underlying this concern is the belief that the visitor notices these blots and blemishes too. Yet this is not a full answer, because if our visitors are properly polite, they will not say anything, and so why should we worry ourselves? Is the answer precisely because this is one of the few times we see the dwelling as it actually is, with a degree of objectivity? Or is the worry caused not by a concern over standards, but rather because the subjectivity of the dwelling – of what it means to us as an object in constant use – is lost because an outsider breaks the taken-for-granted ties behind the dwelling and ourselves? As Martin Heidegger (1962) might have said, they make the dwelling *present-to-hand*. What is now brought sharply into focus is the dwelling itself in its functioning integrity. As a result we see it for what it is – we see it objectively, in that it is literally 'an object' – and not how we ordinarily can and would like to see it, as a mere extension of ourselves. The presence of an outsider gives us a degree of distance and helps us to see what is actually there, rather than allowing us to take it for granted.

Of course, not all observation is a result of an invitation. There are those who enjoy prying into the affairs of others. But why do some people feel the need to watch or look at others from the relative safety of their own dwelling? What does the 'nosey-parker' mentality consist of? Is it an (albeit implicit) statement, or maybe even an exhibition, of their standards and their desire to impose them onto others? Or does it relate to a fear of what others might do? Is it an extended sense of propriety; a belief that our own standards should apply more generally? The key question is whether it is a form of social interaction, or a fear of it? Are these people wanting attention or frightened of it? Is this mentality a defensive reaction to a vague threat to one's morals, or a weak attempt at imposing one's morals on others? Or might it just be a result of boredom?

We know that people react when they feel that their actions might be questioned, when what they think of as private has, by some means, become public. A trite, but convincing, example is given in the first *Harry Potter* novel (Rowling, 1997). When the first Hogwarts letter for Harry arrives, it is addressed to Mr H. Potter, The Cupboard under the Stairs, 4 Privet Drive, etc. Apparently somebody beyond the house knows exactly how Harry's aunt and uncle have treated him. What J. K. Rowling catches here is the sense of panic that people have when they are caught out doing something they know to be improper. For years Harry has been made to sleep in the cupboard under the stairs. More generally, he has been treated as a constant nuisance and drain on the family compared to the way they spoil their own son, Dudley. The Dursleys' reaction to the letter (as well as destroying it before Harry can read it) is to give him a room of his own. It is as if they have been shamed into action by this letter: by the fact that others know of Harry's predicament.[8] What is normal and sustainable within a household can change because of external intervention, or more properly, the perception that outsiders might be witnessing the hitherto unquestioned actions. What makes this more ironic is that the Dursleys are portrayed as being particularly intolerant and dismissive of the lifestyles of others. Perhaps they are so dismissive precisely because matters of lifestyle are so important to them. The characters of the Dursleys, despite being well-drawn and amusing, are, of course, stereotypes. They are there to represent those whose insular, bourgeois, 'me-first' lifestyles lead them to resent difference and eccentricity. They are described as being proud that they are 'perfectly normal', a condition presumably arrived at by self-definition. Yet there is a considerable acuity in this stereotype, in that it demonstrates both that normality begins and ends at home, but also that, once challenged, our sense of normality can be quickly dispelled. We seek to maintain normality through insularity, but consequently, once that insularity is breached, so is the sense of normality. What we seek to achieve above all else in our dwelling is to take it, and our activities within it, for granted. The Dursleys are no longer able to take their treatment of Harry for granted: somebody else knows.

But Rowling also uses the Dursleys' situation as an example of crass commercialism: of the 'ideal home' mentality. This fascination with consumption might itself be linked to anxiety. This occurs where consumption becomes a performance or statement. Consumption, when it is overly conspicuous, becomes a way in which our privacy is actually publicised. It is where our privacy is wilfully turned into a spectacle. In this sense, the dwelling takes on a performative role. Indeed there are many ways in which we publicise our privacy. A high wall or fence, perhaps with wire at the top, states that 'this is mine and you are to keep away'. A burglar alarm also announces that people intend to enjoy what is theirs by excluding those they do not want, likewise for signs warning off salespersons and Jehovah's Witnesses. We might also suggest that net curtains denote a sense of propriety and respectability. Or perhaps we make do with just a hard or challenging stare if others are seen to be looking too closely. This too makes the statement that others are not to get too close. But we also show our desire for privacy through conspicuous consumption, which states that 'we can enjoy the good things' or 'we intend to revel in our privacy'. But the private enjoyment of these finer things must be publicised in order to achieve the right effect: we tantalise with a glimpse, but then squirrel our treats away from prying eyes. In this sense, the dwelling is a spectacle that exists for its effect.[9]

What can explain this attempt to make the dwelling perform? Is it because we want to be distinctive in some way, and we know that what we are doing is only what everyone else can do? We therefore seek to differentiate our dwelling, to show off in a minor way. However, we must do this in a manner that does not destroy the very privacy we need in order to enjoy our purported distinctiveness. Is this where much of the anxiety and desire about dwelling develops? We desire certain things to assuage our anxieties, but are anxious that these desires might not be fulfilled.

Or is it just that we see privacy as in some way competitive? Our consumption and public shows of privacy are merely, therefore, ways of saying that we are more private than our neighbour. Is this what the desire for safety and security really amounts to? Is there an escalation of privacy, whereby we are continually seeking to feel *safer* and *more* secure? So our fences and alarms are there to tell the intruder to choose our neighbour and not us. We must have the highest fence and the most obviously elaborate security devices. But, because of these precautions, we then have to work all the harder to publicise our privacy, before we hide within our fortifications.

This suggests, through our performance, that we still feel pressure to conform and to look out for what 'they' might think. This assumes, of course, that we can locate just who 'they' are and that they really are bothered with us. Why, though, do we presume they might? What if people really were not bothered? What if nobody cared whether or not the Dursleys were normal, but just ignored them and got on with their own lives?

Might not this actually be the case? If consumption is both performative and competitive, what time do we have really to look at the opposition? And if so, is it likely that they are looking at us? So perhaps the Dursleys and their kind anxiously compete to ensure that they are distinguished by their normality, but do not notice that no one is looking (at least someone is only looking under the stairs, but their concern is for Harry and not for them). Would it make them more or less anxious if they realised this?

Mundane comforts

As much as anxiety is found in the mundane, so is its comfort. The precise virtue of dwelling is that it has the facility to protect even when we feel threatened. Even if our taste is ridiculed, or our company shunned, we can find solace in the privacy, security and intimacy of our dwelling. Our dwelling is the one place where we believe we can create our own world in any external (non-mental) sense. We feel we can make dwelling as we want it and personalise it.

But is this correct? Might it not be that this belief, that we have created an external reality, is primarily a mental state itself? Are we not deluding ourselves that we have actually created something? On one level, dwelling does constitute an elaborate illusion based on our own perceptions of autonomy. We are bound by conventions – social norms, or side-constraints, or whatever we wish to call them – that limit us, and by physical, political and social constraints. We are also limited by the very imagination that we use to create our world. We cannot imagine all possible worlds, and can only attempt to create those we can conceive of. But we still believe that we can create a world and that we have done so.

Yet it is precisely the function of dwelling to act as an illusion. It is at this level that dwelling goes beyond the merely quotidian and enters the realm of aspiration. This also means it is the realm of fantasy.[10] In ontological terms, it is not the existential – our sense of being – but the locational – our sense of place – that determines our security (Laing, 1960; Spinelli, 1989). What constitutes our ontological sense of self is our place in the world and our relation to it, not merely our existence within the world. Dwelling helps us to create a sense of place as *the* key locational determinant; hence dwelling is significant as a pre-verbal and non-communicative entity, that exists as much within as without.

So our everyday imperatives within dwelling do not have to relate to objective reality. We can still dwell whether or not we have a firm grip on our 'real world' situation. Many of the personal things that we do in the dwelling we do regardless of whether we are behind with the rent, or we have a further fifteen years of mortgage repayments before we can properly call the dwelling our own. These financial factors do not prevent us from using our dwelling as if no other person's views matter, including the landlord or mortgage lender. What is fascinating here is that we tend to use our dwelling as an important part of the 'armour' or 'carapace' that protects and insulates us from outside worries, including debt. Hence there are many examples of tenants who improve their dwellings whilst neglecting to pay their rent,[11] or tenants who refuse access to the dwelling, even though amenities need servicing or changing according to the normal maintenance cycle. Thus a dwelling can fulfil its role as protection and security even though we are neglecting to pay for it or to maintain it properly. We sometimes use our dwelling to protect us from the very consequences of our misuse of the dwelling. This more than anything shows the crucial distinction between seeing dwelling as an entity or as an activity. A well-maintained dwelling might assist in the activity of dwelling, but is not essential for it: we can still live pretty much how we would like. Likewise, we can persist with our activities even if we neglect to pay the rent or mortgage. Of course, in both these cases, this situation is not sustainable over the long term. However, in the short to medium term we can bear it, and the dwelling itself helps us in doing so. Dwelling then is not merely a cause of anxiety, but it can assuage it through its protective integrity around us.

And what helps us in this are the objects that we use to decorate and ornament our dwellings. Each item in our dwelling is, or becomes, embedded there. It is soaked in meaning and memories. Objects in the dwelling *grasp* us. Martin Heidegger (1993) spoke of things gathering us up, where they take on a meaning through being mixed in with our lives. These things become meaningful precisely because we use them. It is as if these objects take us in, connecting up with a specific memory. So the photograph reminds us of where it was taken and what we did there; the ornament is associated with who bought it for us; the trinket or toy reminds us of who bought it for us; playing a particular CD recalls events from around the time we bought it. Thinking of the object or playing the music replays a loop of memory much like Marcel's madeleine. Some of these objects are shared and others resonate differently for each member of the household. These items offer an intimate, intermittent, episodic and disjointed life history. We can piece together our lives through telling the stories of these objects. What makes that life history more complete, of course, is our own self. These objects, as it were, can be plugged into our history and sense of self. Whether these items are tacky, tasteless or kitsch is irrelevant. Good taste is irrelevant when objects are inhabited by memory. Objects therefore have an associative quality for us, that links us to important life events, such as the birth of a child, or a moment in our relationship. They are the soundtrack and the artefacts of memory.

But it is not a reliable source of memory. Gaston Bachelard (1969) states that we do not experience our dwelling in a narrative or linear manner, but in a cumulative way. It is as much a stock of images and memories as a flow of experience. This means that our remembering is haphazard: we are never sure when we shall knock into a memory or when we will be reminded of an event. Dwelling is thus a random collection of associations and memories, which are irreducible to an essence, and redeemable only through the correct tokens. In this sense, these artefacts of our dwelling are the display of memory, as well as our comfort.

Is this, though, just an adult perspective? Children may not gain the same associations from dwelling. This may be the case, but children still need the complacency of a secure dwelling, even if they use it differently. They need to be able to take things for granted and so use the dwelling as a background, a platform and a springboard. Perhaps in this sense 'growing up' is a series of challenges to this sense of complacency. The important thing is to control it. We, of course, can only be sure we have succeeded in hindsight. Children, being absorbed in their games, their friends and their explorations, never seem to notice the embellishments of a dwelling. They take their own dwelling for granted and see those of others as spaces where they can be with friends or family. They are so lost in their relationships that they cannot care about the container around them.

Dwelling stores the artefacts of memory

Yet at the same time, children view their own dwelling as proto-typical. Theirs is the quintessence of 'home', and matters of tidiness, décor, and so on, do not enter into their perceptions. They have to learn snobbery and status from their elders and betters. This lack of perception may be partly because they lack the experience to make comparisons, but it is also because they are almost totally concerned with use, with, to coin a phrase, function over form. At what point do they lose this innocence and become susceptible to comparisons? Is it when they become self-conscious about themselves and their bodies? Perhaps the home changes as their bodies and minds do: when they themselves become a point of self-reference rather than merely one with functional potential.

It is interesting to see how children react when ill or after an accident. A couple of anecdotes demonstrate this. On one occasion my youngest daughter was sick while staying (along with my wife and other daughter) with her aunt. Her first reaction was to want to return home. Later, she was reluctant to stay at her aunt's house again or indeed to sleep anywhere away from home for several months afterwards. On another occasion she fell off her bike, and cut and grazed herself. Again she demanded to be home. She seemed less concerned with her injuries than that she was away from her refuge. It is difficult to know whether this was a result of just her temperament, or whether these are examples of a more general phenomenon. But is there a sense in which arriving home brings trauma to an end? At home there is security, the known and the certain, which we inevitably contrast favourably with the situation causing us distress and discomfort. Our dwelling is where we will find permanent comfort, rather than the make-do variety by the side of the road or out of a suitcase. How does this plea to be home differ, if at all, from the cry of 'I want my mummy'? It too is a plea for the known, the secure and, above all, the safe.

But, objectively speaking, our home might not help physically in the slightest: wounds do not heal more quickly at home than in hospital, and medicines work just as well in someone else's house. Home might not be the best place – consider those who cannot abide hospital and discharge themselves prematurely. But, of course, we are not considering here the objective and the rational. It is not just a matter of physical symptoms. Our home has a calming, soothing quality to it. There is no placebo effect here, but rather one of emotional and ontological security. It does not necessarily make one well, but it does make one feel better and this means we feel we are moving in the right direction. This feeling appears magnified in the young because their horizons are so much smaller: their dwelling forms a relatively bigger part of their lifeworld than that of an adult.

But then, as we saw with *Panic Room*, it is not the physical structure, no matter what technological feats it can perform, that achieves the relief from trauma, although one cannot have dwelling without this structure. The physical structure is therefore a necessary but not a sufficient condition. What is more important are the emotional and ontological links we form in dwelling. These links are subjective, but in another sense they are common to all who dwell: we all have these feelings to a greater or lesser extent. These are descriptions of common experiences. What differs is the extremity or degree of these feelings, which are dependent on the particular situation.

Dwelling, then, is a source of comfort and relief to us. What we must hope for, however, is that we stay safely within the bounds of the mundane and can keep extremity at bay.

Chapter 8
Loss

We can see dwelling as oscillating between certain poles and rattling up and down continua between these extremes: between privacy and intrusion; between anxiety and desire; even between physicality and affectivity. We can now extend the number of these apparent polarities by a further one. Dwelling, I want to suggest, can oscillate, can shudder violently, between two other existential points. These are on no continuum, but involve the dislocation of effective dwelling. These are true opposites, with no real mid-point or point of connection between the two. At one point is the caring, the sharing, the protected intimacy of 'pure' dwelling – of dwelling as we would have it, or what Gaston Bachelard (1969) saw as the essence of home: 'the really inhabited space' (p. 5) of the ur-dwelling lodged in memory. But at the other is the absolute lack, where inhabitation ceases to be real, but is instead an emptiness caused by loss. This is a de-animated space created by the trauma of separation or death. These two points of difference – of intimacy and loss – can be characterised as love and nothingness. What a discussion on loss shows, perhaps more than anything else, is that dwelling is about far more than housing.

As St Paul states in his so-called 'Hymn to Love', 'if I have all faith, so as to remove mountains, but have not love, I am nothing. If I give away all I have, and if I deliver my body to be burned, but have not love, I gain nothing' (1 Corinthians, 13: 3).[1] The most earnest of sentiments and the most extreme of sacrifices gain us nothing unless we can show love to others. 'Love bears all things, believes all things, hopes all things, endures all things' (v. 7): this contains the veritable heart of what dwelling aspires to. Dwelling is the containment of the other through care, and that care knows no bounds, precisely because it is within bounds. But if we lose it, if the other is taken from us, what is left is the void.

But, of course, St Paul refers not to the void, but to how we respond to it. He is telling us how we should face adversity and with what weapons we can defeat it. For St Paul, facing any adversity will be for nothing unless we have love. We gain nothing from sacrifices we make unless we do this for love. And nor can we recover from the sharp knocks that life can give us.

Krzysztof Kieślowski demonstrates this for us in his film *Three Colours: Blue*, with his depiction of Julie, a widow hollowed out by grief who withdraws from the world as her response to her loss. When asked what she does, Julie replies 'nothing'. She seeks to do nothing and become nothing, to empty herself and thus lose her grief. But the beauty of Kieślowski's film is the manner in which it draws Julie back into life, into generosity of spirit, into love. And whilst this solution is being played out we hear a musical version of St Paul's great 'Hymn to Love'. The film, then, shows the movement from one pole to another: from nothingness to love, from loss to intimacy. The manner in which dwelling and dwellings are used is significant in *Three Colours: Blue*, from the emptiness of Julie's family home to the anonymity and coldness of her Parisian apartment. How she gives her family dwelling away is part of what helps to redeem her loss.

Loss is something we all must bear: it is the inevitable consequence of commitment. We know that at the end of sharing is loss. We push the idea of it away, we refuse to think of it, but, unless we are the one to die or leave, we know it will happen (and just because we run away from it, it does not lessen). This knowledge alters both the space and the affectivity of dwelling. It ceases to be a space of caring and sharing, and becomes a space of gaps. Now at best we see shadows of those who have left us, mere fleeting glimpses of those we once knew so well as to feel almost as one person with them. So what was once a space of intimacy can now be estranged from us, an empty husk instead of a warm nest. And so we react and seek to make something of the dwelling, something that is new because of what it has lost. It may be that we react by changing it and finding somewhere altogether new, but we may feel that we can never now leave. To move would constitute an act of treachery, a cheating of the memory of that person who helped to build the dwelling that surrounds us, that, in some way, it is still theirs. But whatever the response we cannot ignore loss, and how we respond conditions and is conditioned by dwelling as a space and as a (formerly shared) activity.

Kieślowski's film ends with a hymn to love, but it can also be seen as a hymn to animation, to the refilling of a human being and how this creates an outflow to those around her. The film can be seen too as about the re-animation of space, where it again becomes 'really inhabited' through sharing and caring. It is a film that demonstrates how we can begin to cope, and with its epiphanic ending, it is a deeply optimistic vision. Dwelling is an activity that is deeply serious – perhaps the most serious things we can know of are love and loss – yet, at the same time, the caring, sharing and loving nature of dwelling is what shines like a beacon to others, as the fount of generosity and caring that heals the trauma of loss. I shall attempt to explore what loss is, to categorise it as an act of memory and a form of togetherness. I shall then look at how we internalise or externalise our grief, and what the consequences of this are, relying on C. S. Lewis' bitingly honest description of how he came to cope with grief. Through an exploration of Kieślowski's *Three Colours: Blue*, I shall try to see how we can redeem loss, and dwell in peace with ourselves and those we still love, wherever they may be. But there is a more obvious loss that we need to consider, and one that may strike at this optimistic message – the loss of dwelling itself. What does it mean if we lose our dwelling? At the end of the chapter I shall therefore look at the consequences of such a loss. I have left this until last, not because I wish to relegate it or because it is not important, but rather because I wish to show that homelessness is effectively the loss of 'all of the above'. This may dent some of the optimism of Kieślowski's vision, but it also shows why, when we have housing, we are able to do so much that is important to us. It is dwelling that makes us complete. This makes the lack of dwelling a truly savage loss, as if some part of us is missing. A theme that runs through these disparate thoughts is this notion of something missing, a sense of what I choose to refer to as a lack of *animation*. So I want to begin with an exploration of how we animate a place, and how we are the soul of place.

To animate: the soul of place

Aristotle (1986), like other Greek thinkers, used the concept of *psyche*, which we perhaps mistakenly translate as 'soul'. For Aristotle it was that faculty that brought a body to life. As Hugh Lawson-Tancred (1986) suggests, in discussing the meaning of psyche in his introductory essay to Aristotle's *De Anima*, 'the most accurate translation of the term in English would be "principle of life" or "principle of animation"' (p. 12). The translation of soul is therefore conventional rather than accurate for what Aristotle saw as being 'that in virtue of which something is alive' (Lawson-Tancred, 1986, p. 12). So psyche or soul is that which animates the body, which causes it to be alive, to change and to traverse the world: it is what might be seen as the motive force of a body. It is that which differentiates a body from a life.

My aim here is not to conduct a theological discussion on the nature of the soul, nor to get bogged down in any controversy over materialism versus psychologism, nor indeed to consider exactly what the soul might be. Rather what concerns me here is this notion of animation, that there is something – and we might not be able to quantify what this is or even agree if it exists – that brings a body to life. Seeing my mother's body lying in her room mere hours after she had died was to see something empty. It was the same face, the same physical body in its outward form that I had known all my life. I had seen her grow older, but she was always recognisable as that same person. And I could recognise her as that same person still. Or should I say, the same body, for what I saw was not really the same. It was her face, her body, but not she as she was when alive. In some subtle way, that I could notice but not adequately explain as I looked at her, she was different. It was as if she had been deflated, that she was now empty of something. What was there was still a body and what was not there, I now realise, was any sense of animation. There was nothing that constituted life in that body that I knew so well. It could not move itself or think for itself; it could no longer be, if being is anything like Martin Heidegger's 'being there' (Dasein). Yet it was still her.

I do not know what it was that was missing, although 'the principle of animation' seems to me to be a fairly good stab at it. I could not at that moment, and cannot now, hope to quantify that impression I had in any scientific sense. However, it is my experience that many who see a dead person, and particular a loved one, will also see this lack, this deflated sense of a body with something significant being absent.

Likewise her room was still her space, full of her things, as it had been the last time I saw her. It had the same ornaments, the same decoration, yet the space was not the same. It had changed and taken on a distinctly different character. This was because it had lost its animation. The space now had a certain stillness and a quiet that was unnatural. Indeed in a particular sense it was empty, even though she – or her body – was there. A part, again something imperceptible, was missing or had been taken away from the whole. Her space, like the body within it, was both bereft and deflated. It had ceased to be animated by what had previously moved within there and what had made and changed the space.

Subsequent to this loss came the sad imperative, along with my brothers and sister, of clearing our parents' flat. This had until recently been a space full of activity and memory, where three generations could talk and play, within a familiarity that only continuous habitation can bring. Yet now we had to clear it of all its items and decide what we wished to keep, who would have what and what we would dispose of. This cold, calculated and hurried attitude towards objects at the centre of our parents', and our, lives, served to strip away much of that familiarity. What we were doing was de-animating the space. We were calculating whether we should keep certain things and who should have them. Things we had previously taken for granted, that had always been there, were now being analysed and looked at coldly in terms of their utility and sentiment. As we worked, the dwelling became anonymous, empty in more than the conventional sense. It was cleared of all the signs, cues, triggers of memory. We found it harder to locate the memories in this now cold and antiseptic place. The space grew in useable dimension and possibility, but not for us or for our parents. Instead it shrank from a significant place to a shell capable of supporting dwelling ... any dwelling.

Our parents' home was now just another dwelling, that had a future, but with a foreclosed past. It could now be lived in by anyone, and the fact that others were soon to take over possession emptied out the memories in a certain sense. It was no longer a place of possibility for us – a place where we could grow and change – but rather one where access was no longer possible.

The dwelling had now been reduced to its bare function, and its implacability became manifest. It had a clear function, but it was not animated. Its function was as antiseptic as the now unfamiliar smell of the dwelling. It was now ready to accept anyone; it was in stasis, between forms, with only its barest functions now manifest. The dwelling, because we had cleared it and left it neutral, offered tremendous potential for the new user. But for us, who had taken our children to their grandparents, who had talked, argued, laughed, nursed and cried with our parents *in this place*, where we had seen our children read to, as our parents had done to us, the dwelling was now only full of sadness; it was, so to speak, full of loss. It was not empty, so much as containing something unspeakably sad.

An empty dwelling has potential, but it no longer has a past

This sadness, of course, was partly due to the circumstances that led to our standing there in the empty room, of death and its accompanying grief. But it was also a loss of significance, of a place that would be cut off – cut away – from us. A place that could now be accessed only through the portal of memory. Hence it would be a place lacking entirely in possibility, progress and development. It could only be a place without a future for us. Any change in our relationship with this dwelling would be because of what was within us, by our forgetting, by our being too busy or too selfish to remember. The dwelling could offer us nothing now unless and until we left it. This could make it more special, its possession so much more precious, because of this very precariousness. But it could also become ossified or enclosed, as it were, in amber – still visible although not as clearly as before, but inaccessible, out of our touch and perhaps distorted by the very means of its preservation. We could 'hold' it still, but not enjoy it as we used to, as a living, developing thing.

So losing our parents meant losing also that dwelling, that store of memory and possibility, of which they were the keepers. The keeping would now have to be left to us, if we were able to pick through the wreckage caused by the very trauma of loss. This would be possible because we have some of the possessions, but these are really mere triggers to memory: what we keep are mainly memories.

Yet we were also aware that clearing that dwelling was an act of preparation. We were emptying and cleaning it so that it could be used by another. And the fact that we could leave it for someone else was a comfort. We could not resent that another would now be making it theirs. Rather it felt appropriate, that a place lost to us could be remade and a new home created from the barrenness of loss. In this way loss too shows the neutrality and implacability of dwelling. A dwelling, as we have seen, has the quality of equipment (Heidegger, 1962): it is ready-to-hand, there for us to use as part of our ongoing living. It has an instrumentality based on our purposes and ends. But it is also implacable. Anyone can pick up that tool and meld it with their own labour. A tool can work for us or against us; it is simply a means. The meaning of dwelling comes from the use of this tool and therefore depends on us and what is within us. The significance of a dwelling comes from within; it resides in us and not in the place.

This, I believe, sums up much of the significance of loss. The trauma of separation and departure is that it heightens what dwelling does for us. It alters the space and thus makes manifest what it was we held, and why it meant and still means so much. It is we, by our actions and intentions, that animate space, that put the soul into a space. We may not be able to quantify this 'something', but we can recognise its loss. With this in mind, we now perhaps need to try to suggest, in some more programmatic manner, just what loss is.

Weighing the loss

We tend to say that we only know the true importance of something when it has gone. Like all clichés, there is an element of truth to this. Many things do become significant when they are lost to us. When we can no longer see or touch a person, we soon appreciate what they really meant to us: we are now able to see, or rather to feel, a gap in what was hitherto a full life. As a definition of loss this might be a good first attempt: loss is a gap.

But this does not tell us what it is we have lost. We do need to be aware of just what it is that was there. What was it that animated the dwelling and therefore what is lost, and what do we find that is left in dwelling, and left there for us? Nowhere more than in the consideration of loss do we have to face the non-physical but sheer existentiality of dwelling: it is here that it becomes clear what is in dwelling for us. It is through loss that the depth of dwelling becomes clear. In this way, loss shows the complete seriousness of dwelling by showing negatively what we seek dwelling for: what we have now lost is what would make dwelling so good if it were there again.

I have said that loss is the inevitable consequence of commitment. It is commitment that gives loss its weight. What we float in the normal run of life – the sharing and caring – bears down on us when we have lost that link. If this is so, then what does loss depend upon?

First, and crucially, it depends upon the everyday fact that we live with others and need them. We care for others and they care for us. Our plans are also their plans and so what we do does not just depend on us. The only virtue of selfishness is as a guard against loss, for once we start to care for others, we can be hurt by separation from them.

But if we lost everything why would we care? If nothing is there, why does it matter? But, of course, something is still there. Indeed the problem with loss is that our side of the relationship, as it were, still remains. We had a shared intimacy with another, and this is not forgotten by us, but is wistfully and painfully remembered. The trauma arises out of the remembering of intimate moments and shared activities, to which we can no longer gain access, but cannot replace. Therefore loss depends on memory, and particularly a remembering of joint things, of things done together. Loss exists because of the repeated signs of a shared significance. This is important for dwelling,

Loss is intimacy painfully remembered

which is the site of intimacy and thus becomes the site of its loss. Loss then depends on recall and the knowledge that this recall is important.

Loss can be seen as a response or a reaction. If this is so, then how and what we recall matters. This is because we can focus either inwardly on ourselves – on my grief and what I have lost – or we can focus outwards to the other. I wish to explore this distinction by looking at how C. S. Lewis came to terms with his own grief.

Getting over it

C. S. Lewis, in his autobiographical fragment *A Grief Observed* (1961), details how a grief progresses and how we can come out of it. He is grieving for the loss of his wife, trying to understand the loss and reconcile it with his faith in a beneficent God who cares for all His creation. But this brief book, to my mind, contains some of the most pertinent statements on the significance of loss and how we can start to deal with it.

Lewis points to one key element of grief, namely how we become separated not just from the loved one, but from the wider world. It is as if we lose the will to connect once the most fundamental connection has been severed. Yet, at the same time, we still need the security of the known. When we are grieving, we feel we want what is known and to keep it around us, but not to be involved in and with it. We do not wish to be engaged by it, just to have it there. Lewis suggests:

> There is a sort of invisible blanket between the world and me. I find it hard to take in what anyone says. Or perhaps, hard to want to take it in. It is so uninteresting. Yet I want the others to be about me. I dread moments when the house is empty. If only they would talk to one another and not to me.
>
> (Lewis, 1961, p. 5)

We want the known to be there, but do not want it to intrude, to form a dialogue with us. We want a degree of stasis that allows us to wallow – for this is what grieving is, a wallowing in an internal sense, a grasping for certainties to push away the changed engagement with the loved one, who is remembered but now out of reach. We wish to glide through our family and our dwelling, lost in our grief and not prepared to engage with them. Yet they must still be there for us so that we can concentrate on ourselves. Lewis states that 'no one ever told me about the laziness of grief ... I loathe the slightest effort' (p. 7). Grief then can be little more than a wallowing in self-pity, with a complete abnegation of our responsibilities. This is why we still need the dwelling and others around us. We depend on them, but only in a selfish way: we lose the capacity for reciprocity when we grieve.

Grief, Lewis suggests, is like suspense or waiting:

> just hanging about waiting for something to happen. It gives life a permanently provisional feeling. It doesn't seem worth starting anything. I can't settle down. I yawn, I fidget, I smoke too much. Up till this I always had too little time. Now there is nothing but time. Almost pure time, empty successiveness.
>
> (Lewis, 1961, pp. 29–30)

But Lewis discovers that his loss does not depend on place. He recounts how he feared going to the places he enjoyed visiting with his wife, as if the loss would there be greater. He feared that the significance of the place would bear down more heavily on him. Yet he found it no different: 'Her absence is no more emphatic in those places than anywhere else. It's not local at all ... The act of living is different all through. Her absence is like the sky, spread over everything' (p. 12). This indicates that grief is not connected to a place, but is carried within. What matters then is how we internalise the loss and seek to externalise its effects.

But this is something Lewis is not prepared to do. When trying to encapsulate what he had, and therefore lost, he says, 'The most precious gift that marriage gave me was this constant impact of something very close and intimate yet all the time unmistakably other, resistant – in a word, real' (p. 17). This is, I believe, a key statement, not because it advocates marriage, but because he is able to see his wife as someone capable of closeness and intimacy, yet still a distinct person. She existed beyond him, and importantly, still can. She is not someone he can control – we can never do this with real people – but an entity beyond him whom he can love. What differs, as time passes, is that he is capable of seeing beyond the pain to the person, and this involves coming out of himself, of concentrating not on the pain inside so much as the relations that exist between him and the outside world. His wife was, and is, part of that outside world.

So as time goes by, he believes he remembers his wife better '*because* he has partly got over it' (p. 39, original emphasis). He goes on: 'You can't see anything properly while your eyes are blurred with tears' (p. 39), and questions 'Is it similarly the very intensity of the longing that draws the iron curtain, that makes us feel we are staring into a vacuum when we think about our dead?' (p. 40). As he suggests, 'Thought is never static; pain often is' (p. 36), and once the pain starts to dim he can begin to think and then move again. He can start to re-animate his life.

What achieves this is not revelation, on the nature of God or anything else, but rather the simple passage of time that allows him to get over it. It is simply by getting on with his life, in its dull everydayness, that he achieves this re-animation. By doing this Lewis comes to see his wife more clearly: 'It is just at those moments when I feel least sorrow … that H. [his wife] rushes upon my mind in her full reality, her otherness … as she is in her own right' (p. 47). It is when he is able to carry on living fully and doing the usual things, that he thinks of his wife as she was and not of the loss of her: when he thinks of her and not of himself. Perhaps this is what getting over loss is about – of learning to think of the loved one as other, and not just as part of oneself. What is needed is to shift from loss to memory: from nothingness back to love. As the pain dims, thought can start to move again.

This leads Lewis to criticise the rituals of death as a means of preventing the development of proper memory:

All that (sometimes lifelong) ritual of sorrow – visiting graves, keeping anniversaries, leaving the empty bedroom exactly as 'the departed' used to keep it, mentioning the dead either not at all or always in a special voice, or even (like Queen Victoria) having the dead man's clothes put out for dinner every evening – this was like mummification. It made the dead far more dead. Or was that (unconsciously) its purpose? ... Certainly these rituals do in fact emphasise their deadness.

(Lewis, 1961, p. 48)

He is critical of the practice of placing the dead in museums for grieving. He sees this as an insistence that nothing has changed and that the life before loss can continue. But this merely means that one never gets over the loss. Putting out someone's clothes does not bring them back. Indeed all it does is to show a lack of animation: it merely advertises the loss. What Lewis appears to advocate is a re-engagement with the world, with getting on with the everyday activities that make up our lives. In doing this, we are then able to see the person as they were, and are. This takes time, for the pain to ease and the eyes to clear of tears, but once it is achieved we can appreciate the person as other, as external to us, but remembered. Thus Lewis can state, 'The less I mourn her the nearer I seem to her' (p. 48).

Love or nothing: Kieślowski's *Three Colours: Blue*

One of the greatest achievements in European cinema in recent years has been Krzysztof Kieślowski's trilogy *Three Colours*. Each film takes one of the three symbols of the French Revolution – liberty (*Blue*), equality (*White*) and fraternity (*Red*) – and explores these through the lives of three ordinary people facing loss, loneliness and rejection. One of these films, *Three Colours: Blue*, tells how a widow comes to terms with the loss of her husband and daughter in a car accident. The film explores the theme of liberty, showing how the widow, Julie (played by Juliette Binoche) seeks to deal with her loss through withdrawing from all commitments – she sells the family home and moves into an anonymous Parisian apartment, cutting off contact with all her friends – and how she is forced, against her will, to commit herself to others and to the world. It is this re-attachment that liberates her from her grief and loss. It is through her generosity to others – her giving of herself – that she finds some freedom for herself.

But what also interests me in this film is the manner in which dwelling plays a part. Julie flees the family home in preference for an anonymous apartment. She responds to grief by trying to close down her former life, by turning away from it. She does not appear interested in creating anything new, merely in being away from her old life: she tries to wipe out all memory. Julie closes down any sense of home and rejects all sense of the maternal, until the end of the film when she acts as 'mother' to her husband's unfinished oratorio. We only see the family house after it has been emptied and we see that she intends to sell it. At the end of the film, however, she does not sell it, but gives it to her husband's pregnant mistress. She comes to recognise the needs that come from motherhood. This is merely one of the acts of generosity Julie performs, and it fully signifies her re-entry into the world. She recognises the needs of motherhood and acts accordingly.

It is interesting in this regard to see her watching the joint funeral on television (her husband is a famous composer). Julie concentrates on her daughter as she watches from her hospital bed. She tries to touch the child-size coffin and commune with her child, all whilst her husband is being praised as a great man. So we have this desperate attempt to connect mother and daughter whilst the father is being extolled. Indeed we see the child face on – the first human we encounter directly in the film – as she stares out of the back of the speeding car at night. However, we only see the husband from the rear and we see his face later only in photographs, and then with his mistress. The husband is a blank space, yet the action takes place around this empty space where something once dwelt – the music, the mistress, the house. There is an ambiguity about the relationship between husband and wife that complicates the nature of Julie's loss. There are, indeed, many blank spaces in this film: the old house is a mere shell, but so is Julie's apartment. One might also suggest that Julie herself also seeks to hollow out herself. Her aim is to re-create herself as a blank, de-animated space.

Julie seems to be punishing herself, but can only go so far. She cannot kill herself. Her self-punishment is not out of any sense of losing a pure marriage. Is it then to expunge the paucity of her marriage? It is clear that it was she who was the musical talent not her fêted husband. At least it was a collaborative effort and so she sacrificed herself for him and his reputation, but for what? Was it merely so she would feel loss? So she is now trying to free herself, to liberate herself from the marriage and its vestiges that persist even after death. She attempts to do this by breaking up the family home and isolating herself from her past. Julie seeks a selfish freedom, as if she can rid herself of loss by ending all commitment and engagement, shown by the desolate and empty house. She will not permit intimacy and closeness.

But if this is the case, why at the end of the film does she feel she has to finish her husband's composition? A clue is that throughout the film we are shown a blank screen and hear music. This is meant to be in her head, as is shown when she is in the swimming pool. It always comes at times of heightened emotion, as if it is an expression of something within her that is more permanent and of greater longevity than her loss. This something else is *love*. These should be read as hints that she (and we) cannot cut herself off completely from her past or from those now around her, no matter how hard she (and we) might try.

We see a trace of this with the only thing she retains from her house, a blue crystal lamp hanging in what is described as 'the blue room'. And the first action in her new flat is to hang it up. As Janina Falkowski (1999) suggests, the blue lampshade is further proof that one cannot cut oneself off from the past. Julie thinks that once she has got rid of everything, she can be herself and compose herself. But she cannot get rid of everything, and what she keeps is a store of memory, an association with her past.

But even in her new apartment she cannot escape motherhood, when she comes across a mouse and its babies. She tries to rent another flat but cannot, and so she has to take action and borrows a neighbour's cat to kill the mice. One feels it is not just the mice themselves that trouble or frighten her, but the role of the mother and the dependence of the blind and incapable babies. Julie cannot abide any sense of nurturing because it is not her, it now excludes her, and makes manifest her loss. But this is another occasion when she has to act and, in doing so, comes into contact with others. So whilst it shows her attempt to isolate herself from any sense of the maternal it also helps to re-integrate her.

This incident also indicates that, even in the midst of loss and disengagement, Julie still cares about how she lives. She does not want vermin in her apartment and seeks a practical solution to this problem. One might see this as being selfish, and it certainly is. But it is no more selfish than the actions of anyone else in the same circumstances. And, as with most of us, it is a problem that can only be solved by interaction with others, even if this is by buying mousetraps. This apparently banal episode demonstrates how everyday actions involve co-operation, and that if we seek to live normally we must come into contact with others. There is no such thing as a normal hermetic life.

The lack of any sense of nurturing extends to the relationship that Julie has with her mother who is in a residential home. She cannot remember Julie's name and confuses her with her sister. She can retain no knowledge of her daughter and her life. Her life is centred on the television and she has to tear herself away to converse with her daughter. Julie tries to open up and explain her situation, but her mother merely responds with banalities. Thus, for most of the film, normal family relations, and particularly those between mother and child, are seen as either doomed or failing.

In the early part of the film any sense of home has been killed off along with Julie's family. When we see the house for the first time we see it as cold, as leached of light and already empty despite the presence of furniture. The predominant colour, as it is throughout the film, is blue. She cannot seek any intimacy and comfort. She deliberately removes all the artefacts of her life, including the crucifix found at the roadside after the car crash. In the house Julie is cold and unemotional. Julie asks her housekeeper why she is crying: 'Because you're not', is the response.

She makes love with Olivier, her husband's assistant, in the now empty house, but it is matter-of-fact, and no real intimacy is being offered by Julie. The sex between them is unloving, at least on her part. She thanks him afterwards and brings him a coffee, and then leaves whilst he is still in bed. It is as if she wanted to defile the memory of family and intimacy. She wishes for a complete break with her past, and this can be achieved by lovemaking with another person in the now empty dwelling which had contained her as a mother and a wife. She uses the dwelling for a purpose that is the very opposite of protected intimacy. There is no nurturing, closeness or search for permanence. The nurturing of motherhood and family is replaced with the mechanics of sex. This, like other actions, can be seen as a form of self-mutilation, as when she sells all her belongings, or when she deliberately rubs her hand against a stone wall. She is trying to hurt herself, to cause herself pain, as if this will aid her withdrawal.

She attempts to withdraw completely, both from her past life and the world around her. She seeks to end all commitment. No one knows where she has moved to, she reverts to her maiden name and does no work. She tries to become a non-person. In fact, when asked by the estate agent what she does, she says 'nothing'. She wallows in this nothingness, this abnegation of any commitment to the world. But she cannot achieve it. She mistakes what it is that liberates. It is not isolation, but commitment; not coldness, but generosity.

All the routines we see her having are external to her home, such as swimming and going to the same café, where she is clearly such a regular that she does not need to order. It is as if all the important things in her life now take place in the anonymity of public space. We see mere glimpses of her flat, but only when her privacy and non-commitment are being challenged. She sees someone being beaten up and goes to the stairs to see if he is there (causing her to lock herself out); she is then visited by a neighbour with a petition to evict another tenant, Lucille, who is a prostitute; and she is visited by Lucille herself, who thanks Julie for not signing the petition (even though this was due only to a wish on Julie's part not to get involved).

Lucille's entrance into Julie's apartment is interesting, if only for her first words on crossing the threshold: 'Your place is cool'. We should assume here that this phrase has two meanings. First, there is the conventional compliment meant by Lucille, but also the fact that there is no emotion, no comfort in the dwelling: the place is cold and without human warmth. We see little or no engagement between Julie and the dwelling. As a place it is neutral. Julie is obviously not committed to this place any more than any other. What matters is merely that she can bolt the door and keep others out.

However, the character of Lucille is quite pivotal to Julie's re-emergence in the world. The two women begin to develop some sort of friendship and support each other. Lucille offers to clean up Julie's flat after the cat has done its work of dispatching the mice, and Julie comes to Lucille's sex club to listen to her and support her when she sees her father in the audience.[2] It is also at the club that Julie sees a television programme about her husband and discovers that he had a mistress. So it is this relationship, more than anything, that pushes Julie back into the world. It is her inability to withdraw from her neighbours and the reciprocity that comes from proximity that is important here. No matter how hard she tries, she cannot disengage from those around her.

These commitments bring a gradual re-engagement with the world, and in ways not of her choosing. She finds that she can no longer just do nothing. As Janina Falkowski suggests, 'Julie slowly re-enters the world not because she wants to, but because life's events pull her into it. She must make certain decisions, some of them practical, and others of a more moral nature' (1999, p. 143). She is forced into making decisions, about whether to help Lucille, to rid the flat of the mice, to find her husband's lover. The film shows two meetings between these two women. The first is in the toilets of the law courts (the lover is an advocate), where Julie finds the other woman is pregnant. The second meeting is at Julie's old house, which she has taken off the market and now offers to the mistress. We now realise that Julie has reconnected with the world and this has occurred because of motherhood. It is the fact that the mistress is pregnant and soon to be a mother that opens Julie up to the love and care of others. It is here we see that she has rejected nothingness. Falkowski (1999) suggests that, 'Julie replaces envy, hatred and grief with generosity and love' (p. 144), and accordingly she agrees to help Olivier finish her husband's oratorio for the EU. This is the piece that has been circling around in Julie's head throughout the film, but only here do we find it is a setting of St Paul's 'Hymn to Love'. As Falkowski says, 'Through this humility and renunciation of her own egoistic right to submerge herself in mourning, Julie reaches a state of spiritual and emotional liberation, a state of grace which puts a faint, almost indiscernible smile on her face' (p. 144).

The film ends with a long panning shot of the main characters in the film, whilst we hear St Paul's hymn about being as nothing if we have not love. This shot begins and ends showing Julie with the barest trace of a smile on her face. She has rejected her intention of doing nothing and has chosen love, and the music behind the images amplifies this beautifully:

> The predominant theme in the hymn is love: humble, powerful and selfless. This love offered by Julie makes life meaningful to all the film's protagonists. Moreover, her act of generosity towards them brings a final liberation to Julie herself ... an emotional and spiritual closure.
>
> (Falkowski, 1999, p. 144)

Julie has re-animated her own life, as well as bringing life to others. She has also re-animated her family home, by installing a new family. What we feel is that Julie is finally *at home*. She will still feel the pain of her loss, but she has found some consolation, and she has done this through an engagement with the needs of others.

Kieślowski's film talks to us about how we cannot console ourselves, but need the comfort of others, and that through mutuality we find some resolution and liberation. We can get consolation through others, by expressing love for others, by translating from 'nothing' to loving. We cannot dwell *in* our loss, as Julie initially seeks to do, but only by dragging things out, perhaps painfully, by bringing things forward from out of it, such as the joy of music and the knowingness of maternity. What we must do, as Lewis suggests, is to live our lives, and in this way the other will show themselves, when we least expect, but as they are.

There is indeed a similarity between the manner in which Kieślowski resolves the pain of loss and C. S. Lewis' rise from grief. Both begin with the pitch black of despair, of a questioning of all relations, but end with a reconciliation and a coming back to the world. I would suggest that the slight smile on Julie's face be seen as a signal of some form of recognition that her life will and should go on. But it also reminds us that there is still a loss. Those we love are still not there. But all we can do is remember and not mourn.

Dwelling animates us

I would like to think that what Lewis is inviting us to do is to get on with dwelling, to do those normal things we have to do in order to live. We can sink into bleak despair or we might feel like giving it all away, as Julie attempted. Yet there is no remedy here, and this is what Kieślowski is telling us too. We cannot live without commitments. Importantly these commitments are not just to others, but to ourselves as well. We have a duty of care to ourselves, and this means re-establishing the routinisation of life. These routines, I would suggest, are what using dwelling amounts to.

I have never been in Julie's situation of losing my partner and children, and it is something one cannot properly imagine. Yet like many, I have faced the loss of loved ones, and I have tried to discuss what this meant and how it affected the sense of dwelling I had shared and experienced with my parents. There is a loss of place, a feeling that the space which had contained such love and caring is now but nothing. I, too, along with my sister and brothers, emptied out a home full of memories and familiar objects. But there was a difference between Julie and myself. This was not that it was the death of my elderly parents, as death is seldom welcomed even if it might be half-expected. The difference was that I, unlike Julie, had a place to go. By this I mean not just that I could afford a new place, but that there was a place I *wanted* to go to. I had a place that was beyond that loss I had experienced. I could return to my wife and children and the home that we had built, and to this I could add some of the familiar objects taken from my parents' home.

My point is that I was able to use the dwelling I had and that I shared with others to help to insulate and cure me of the pain of loss. Julie's mistake was in withdrawing from this insulation, breaking up her home and removing all memory and familiarity. Her redemption was through allowing memory and commitment to push back in. For most of us who have suffered loss there is this possibility of reconnecting through the familiar: we have somewhere to go. In this sense, it might not always be a mistake to retain the dwelling that we shared. C. S. Lewis does not talk of moving out or changing how he lived. He tells us that he initially dreaded being alone in the house, but he soon moves back to his routines, and it is through these that he best remembers his wife as she was. We do not cease to mourn by running away but through engaging with life as we find it. In this way it is our dwelling, with its mundane routines, that can animate us and help to put the soul back into us.

Losing it all

But what does it mean to lose our dwelling? What does it mean not to have a place to animate, or to be de-animated because we have no place? What impact does being homeless – *dwellingless* – have on us? Surely this is the most important element of loss that we need to consider, and therefore something which should have a greater prominence that I have chosen to give it. However, I have taken this approach because I believe that homelessness is the loss of *all of the above*. Losing our dwelling denies us all that we have considered in these speculations: the privacy, intimacy, sharing, loving, caring, and the ability to grieve in solitude, and leaves us merely with anxiety, unrequited desire and loss. To be homeless is to lack private dwelling and thus to be bereft of our most existentially significant activity. We might say that if we summate all the qualities I have ascribed to private dwelling, and then deny them or take them away, this is what homelessness means.

Yet this sounds dismissive and straightforward. We ought not to be able to encapsulate the full effects and implications of homelessness in this rather glib manner. The effects of homelessness are considerable and consequential. It makes a normal life impossible and we really need to give it more thought and indeed more space, to try and place it as a singular event for each and every individual who suffers it.

But this is precisely my intention. I see, and have sought to show, dwelling as a deeply serious activity – of considerable and consequential import – and therefore to say that homelessness is the loss of 'all of the above' is not to try and diminish it with a trite phrase. Homelessness is where dwelling is reduced to *nothing*. But I would prefer to say that it is *negative dwelling*. It is where there is the opposite of dwelling. By this I do not intend that there is a void where dwelling should be, for we have memories and images of past places. However, these memories and images cannot be located. They are not stored, but float free, like the wreckage left after a storm. We can still see them as they drift past, but we cannot put them into any coherent and meaningful structure.

That this is negative dwelling is publicised by our inability to withdraw. This is unlike Walter Benjamin's bourgeoisie, who were able to use the domestic interior as a theatre box, where they can spectate on the world, but with themselves free from observation (Morley, 2000 and see chapter 2). Homeless persons are themselves the spectacle. They are on view and open to the criticism and opinions of all that pass.

We can therefore concur with the title of a government publication that described homelessness as *More Than a Roof* (ODPM, 2003). This report recognises that homelessness entails the lack of a suitable physical structure. But it also demonstrates that homelessness is not just a lack of shelter. Lacking a dwelling has multiple effects: on education, employment, our relations with partners and children, our self-esteem, and our health. We cannot lead a complete and fulfilling life without housing. But, of course, British homelessness law goes further in accepting the qualities that constitute effective dwelling. The law does not equate homelessness with rooflessness. We can be considered homeless even when we have a roof over our head. What is at issue is whether the housing is permanent or secure. We might see homelessness as where our privacy is either impossible or seriously compromised.[3]

In this sense then, it is truly the very opposite of what this book has considered. Homelessness is where we lack the capability to love, care for, share with, and educate our children, all secure in our privacy. It is where there is no possibility of tranquillity, merely the constant threat of transform-ation, flux and change. It is where there is no peace and no complacency. It is where there is anxiety about the unknown, the unlooked-for change. Homelessness is where we cannot exercise sufficient control over our environ-ment, because we lack the ability to exclude. We are therefore unable to repel intrusion, to stave off change and to create a stable environment that allows us and our intimates to thrive. At best, and if the law allows, this capability may merely be temporary, which in itself is a serious diminution in our security.

All our actions, be they public or private, are situated (King, 2003). There is little meaningful that we are able to do which does not entail the use of some place. If we are able to control this place, to exclude unwanted others and secure it, we can achieve much of what is possible for us. Homelessness is then that condition where all places are closed to us. We may only be in any place on the sufferance of others.

Many of the actions we wish to undertake are personal to ourselves and those intimate with us. These are activities we would wish to conduct in a secure environment free from intrusion. We wish to be able to close *our* door to *our* place and to allow access only on *our* terms. This is what private dwelling centres upon and is what a private dwelling allows us to do. We wish to be situated with those we care for and who care for us, and away from those we do not know and who have no legitimate interest in what we do and why.

This clearly politicises these speculations, as they seek to tell us why we need to be situated: why we need private dwelling free from insecurity, impermanence and unwanted publicity. These speculations demonstrate that the lives we wish to lead are impossible without that place we call dwelling: they are a manifesto for a civilised life. We can see this every time we walk past someone homeless sitting in a shop doorway or a subway. We see a lack, something that is missing. Homeless people are de-animated by their plight, by the daily struggle to stay alive. This, without doubt, is a physical debilitation, but there is also a psychic loss caused by this inability to lead any part of their lives in private.

Perhaps, then, we should see homelessness as a form of mourning. The homeless are mourning for the loss of control over their lives, of the ability to maintain themselves in security and permanence. What they have is a sense of loss and they lack much more than a roof. They lack the very soul of what it is that constitutes our civilised lives: a private dwelling.

Conclusions
The stopping place

These speculations have looked at the personal use of housing, and what our housing means to us. What I have tried to do is consider the manner in which we relate to our housing, not as a commodity with a price attached, and not as a collective entity, but as something we use. We may need to look at housing in these terms, and many do, but I have focused here on the subjective sense of housing. Housing has an objective quality to it. It can be touched and measured, but this is not all that is important. What I have tried to build up is a picture that encloses both the palpable, quantifiable objects and the meanings we attach to them. The result may be somewhat less straightforward and clear than other perspectives on housing, but this, I would suggest, merely points to the very nature of dwelling as a practice that is both rather diffuse and at the same time particular to each and every one of us. I have frequently used this word 'dwelling' in place of housing, and hopefully the reasons for this are clear. Indeed an understanding of the distinction between housing and dwelling is at the core of my speculations: the physical entities called houses are just a part of what is involved in what we have and do when we dwell, when we live in enclosed spaces with others. Dwelling helps to explain why we do this, as well as just detailing what it is we are doing. The answers I have given may be vague, but this is precisely because I am trying to discuss a universal condition – something we all do, but do differently. There is thus a rather unsteady mix of universalism and relativism within this concept of dwelling.[1]

But this very quality presents us with a problem: where can we end these discussions? Is not dwelling immune to neat narratives, with a beginning, middle and an end? On the one hand, we can never say enough about dwelling, simply because it is so ubiquitous. Yet, as dwelling is also so unique – my dwelling is not your dwelling; my experiences are mine and mine alone – what can we say that is conclusive? Dwelling is so common that we really ought to know everything that needs to be known already. But what is so particular to each individual surely cannot be fully generalised upon. So either way we appear to be stymied. Yet, of course, I have found much to say about how we use housing and what to dwell therefore means to us.

But what I cannot claim is that I have said all that there is to say, nor that I have said it correctly, nor even that I have picked out the most important things. So the question remains: can we come to any conclusions? If there is so much more to say and explore, and so many different ways of doing it, should we not be extremely wary of trying to pull all this together? Perhaps this is so, but for the sake of the completeness of this particular project I wish to make some, albeit brief and tentative, conclusions, so long as these are seen neither as definitive nor as an act of closure.

But I have no wish to be programmatic here, to suggest that by a series of policy interventions, some new tax or change to the planning system, education programme or government roadshow we can alter the perspective we have on dwelling. As I said at the beginning of this book, I have no particular wish to change anything. I merely seek to open up a new series of questions. The most crucial understanding is that dwelling is not necessarily, or even frequently, about change or transformation, either social or personal (although it can be the latter, as I have discussed at several points in this book: think of becoming a parent or losing a partner). Normally speaking, dwelling allows us to mitigate change, to fight against it and hold it off. It allows us to control our environment, to some limited extent at least, and this involves much more than just altering the thermostat. It is about what we do and when, who we are intimate with, how we raise our children, whom we see and relate to, and how we view ourselves and others around us. Dwelling allows us to insulate ourselves from those influences we do not like. It can keep us blissfully unaware, as we can control what comes in (and that means any fault lies with us). We *can* turn over or turn off. It is where we can ignore and be indifferent to the histrionics of ideologues, the inanities of entertainers and the offensiveness of artists; where we can fill the house with cuddly toys or cut glass; where we can listen to the Eurovision Song Contest or Shostakovich symphonies, read Céline or Barbara Cartland. We can have the radio on as background whilst we wash up, or change a nappy, regardless of what the presenter thinks. We can put those things we want into the background. Dwelling means that things do not dominate us, but we control them. This does not happen perfectly, but it happens well enough. And if households are influenced by what they watch and read, who is to say that is all bad or wrong? They still had, and still have, a choice, and by not turning off they are exercising it. The worst couch potato is as free as anyone else and would quite legitimately resent anyone telling him[2] otherwise. We should not ignore the intrusions of media and new technologies into the domestic sphere, but we should also admit, along with David Morley (2000), that debates on globalisation, mobility and de-localisation are debates amongst and about elites. Most of us are unaware of these changes, and can in fact use our dwelling to insulate us from them. At best we sit in the comfort of our four walls and somewhat bemusedly watch these changes going on around us. Many people may now speak with Australian vocal inflections due to the influence of soap operas, but the only way we notice this is by talking to our neighbours about the weather and what the local kids are up to.

What compounds the difficulty of discussing dwelling is that we often cannot or do not articulate its meaning and importance to us, nor do we need to be able to do so. It works just as well whether we can explain it, describe it, understand it, or do none of these things. Dwelling is based on habit and is therefore a tacit relation. We have no contract between ourselves and our dwelling, nor do we have a contract with our intimates and families. This perhaps suggests we only notice it when it is gone, or at least when it ceases to function as we expect. Of course, that means that these speculations in themselves will not make any difference. We will not live better, enjoy it more (or less), or be any happier because of any insights that I might have found. So, then what has been the point of it all? Why write about something we cannot change or even influence?

The most obvious, yet profound, reason is so that we can understand dwelling better. These speculations might then be seen as something of a corrective to the vast majority of the literature about housing and its importance. They might have an, admittedly small, effect on those who plan and try to control housing, and who think they can and do understand housing in a programmatic way. These discussions might cause them to pause and to question their certainty that they already know what housing is about. Those academics and commentators who still seriously suggest that housing is just about production and consumption, and nothing else, might stop for at least a second and make the connection between what they talk and write about and the place they go home to at night. More broadly, these ideas might make us question what we actually mean when we throw out glib phrases such as 'anti-social behaviour' and 'affordable housing', and the cavalier use of 'home' in the thoroughly discrediting and inappropriate manner that has become so common. They might encourage us to be circumspect in our language and more considered in our thinking. So I may not be able to affect dwelling as such, but I can hope to influence those who think they know what they are talking about.

The purpose of these speculations has been to show that what is really important with regard to our dwelling is neither physical, material or related to standards. Housing is important because of how we use it. But 'usefulness' is not an intrinsic quality. Things are not useful as such: usefulness is not an abstract quality. Something is useful in terms of how it relates to a specific purpose and in relation to certain conditions, and not merely on its own. If we have empty lives a four-bed detached house will not fill them: we might be more comfortably empty, but empty we still are. So it follows that issues like tenure and house prices do not of themselves matter. What matters is how we use the space we have. Dwelling has an ontological meaning as well as an economic one. Subliminally we know this, even as we fret over house prices and colour schemes, but we need to make it more explicit. We need to make it clear that whatever the economic value of the house we live in, its *real* value lies in who we share it with and what we use it for. So there is a need to separate out 'owning' and 'using'. One might be able to use it better because we own it, but this is not a necessary condition. There is some purpose in the old Marxist distinction between use value and exchange value.

But this sounds too glib, as if we are reducing the discussion to slogans. We need to be a little more specific about what private dwelling can and does do for us. Just what does it mean, in this case, to say housing has a use value? Or put another way, why is private dwelling so useful? I would point to three facets of private dwelling that I consider are the most important.

First, with private dwelling there is the possibility of intimacy. We are able to be close to those we choose to share with. But it is also where this intimacy can be regular, expected and normal. So second, private dwelling is where intimacy can be protected. Not only can we express ourselves fully with those we love and care for, but these relationships are nurtured and allowed to grow stronger. Dwelling is that which provides the right conditions for intimacy to develop. It does not just allow it but feeds it. Third, private dwelling is that place where we can be complacent. It is where we can take what we have, and take it for granted. We may normally consider that taken-for-granted means taken lightly. But with dwelling, as well as other things we use as equipment ready-to-hand, it is precisely this quality that allows us to use it fully. This is because a dwelling is a means; it is something we use for its instrumental effect. What we might say therefore is that, if we cannot take dwelling for granted – if we cannot sink into complacency – it is failing for us.

This, of course, has its negative side, and we should not shy away from this. Gaston Bachelard (1969) always, and deliberately, emphasises the optimistic and benevolent role of dwelling. Home for Bachelard is dependent upon childhood memory and thus has a benign, calming quality. It is always a reverie and never a nightmare. But, of course, this need not be so: the very

Dwelling is space we use rather than measure

privacy of dwelling can repress and reject. So we need to remember that there is an implacability to dwelling. It can equally well work for us as against us. It has the neutrality of the tool. At several points I have shown how this tool can turn against us, when it breaks or fails, when we have power over others, or when we wish to connect with someone who does not wish it. The separated nature of dwelling allows us to behave towards others in a way that may not respect their autonomy and freedom. So what allows us to be intimate with those we love allows us to shun the outsider and to abuse others.

I do not wish to overplay this aspect of dwelling, but any description of dwelling cannot ignore these facets. If we are to understand dwelling to its full extent, we have to be aware of its dangers. Yet just as car accidents do not lead us to ban cars, merely to control them better, so we need to keep in proportion what dwelling does, and to balance its positive and negative effects. It is my view that we can deal with the negatives without destroying the positives. Indeed we cannot, properly speaking, live without it: dwelling, after all, is merely another way of describing how we live.

Dwelling is about activity within a given space. It is the controlling of space, but also where the space itself becomes implicated in the activity. The space, in effect, becomes part of the mechanism of control itself. This is why it is such a difficult, and perhaps a redundant, exercise to distinguish between dwelling as a thing and as an activity. Even though dwelling is more than an object, we still need that object, and without it we have nothing at all. The thing takes on a meaning because of what we can do in it, and we can use it because of its fastness and other physical qualities. This is truly a circular process: one cannot have use without a dwelling, but it is using the dwelling that we aim to achieve.

The problem comes when we try to translate this into a language that is useable for policy makers, politicians and planners. The difficulty is essentially that one aspect of this process is quantifiable, measurable and controllable – we can count dwellings, measure standards, estimate supply and demand, and try to alter prices – whilst the other aspect is almost beyond prescription. It is difficult to regulate what goes on behind closed doors. The only way is probably to remove the doors, but in doing so we would also take away much of the very purpose of dwelling. It is therefore not surprising that we concentrate on what we can count, and try to persuade ourselves that these are the things that really matter.

But just because something comes with a price tag and can be measured does not mean it is the most important. What we need to appreciate is that once we have a dwelling, our 'project' then starts, rather than ends. We should not mistake the production of dwellings for the activity of dwelling. To describe the activity of dwelling merely in terms of production and consumption is to delimit the concept to only a cipher, to just the easy, describable, quantifiable part alone. The fuller meaning is derived from the 'protected intimacy' of dwelling itself. It is not that we can just consume, but that we can nurture, love and grow as individuals, couples and families. Of course, we know this, and this is because we live in this way: we all go home at night. But we take it for granted. Perhaps, somewhat perversely, it is precisely because it is private to us that we can seemingly ignore its significance. We do not consider what we do with our partners and children as a matter for public discourse, and, most assuredly, it is not. Yet this should not negate its significance. We do not discuss it precisely because it means so much to us, and to discuss it would be to belittle or even destroy it. So we concentrate on those matters that are so general that they are shared: that we consume, that housing must be produced, that we can see certain notions of house and home as 'ideals'.

Yet we should not assume that what we share, that what we have in common, is all that there is. It is perhaps not surprising that we concern ourselves mainly with what we can quantify and measure, rather than those personal, mundane, quotidian, banal things we have and choose to do day by day. These things cannot easily (if at all) be translated into a monetary value. Properly speaking they are priceless, in the sense of being without or beyond price, and perhaps we would only fully notice and appreciate them if they were lost or taken away. Yet, nevertheless, they do still matter. They would still matter if house prices fell, if interest rates rose, if the green belt were built on, or if VAT were not charged on brownfield development. It may be a comfort to stay with the herd and to congregate in just one corner of the field. We might find solace and support in doing what others do. But we should not assume that because the herd moves in one particular direction, it is the correct one. Perhaps sometimes we should try to put a little distance between ourselves and the herd and give ourselves the space to see what is going on around us, and reflect on what we might ourselves want when we are not being pushed and pulled within the crowd. Perhaps we need to look over the fence and see what is there in the bigger world. There is, to coin a phrase, 'a herd mentality', and this is nowhere more apparent than with housing, not particularly on the part of academics, but in popular consciousness and the press. It is not that we should expect the grass to be greener on the other side, but rather that there is much more to the world than mere grass.

What the commodification of dwelling creates is an ideology of displacement, a churning of anxiety and desire that insists always on change, on bigger

It's time we looked around more

and better, on the possibility of the ideal, on that place that is always just over the horizon, near but tantalisingly out of reach. But the thing is, if we wish to use our dwelling fully and to accomplish what it can achieve for us, *we have to stop*. We have to see dwelling as a form of stasis, as tranquillity and not transformation: *as a filling-up and not as a flow*. Once we have done this we are then able to put our heads up and look around, to reflect on what and where we are, free of any sense of competition or any anxiety at being in the 'wrong' place.

What matters then is where and how we stop. What is the stopping place like and how does it fit us? Did we choose it or did we fall there? How have we arrived at this point? Were we dumped there by circumstance, or duped by our own desire, by our search for a transient fix of consumption? Or are we now in a place of our choosing where we can look up and take in our fill from around us?

The meaning of dwelling – its existential significance – is based around these two ideas of *filling-up* and *the stopping place*. We fill up the dwelling with memories, happenings, with loving and caring, with sharing with those we love. We do all these things by stopping still: we stay in one place so that we can love and care, share, dream and remember. Stopping in this sense brings with it familiarity, quietude, permanence and stillness. But most of all it brings a sense of belonging. And so it is important that we are the ones who say 'no further', that we call time on our travels, our climb up the ladder, and stop at the place of our choosing. Here we cling on and have what we need, namely, dear life itself. However, we have to want to stop in this place and be content with it.

What we need to realise is that for dwelling to work as we would like it to, we have to be able to exercise some control: we need to be able to make choices. If we are to choose our stopping point we have to be in control of our dwelling and not let it control us. Now this perhaps ought to lead us on to a series of policy statements by way of conclusion. We may indeed be able to come to some prescriptions about how we enhance choice, how we ensure that some are not left behind, and how all choices come to matter equally. But this has not really been my aim in this book. What I have sought to do is consider what housing means to us. To extrapolate from these speculations into the realm of policy would be fascinating, but would, I believe, distract from my main themes. All policies are limited to a given time and place, and all are controversial. My worry is that by advocating one particular approach, I take the risk that my whole argument will be dismissed by those who feel an alternative policy would be more appropriate. This may lead to a charge of copping out, but I would rather risk that. At least readers will have reached this point before realising that I have not really come to a conclusion.

The issue for me is that there have been many attempts to consider policy, to try to determine what we do with housing, and to pick out the key problem and the all-encompassing solution. Some of these prescriptions have even been tried, and there may even be some that might have worked, at least for a time.[3] But what is missing is an attempt to understand just why housing is so important to each and every one of us: what is it about dwelling that makes it so significant at the subjective level? Dwelling is both ubiquitous and unique. We all do it and need to keep on doing it, yet we all do it differently. Dwelling is both universal and relative, and this is neither a paradox nor a contradiction. Perhaps the way we should see this is that, in general terms, the outcomes – the things we all want from our dwelling – are the same. We all want to have privacy, security and intimacy. But what we want these things for, and hence how the particulars of dwelling are configured, and how they develop, will change relative to our ends and the constraints that impinge upon us. We literally can have our cake and eat it, and because no one is looking, we can even have a second helping!

Indeed I would go so far as to suggest that it is the very qualities we prize in dwelling that lead housing to be so low on the political agenda. The fact that we *can* control what we do in and with our dwellings, and therefore lead quiet predictable lives, allows us to ignore much of what occurs outside. Being in control means that we do not have to rely on others to provide for us. This does not mean that there is no need for planning, but rather that there should be limits. Policy should be about creating tranquillity and not transformation: calls for a 'step change' will merely persuade people to put an extra bolt on the door.

There is nothing more particularistic than our housing, yet it is this very private activity that we hold in common. Regardless of house type, location, value, tenure, indebtedness or whatever, we can still use the dwelling the same way. We are just as secure, just as capable of intimacy, just as private, as much in control over what we can say, watch and do alone and together; we can love as much, and we can share as much. There is then a very important political point in here after all, even if we do not delve into policy as such. What we appear to have forgotten is that what we all share is a common interest based on the shared experience of housing itself. What is never called upon as a means of social solidarity is the very ubiquity of housing as a lived experience.

So, my final point, based on the preceding discussions of how we live, is that there needs to be some attempt to build up this notion of a common interest. In other words, we need to explore what is common to all households through their ubiquitous relationship with their housing. These speculations apply to us all, they apply all the time, and always will: what brings us together – what gives us a real chance of solidarity – is that we all, as human beings, dwell. The simple act of dwelling as separate households, then, can and ought to be a source of solidarity. And in so doing, we will conserve what we hold most dear.

Notes

Preface

1 I fear sometimes that many just consider this idea of housing too banal and uninteresting in their search for research grants and policy influence.
2 See Robert Nozick's *Invariances* (2001) for an illuminating discussion on this subject.
3 I discuss the idea of use and usefulness in the introduction.
4 See Stanley Cavell (1979), Arthur Frank (1991), Donna Haraway (1997) and Slavoj Žižek (1999, 2000) respectively.

Introduction

1 What is interesting, as I discuss in chapter 4, is that many housing professionals have now replaced the term 'house' with 'home'. Thus they go home after working on homes all day! One hopes that at least some might see the irony here.
2 Having said this, it does raise some interesting general methodological issues that create doubts about housing research more widely, if only because the whole point of building houses is for people to live in them.
3 I discuss Wittgenstein's notion of philosophical description, and my methodology more generally, in more detail in chapter 1 in the section 'Transformation and tranquillity'.
4 Having said this, of course, Wittgenstein has been perhaps the most significant academic philosopher in the English speaking world over the last fifty years.

Chapter 1

1 Although Kemeny (1992) notes the ambiguity of the term, as demonstrated by the UK Census in 1991, which defined a dwelling in terms of a household and a household in terms of a dwelling!

2 But see David Fincher's *Panic Room* for an evocation of how these notions are double-coded: there are occasions when we can only be secure by effectively entrapping ourselves. Thus an intruder cannot get in, but we cannot safely come out. In a different manner, prisons offer safety and security, but on this occasion not for the inmates so much as those outside the gates. *Panic Room* is discussed more fully in chapter 7 on anxiety.

3 Hence we can make, an admittedly banal, connection between Norberg-Schulz's four modes of dwelling and what we might call 'civilisation'.

4 See Archer (2000) and Ellis and Flaherty (1992) for examples of this trend.

5 Of course, this ignores the very real problem of whether we can describe phenomena fully without changing them as part of the process. See Nozick (2001) for a detailed discussion of this problem.

6 See Williams (1997) and the discussion of this epistemological conceit in King (1998, pp. 35–7).

7 We should remember that Popper saw no reason why the social sciences could not aspire to the same rigour as the natural sciences.

8 Margaret Archer (2000) offers a particular example of this when she states that 'agents are not infallibly right about their agency. Indeed they are not, or there would be less discrimination, injustice, alienation, oppression, materialism and consumerism around, and much more emancipatory collective action' (p. 2). If only they would listen to the good professor.

9 I discuss this side-constraint argument in some detail in *A Social Philosophy of Housing* (King, 2003).

10 This is similar to the argument that theorising about housing is a distraction from the imperative of housing people. It can be answered in the same way, that one is unlikely to succeed in housing policy unless one understands the manner in which housing relates to households. Theories can help in achieving this (King, 2003), but also there is much about this condition that is universal and thus applies equally to all.

11 One can, of course, criticise the Right to Buy for other reasons. In *A Social Philosophy of Housing* (King, 2003) I argue that the Right to Buy is an illegitimate policy because of its lack of universality, that it is not and cannot be applied to everyone equally. Having said that, we need to appreciate its popularity. The effect of the Right to Buy is to extend the effective control that the household has over their dwelling.

12 Of course if the aim is simply to achieve equality, then this practice will have succeeded in achieving it.

Chapter 2

1   Only one transfer took place in the London Borough of Westminster. The policy was repealed in 1996.

2   This type of bracketing out is, of course, the very opposite of that of Edmund Husserl's transcendental phenomenology, which sought to bracket out the subjective to gain a grasp on the essences in all their purity.

3   The word private is derived from the past participle (*privatus*) of the Latin word *privare* meaning to deprive.

4   I take animation as a major theme in my discussion of loss in chapter 8.

5   As we shall see in chapter 4, the phrase 'make yourself at home' is particularly ambiguous.

6   So instead of talking to her, I wrote this very note in my notebook, without knowing if it would lead to anything, instead of spending part of a sunny day talking to an interesting person. This would seem to be a good definition of the academic – a preference for intense insularity in lieu of conversation with others!

7   There is an interesting literature developing on the issue of relative privacy in the dwelling. See in particular Craig Gurney (2000).

8   This relates again to the discussion of the lifeworld concept in chapters 1 and 5.

9   If we were to take this idea of a duty far enough, might we not say we ought to purchase the product or accept the offer so that they can receive their commission? Do we not have a duty to ensure that they earn a decent living?

10   For someone to offer without having been asked would be another matter altogether, of course. My point here is entirely about the ethics of asking or expecting the help and not whether help might be reasonably offered should it come about through other means.

11   Ben Elton, in response to being criticised for being a celebrity lefty, summed up this form of criticism with the reply, 'Call yourself a socialist and you've got shoes!' The often bitter debate about the responsibility of Christians to accept poverty and live like Christ is evoked wonderfully in Umberto Eco's *The Name of the Rose* (1983). Perhaps the fact that the debate is described as taking place in a monastery on the top of a mountain in the middle of winter should be taken as an indication of its relevance for the rest of Christendom.

Chapter 3

1 See chapter 8 for a fuller discussion of animation.
2 See King (1996) for a discussion of how this concern came to dominate housing policy in the late twentieth century, driven by an obsession with tenure.
3 The notion of property is discussed further in chapter 5.
4 This is discussed further in chapter 4 on language.
5 See the discussion of David Fincher's *Panic Room* in chapter 7 for a fuller consideration of this apparent paradox.
6 But see Slavoj Žižek's interesting and amusing discussion of the ideology of toilet design in the opening pages of *The Plague of Fantasies* (1997).
7 The machine metaphor, whilst carrying generally unfortunate connotations, carries with it some interest when used by thinkers such as Manuel De Landa (1991, 1997, 2002). De Landa takes the machine metaphor of Deleuze and Guattari (1983, 1988) to present a materialist conception of history. Such a metaphor, I believe, could be used to show the objective nature of housing, but as De Landa is keen to argue, in a manner that does not neglect methodological individualist principles and, crucially, the importance of spontaneous or non-organised phenomena.
8 There is an important caveat to this statement, namely that we are unlikely to view the dwelling in this manner when it is our principal place of work.

Chapter 4

1 See for example Hastings (2000); Marston (2002); Saugeres (1999); and Watt and Jacobs (2000).
2 This links to the discussion on socialisation in chapter 5.
3 Oscar Newman's (1973) arguments about public space being no one person's responsibility are relevant here.
4 Turner (1976) compares the street system in London, which is limited by the proscriptive Highway Code but allows multiple routes to a destination and several means of getting from A to B, with the prescriptive London Underground which offers one route and one means of travel.
5 This does not mean that there might not be a dominant ideology, merely that the term 'common sense' is not a particularly apt description for it.
6 See Anthony O'Hear's book *After Progress* (1999) for an elegant and cogent summary of this argument. However, it dates back to contemporary critics of Rousseau, such as de Maistre (1996), who quickly saw through the illogic of the social contract.

Chapter 5

1 I discuss this, and the whole issue of loss, more fully in chapter 8.

2 I mean this only in the material or practical sense of sharing tasks in the dwelling. No one would seriously deny that a new baby brings much into the world.

3 During the six years I lived without a television I was frequently told by friends and family that I would be welcome to have their spare set. It apparently did not occur to them that I might not have a television by choice.

4 I ignore here the issue of whether one is becoming depraved by the act, or the traditional conservative argument that one poisoned limb can destroy the whole organism. I also leave aside for the moment the strong, but separate, general argument, that the demand for child pornography encourages further abuse. In any case, whilst the total irradication of web-based activity might significantly diminish the amount of child abuse, it is hard to believe that the practice itself would stop. Child abuse was not invented along with the Internet.

5 This is, indeed, technically possible with Internet service providers that are able to check the use of the system by their clients. Whether policing the vast number of connections is viable, or desirable, is another matter. Additional to this, liaison between the police and credit card companies has made it possible to trace those who do just watch without downloading, as the case of Pete Townshend in 2003 showed.

6 As an aside, we could question whether surfing the Internet is a public or private act, or is it both? It is now perhaps the most common example of the phenomenon of how we do many common activities together in private. Hence the appeal, and the danger, of Internet chat rooms. We can be intimate with minimal risk (if we do no more than tap on a keyboard), but without really knowing the truth of what is being told us.

7 See the discussion on temporary dwellings in chapter 3.

Chapter 6

1 We would have to admit that different people have different horizons, and therefore what is just beyond the reach of some might be considered completely beyond attainment by others and thus not worth even considering.

2 Yet, on the other hand, there is also no means to test one's position to gain the necessary sense of proportion.

3 I have considered the idea of authenticity and how it is linked to autonomy and dwelling in *The Limits of Housing Policy* (1996).

4 Presumably many intellectuals do this in part by reading Žižek. Žižek does it by writing his books.

Chapter 7

1 This is an issue that has come to the fore in the UK with the case in 2000 of Tony Martin, a Norfolk farmer found guilty of fatally shooting a burglar in the act of robbing his house. The debate between those who consider we have a right to protect ourselves and our property in the face of unknown invaders, against those who consider that we must act reasonably and proportionately has been lively and will go on.

2 Of course, this enframing operates on at least two other levels. First, nearly all the film takes place within the strict confines of one dwelling. Second, as Mulhall (2002) has noted, the technology of filmmaking is itself the enframing of images to be projected onto a screen.

3 It is therefore perhaps not coincidental that the inhabitants of the house are just mother and child.

4 One might, however, suggest that this situation arose out of the vanity of the previous owner of the house.

5 This is why films such as *The Blair Witch Project* have such an effect. It is not despite the lack of special effects that this film is effective in unsettling us, but precisely because much is left to our imaginations.

6 One is reminded here of the urban myth of people tidying up *before* the cleaning lady comes, so as not to feel too ashamed or inadequate.

7 But are we the best ones to ask? Will we be honest with ourselves?

8 There is another, more serious, example of this form of behaviour. Amnesty International's policy of encouraging groups to send letters continually pleading for political prisoners is predicated precisely on this principle of shaming political leaders into acting properly, on the basis that so many people across the world know they are acting improperly.

9 Of course, this effect is always assumed. One could not ask about another's reaction!

10 See the discussion on fantasy in chapter 6.

11 I had occasion as a housing officer in the early 1980s to visit a tenant in arrears in order to serve them a notice of seeking possession, to find they had installed a new heating system and knocked down a partition wall in their property. All this work had been done professionally and well, albeit without permission. I refrained from asking if they had paid the builder.

Chapter 8

1   Revised Standard Version.
2   This offers a further hint of the troubled relationship between parent and child.
3   I do not suggest here that UK homeless legislation is in any sense the ideal. Indeed the refusal to help certain groups seriously compromises its effectiveness. It is merely that the legislation appears to enshrine some of the fundamental principles I have uncovered in these speculations.

Conclusions

1   This may, of course, point to the redundancy of the apparently absolute distinction between relativism and universalism: between those who wish to assert the nature of essences and those who suggest there is no presence. There is, of course, an increasing body of theorists, such as Alain Badiou (2001, 2003), Manuel De Landa (1997, 2002) and Slavoj Žižek (1999), who take this same view. One might also suggest that Ludwig Wittgenstein would have found this debate an example of philosophers and social scientists asking the wrong sort of questions.
2   My wife subscribes to the theory that only men are couch potatoes, and I cannot raise myself up to disagree.
3   I have no wish to denigrate those who do concentrate on the sharp end of policy-making and the issues of implementation. I merely wish to suggest that there is the need sometimes to consider the basics, the foundation upon which we then build.

Bibliography

Archer, M. (2000): *Being Human: The Problem of Agency*, Cambridge, Cambridge University Press.

Arias, E. (Ed.) (1993): *The Meaning and Use of Housing: International Perspectives, Approaches and Their Applications*, Aldershot, Avebury.

Aristotle (1986): *De Anima*, London, Penguin.

Austin, J. L. (1962): *How to Do Things with Words*, Oxford, Clarendon.

Bachelard, G. (1969): *The Poetics of Space*, Boston, Beacon.

Badiou, A. (2001): *Ethics: An Essay on the Understanding of Evil*, London, Verso.

Badiou, A. (2003): *Saint Paul: The Foundation of Universalism*, Stanford, Stanford University Press.

Bengttson, B. (1995): 'Politics and Housing Markets: Four Normative Arguments', *Scandinavian Housing and Planning Research*, Vol. 12, pp. 123–40.

Benjamin, W. (1999): *The Arcades Project*, Cambridge, MA, Belknap/Harvard University Press.

Bruner, J. (2002): *Making Stories: Law, Literature, Life*, New York, Farrar, Straus and Giroux.

Cavell, S. (1979): *The World Viewed: Reflections on the Ontology of Film*, enlarged edition, Cambridge, MA, Harvard University Press.

Céline, L.-F. (1954): *Guignol's Band*, New York, New Directions Publishing.

Cioran, E. (1998): *The Trouble with Being Born*, New York, Arcade.

Cioran, E. (1999): *All Gall is Divided: Gnomes and Apothegms*, New York, Arcade.

De Landa, M. (1991): *War in the Age of Intelligent Machines*, Cambridge, MA, Zone Books.

De Landa, M. (1997): *A Thousand Years of Nonlinear History*, Cambridge, MA, Zone Books.

De Landa, M. (2002): *Intensive Science and Virtual Philosophy*, London, Continuum.

Deleuze, G. and Guattari, F. (1983): *Anti-Oedipus: Capitalism and Schizophrenia*, Minneapolis, University of Minnesota Press.

Deleuze, G. and Guattari, F. (1988): *A Thousand Plateaus: Capitalism and Schizophrenia*, London, Athlone.

de Maistre, J. (1996): *Against Rousseau*, Montreal, McGill-Queen's University Press.

Derrida, J. (1976): *Of Grammatology*, Baltimore, Johns Hopkins University Press.

Derrida, J. (1978): *Writing and Difference*, London, Routledge.

Eco, U. (1983): *The Name of the Rose*, London, Picador.

Elliott, A. (2000): 'Psychoanalysis and Social Theory', in Turner, B. (Ed.): *The*

Blackwell Companion to Social Theory, 2nd edition, Oxford, Blackwell, pp. 133–59.

Ellis, C. and Flaherty, M. (1992): 'An Agenda for the Interpretation of Lived Experience', in Ellis, C. and Flaherty, M. (Eds): *Investigating Subjectivity: Research on Lived Experience*, London, Sage, pp. 1–13.

Elster, J. (1989): *The Cement of Society: A Study of Social Order*, Cambridge, Cambridge University Press.

Fairclough, N. (1992): *Discourse and Social Change*, Cambridge, Polity.

Falkowski, J. (1999): '*The Double Life of Veronique* and *Three Colours: Blue*, and the Escape from Politics', in Coates, P. (Ed.): *Lucid Dreams: The Films of Krzysztof Kieślowski*, Trowbridge, Flick Books, pp. 136–59.

Foucault, M. (1977): *Discipline and Punish: The Birth of the Prison*, London, Penguin.

Francescato, G. (1993): 'Meaning and Use: A Conceptual Basis', in Arias, E. (Ed.), pp. 35–49.

Frank, A. (1991): *At the Will of the Body: Reflections on Illness*, Boston, Mariner.

Franklin, B. (2001): 'Discourses of Design: Perspectives on the Meaning of Housing Quality and "Good" Housing Design', *Housing, Theory and Society*, Vol. 18, no. 1–2, pp. 79–92.

Frege, G. (1997): 'On *Sinn* and *Bedeutung*', in Beaney, M. (Ed.): *The Frege Reader*, Oxford, Blackwell, pp. 151–71.

Gurney, C. (1999): 'Lowering the Drawbridge: A Case Study of Analogy and Metaphor in the Social Construction of Home-Ownership', *Urban Studies*, Vol. 36, no. 10, pp. 1705–22.

Gurney, C. (2000): 'Transgressing Public/Private Boundaries in the Home: A Sociological Analysis of the Coital Noise Taboo', *Venereology*, Vol. 13, pp. 39–46.

Haraway, D. (1997): Modest_Witness@Second_Millenium.FemaleMan©_Meets _Oncomouse™:*Feminism and Technoscience*, London, Routledge.

Hastings, A. (2000): 'Discourse Analysis: What Does it Offer Housing Studies?' *Housing Theory and Society*, Vol. 17, no. 3, pp. 131–9.

Heidegger, M. (1962): *Being and Time*, Oxford, Blackwell.

Heidegger, M. (1971): 'Building, Dwelling, Thinking', in *Poetry, Language, Thought*, New York, Harper and Row, pp. 145–61.

Heidegger, M. (1993): 'The Origin of the Work of Art', in *Basic Writings*, London, Routledge, pp. 139–212.

Hodder, I. (1990): *The Domestication of Europe: Structure and Contingency in Neolithic Societies*, Oxford, Blackwell.

Husserl, E. (1970): *The Crisis of European Science and Transcendental Phenomenology: An Introduction to Phenomenological Philosophy*, Evanston, IL, Northwestern University Press.

Illich, I. (1992): *In the Mirror of the Past: Lectures and Addresses, 1978–1990*, London, Marion Boyars.

Kemeny, J. (1992): *Housing and Social Theory*, London, Routledge.

King, P. (1996): *The Limits of Housing Policy: A Philosophical Investigation*, London, Middlesex University Press.

King, P. (1998): *Housing, Individuals and the State: The Morality of Government Intervention*, London, Routledge.

King, P. (2003): *A Social Philosophy of Housing*, Aldershot, Ashgate.

Lacan, J. (1977): *Ecrits: A Selection*, London, Routledge.

Laclau, E. (1993): 'Discourse', in Goodin, R. and Pettit, P. (Eds): *A Companion to Contemporary Political Philosophy*, Oxford, Blackwell, pp. 431–7.

Laing, R. D. (1960): *The Divided Self*, London, Penguin.

Lawson-Tancred, H. (1986): 'Introduction', in Aristotle: *De Anima*, pp. 11–116.

Le Corbusier (1927): *Towards a New Architecture*, London, Butterworth.

Le Corbusier (1929): *The City of Tomorrow*, London, Butterworth.

Lewis, C. S. (1961): *A Grief Observed*, London, Faber and Faber.

Lewis, D. (2002): *Convention: A Philosophical Study*, Oxford, Blackwell.

Macey, D. (1994): *The Lives of Michel Foucault*, London, Penguin.

Madanipour, A. (2003): *Public and Private Spaces of the City*, London, Routledge.

Marston, G. (2002): 'Critical Discourse Analysis and Policy-Orientated Housing Research', *Housing Theory and Society*, Vol. 19, no. 2, pp. 82–91.

Milgram, E. (2002): 'How to Make Something of Yourself', in Schmidtz, D. (Ed.): *Robert Nozick*, Cambridge, Cambridge University Press, pp. 175–98.

Morley, D. (2000): *Home Territories: Media, Mobility and Identity*, London, Routledge.

Mulhall, S. (2002): *On Film*, London, Routledge.

National Housing Federation (2003): *In Business for Neighbourhoods: Action for Change*, London, National Housing Federation.

Nehamas, A. (1998): *The Art of Living: Socratic Reflections from Plato to Foucault*, Berkeley, University of California Press.

Newman, O. (1973): *Defensible Space*, London, Architectural Press.

Nietzsche, F. (1996): *Human, All Too Human: A Book for Free Spirits*, Cambridge, Cambridge University Press.

Norberg-Schulz, C. (1985): *The Concept of Dwelling: On the Way to Figurative Architecture*, New York, Rizzoli.

Nozick, R. (1974): *Anarchy, State and Utopia*, Oxford, Blackwell.

Nozick, R. (1989): *The Examined Life: Philosophical Meditations*, New York, Touchstone.

Nozick, R. (2001): *Invariances: The Structure of the Objective World*, Cambridge, MA, Belknap/Harvard University Press.

Office of the Deputy Prime Minister (2003): *More Than a Roof: A Report into Tackling Homelessness*, London, ODPM.

O'Hear, A. (1999): *After Progress: Finding the Old Way Forward*, London, Bloomsbury.

Pepper, D. (1984): *The Roots of Modern Environmentalism*, London, Routledge.

Popper, K. (1989): *Conjectures and Refutations: The Growth of Scientific Knowledge*, London, Routledge.

Putnam, R. (2000): *Bowling Alone: The Collapse and Revival of American Community*, New York, Simon and Schuster.

Putnam, T. (1999): ' "Postmodern" Home Life', in Cieraad, I. (Ed.): *At Home: An Anthropology of Domestic Space*, Syracuse, Syracuse University Press, pp. 144–52.

Rapoport, A. (1995): 'A Critical Look at the Concept "Home"', in Benjamin, D. (Ed.), *The Home: Words, Interpretations, Meanings, and Environments*, Aldershot, Avebury, pp. 25–52.

Rowling, J. K. (1997): *Harry Potter and the Philosopher's Stone*, London, Bloomsbury.

Saugeres, L. (1999): 'The Social Construction of Housing Management Discourse: Objectivity, Rationality and Everyday Practice', *Housing Theory and Society*, Vol. 16, no. 2, pp. 93–105.

Saunders, P. (1990): *A Nation of Home Owners*, London, Unwin Hyman.

Schmidtz, D. (2002): 'The Meanings of Life', in Schmidtz, D. (Ed.): *Robert Nozick*, Cambridge, Cambridge University Press, pp. 199–216.

Shonfield, K. (2000): *Walls Have Feelings: Architecture, Film and the City*, London, Routledge.

Spinelli, E. (1989): *The Interpreted World: An Introduction to Phenomenological Psychology*, London, Sage.

Stroll, A. (2000): *Twentieth Century Analytical Philosophy*, New York, Columbia University Press.

Stroll, A. (2002): *Wittgenstein*, Oxford, One World.

Studer, R. (1993): 'Meaning and Use: A Basic Understanding', in Arias, E. (Ed.), pp. 29–34.

Torfing, J. (1999): *New Theories of Discourse: Laclau, Mouffe and Žižek*, Oxford, Blackwell.

Turner, J. (1976): *Housing by People: Towards Autonomy in Building Environments*, London, Marion Boyars.

Watt, P. and Jacobs, K. (2000): 'Discourses of Social Exclusion', *Housing Theory and Society*, Vol. 17, no. 1, pp. 14–26.

Williams, P. (1997): 'Introduction: Directions in Housing Policy', in Williams, P. (Ed.): *Directions in Housing Policy: Towards Sustainable Housing Policies for the UK*, London, Paul Chapman Publishing, pp. 1–6.

Wittgenstein, L. (1953): *Philosophical Investigations*, Oxford, Blackwell.

Žižek, S. (1997): *The Plague of Fantasies*, London, Verso.

Žižek, S. (1999): *The Ticklish Subject: the Absent Centre of Political Ontology*, London, Verso.

Žižek, S. (2000): *The Fragile Absolute – or Why is the Christian Legacy Worth Fighting For?*, London, Verso.

Žižek, S. (2001): *Did Someone Say Totalitarianism? Five Interventions of the (Mis)Use of a Notion*, London, Verso.

Filmography

Alien3 (1992): directed by David Fincher, with Charles Dutton and Sigourney Weaver.

Cathy Come Home (1966): directed by Ken Loach, with Ray Brooks and Carole White.

Fight Club (1999): directed by David Fincher, with Edward Norton and Brad Pitt.

Panic Room (2001): directed by David Fincher, with Jodie Foster and Forest Whitaker.

Seven (1995): directed by David Fincher, with Morgan Freeman and Brad Pitt.

Three Colours: Blue (1993): directed by Krzysztof Kieślowski, with Juliette Binoche.

Index